T0320831

The Myth of the Ethical Consumer

Do consumers really care where products come from and how they are made? Is there such a thing as an "ethical consumer"?

Corporations and policy makers are bombarded with international surveys purporting to show that most consumers want ethical products. When companies actually offer such products, though, they are often met with indifference and limited uptake. It seems that survey radicals turn into economic conservatives at the checkout. This book reveals not only why the search for the "ethical consumer" is futile but also why the social aspects of consumption cannot be ignored. Consumers are revealed to be much more deliberative and sophisticated in how they do or do not incorporate social factors into their decision making. Using first-hand findings and extensive research, *The Myth of the Ethical Consumer* provides academics, students, and leaders in corporations and NGOs with an enlightening picture of the interface between social causes and consumption.

TIMOTHY M. DEVINNEY is Professor of Strategy at the University of Technology, Sydney. He is a Fellow of the Academy of International Business, a recipient of an Alexander von Humboldt Research Award, a Rockefeller Foundation Bellagio Fellow, an International Fellow of the Advanced Institute of Management (UK), and a Distinguished Member (Fellow) of the Australian and New Zealand Academy of Management. He has published six books and more than eighty articles in leading academic journals.

PAT AUGER is Associate Professor of Information Systems and e-commerce and Director of the Executive MBA program at the Melbourne Business School, the University of Melbourne. He has published extensively in leading academic journals in a variety of disciplines, including information systems, marketing, business ethics, and strategy.

GIANA M. ECKHARDT is Associate Professor of Marketing at Suffolk University, Boston. She has published widely on issues related to consumer behavior in China, branding, culture and globalization in Asia, and consumer ethics. Her research has been funded by and won awards from the Sheth Foundation and the Marketing Science Institute.

The Myth of the Ethical Consumer

TIMOTHY M. DEVINNEY
University of Technology, Sydney

PAT AUGER
Melbourne Business School

GIANA M. ECKHARDT
Suffolk University

CAMBRIDGE
UNIVERSITY PRESS

CAMBRIDGE UNIVERSITY PRESS
Cambridge, New York, Melbourne, Madrid, Cape Town, Singapore,
São Paulo, Delhi, Dubai, Tokyo

Cambridge University Press
The Edinburgh Building, Cambridge CB2 8RU, UK

Published in the United States of America by Cambridge University Press, New York

www.cambridge.org
Information on this title: www.cambridge.org/9780521747554

© Timothy M. Devinney, Pat Auger, and Giana M. Eckhardt 2010

First published 2010

Printed in the United Kingdom at the University Press, Cambridge

A catalogue record for this publication is available from the British Library

Library of Congress Cataloguing in Publication data
Devinney, Timothy M., 1956–
The myth of the ethical consumer / Timothy M. Devinney, Pat Auger, Giana M. Eckhardt.
    p.   cm.
Includes bibliographical references and index.
ISBN 978-0-521-76694-4 – ISBN 978-0-521-74755-4 (pbk.)
1. Consumption (Economics) – Moral and ethical aspects.   I. Auger,
Pat.   II. Eckhardt, Giana M.   III. Title.
HB835.D48   2010
174–dc22
                                                                          2010008741

ISBN 978-0-521-76694-4 hardback
ISBN 978-0-521-74755-4 paperback

For our spouses:
Sandra Brandt Devinney
Daphne Ng
Worth Wagers

By pursuing his own interest [the individual] frequently promotes that of the society more effectually than when he really intends to promote it. I have never known much good done by those who affected to trade for the public good.

Adam Smith, *The Wealth of Nations*, Book IV, sect. I, chap. 2, para. 9.

How selfish soever man may be supposed, there are evidently some principles in his nature, which interest him in the fortune of others, and render their happiness necessary to him, though he derives nothing from it, except the pleasure of seeing it.

Adam Smith, *The Theory of Moral Sentiments*, Part I, sect. I, chap. 1, para.1.

Contents

List of figures	*page* xii
List of tables	xiii
Preface	xv

1	The appeal and reality of ethical consumerism	1
	The ethical consumer and myth	1
	Ethical consumerism versus consumer social responsibility	9
	Moving from ethical consumer to C_NSR	11

2	Social consumerism in the context of corporate responsibility	16
	Social consumerism and firm profitability	16
	Economic profit	17
	Willingness to pay and C_NSR	18
	Economic profit in light of C_NSR	23
	Firm and market reactions to social consumption	24
	Firms and the social consumption context	28
	The evolution of preferences and the role of the firm	33
	The ethical consumer and CSR	35

3	Are we what we choose? Or is what we choose what we are?	37
	Radical attitudes, conservative behaviors	37
	Understanding the nature of consumer choice	40
	Archetypes of consumer behavior	41
	Consumers as rational informed processors	41
	Consumers as quasi-rational reactive purchasers	41
	Consumers as quasi-rational co-producers of value	42
	Consumers as actors for the adaptive unconscious	42
	The consumer as *vox populi*	43
	The consumer as evolved ape	46
	Two meta-models of social consumer behavior	48
	A linear model of social consumption	48

A recursive model of social consumption   51
Implications of the models   53
The attitude–behavior gap and its implication
    for measurement   56
    The four methodological flaws: incentive compatibility,
        comparability, inference, and context   56
    Increasing the predictive validity of intentions   59
The myth of ethical consumption; the reality of social consumption 60

4   Ethical consumers or social consumers? Measurement
    and reality   64
    The importance of the consumer   64
    Experimentation and consumer social behavior   67
    Are we willing to put our money where our conscience is?   72
        Discrete choice experimentation   72
        The components of study no. 1   74
            Ethical disposition inventory   76
            The MORI poll   79
        The study sample   79
        Willingness to consider/purchase; willingness to pay   79
        How valuable is providing information?   86
    Can we believe what consumers say when not constrained?
        The link between surveys and experiments   87
    Will consumers sacrifice functionality?   94
    Global segments of social consumers   98
        The structure of study no. 2   98
            The sample   99
            Product features and structure of the experiments   99
        Global segments   102
            Demographics again   106
        Does "social" segment position exist independent of product
            context?   106
        Segment size and country differentiation   108
        The importance of recall   109
    Ethical consumerism in light of experimental reality   112
        Assessing the myth   116

5   Rationalization and justification of social
    (non-)consumption   117
    The contribution of interpretative methods to understanding
        $C_N SR$ 118
    An interpretative approach   120

	Understanding varying social consumption rationales	123
	The economic rationalists	124
	The governmental dependents	126
	The developmental realists	128
	Currents of logic and justification	132
	Interpreting the myth	134
6	**The ethical consumer, politics, and everyday life**	**137**
	From the consumer context to the perspective of the citizen	137
	A pound for human rights, a penny for genetically modified food: a glimpse at measuring social issue priorities	140
	Seeing the citizen: estimating general societal preferences	152
	The consumer as citizen: linking social and consumer preference	162
7	**Tastes, truths, and strategies**	**166**
	De gustibus non est disputandum	166
	The inconvenient empirical truths	172
	The convenient empirical truths	176
	Strategies for enhancing C_NSR	179
	Jettisoning the myth	183
Appendix 1	Description of country choices and participant sampling	188
Appendix 2	Ethical disposition survey: the MORI poll and ethics scales	195
Appendix 3	Latent class finite mixture modeling	201
Appendix 4	Semi-structured interview guide used in all countries	203
Appendix 5	The logic of best–worst scaling	206
Appendix 6	Australia omnibus social, economic, and political preference study	209
Notes		216
References		219
Index		232

Figures

2.1 A stylized test of social versus conventional
consumption   *page* 22

2.2 Market characterization with different assumptions
about social consumption   25

3.1 A linear model of social action   49

3.2 Values, beliefs, and attitudes   50

3.3 A recursive model of social action   51

4.1 Structure of study no. 1   73

4.2 Mocked-up news article for athletic shoes   76

4.3 Example of the choice task for athletic shoes   78

4.4 Design of social and function product feature mix
in study no. 1+   95

4.5 Pseudo-demand curves for athletic shoes with good
social features   96

4.6 Pseudo-demand curves for bath soap with good
social features   97

4.7 Impact on choice by athletic shoe segment   103

4.8 Impact on choice by AA battery segment   104

4.9 Overlap of segments for the product categories   107

4.10 Percentage of consumers recalling features from
last purchase   110

4.11 Influence of feature recall on focal product feature   111

6.1 Experiment instructions and example of the
best–worst task   145

6.2 Mean best–worst scores across six countries   146

6.3 Mean best–worst scores by country   147

6.4 Mean best–worst scores for sixteen social, economic,
and political issues   156

6.5 Mean best–worst scores for sub-issues in four categories   158

6.6 Social, economic, and political preferences by party vote   159

7.1 The components of a C_NSR strategy   182

Tables

2.1	Changes in value based on scenarios	*page* 28
4.1	Product features and social attributes used in study no. 1	77
4.2	Sample characteristics for study no. 1	80
4.3	Probability of considering a product based on social product features	82
4.4	Willingness to pay for social product features	84
4.5	Probability of buying a product based on whether or not social product features are mentioned in the news article	87
4.6	MORI poll responses by sample and in total	88
4.7	Correlation matrix of MORI poll responses (all respondents)	90
4.8	MORI poll responses by extreme segments	92
4.9	Sample characteristics for study no. 2	100
4.10	Product features and social attributes used in study no. 2	101
4.11	Distribution of country and segments	109
5.1	Scenarios used for interviews	121
6.1	Sixteen issues considered in the six-country best–worst experiment	143
6.2	Mean best–worst scores by country	148
6.3	Mean best–worst scores by product category segment (AA batteries)	151
6.4	Mean best–worst scores by product category segment (athletic shoes)	151
6.5	Categories of social issues	154
6.6	Best–worst scores based on human rights activities	160
6.7	Best–worst scores based on animal welfare activities	161
A2.1	Correlation matrix of MORI poll responses (all respondents)	198
A6.1	Socio-demographics of the Australia omnibus study	210
A6.2	Sub-issues by category with mean best–worst score	211

Preface

Any project like this one takes enormous efforts over an extended period of time. This project started in 1997 with what can be considered a random event: we were involved in an external project and a simple question was asked: "Do consumers really care?" Not having the answer at the time – and being surprised that there was nothing approaching an answer – we began what ended up becoming a quasi-systematic investigation of this question. None of us knew at the time that, ten years later, we would still be working out the answer.

No one in the team would characterize him- or herself as being involved in research on business ethics or in an academic area in which one would expect this question to be of interest. Timothy Devinney is trained as an economist (with a bit of psychology). Pat Auger is trained in management. Giana Eckhardt is a consumer behavior marketing scholar. However, what we bring to bear on this topic (along with our many collaborators) is a perspective that is untainted by a normative predisposition. It is our concern only to try and understand the phenomenon, not to change it. This book is not an advocate's manifesto, except in wanting to bring clarity to a contentious topic. We do not deny the importance of many of the issues that we are investigating, nor that advocates for these issues have a justification in promoting them as a natural process of social, cultural, and political debate and change. However, we are operating under the belief that to understand the facts about individual social consumption behavior and to attempt to do so via the use of multiple methods in different locations is important to inform that debate. It is our role to be independent observers and arbiters.

Over the years we have had much support and many collaborators. First and foremost, the major portions of this work involved collaboration with Jordan Louviere and Paul Burke at the University of Technology, Sydney, and Russell Belk at the Schulich School of Business, York University, Toronto, without whom the work would have been less scientifically rigorous and certainly less interesting. In addition, individuals such as Joachim Schwalbach and Anja Schwerk played a part in helping our thinking and giving us outlets through involvement with their conferences in Berlin and a home at Humboldt University. Grahame Dowling and various colleagues played a part in reading many drafts of the chapters and related materials, honing our thinking and making sure that we did not digress too far from the important points. Many individual research assistants were involved at different stages: Thomas Birtchnell, Carolyn Dorrian, Omer Konacki, Christina Li, Maria Mikirtumova, Sandra Peter, Michal Ulrych, and Verena Vellmer. Michael McGee, Steve Cook, and Joelle Baudet from Future and Simple provided programming support and were also involved in the making of the documentary film *The Social Construction of Consumption*, by Belk, Devinney, and Eckhardt. A copy of this documentary is included with the book. Anne Fitzsimmons, Pauline Olive, Fran Prior, and Linda Camilleri were there to keep the administration working, and also keep the administration off our backs (and warn us about money!). Rachael Weiss provided a much-needed literary and human addition to our academic prose. Paula Parish and the team at Cambridge University Press were very patient, as one must be, with academic writers such as us, who have a very different perception of time and deadlines. We would also be remiss if we did not mention the – literally – thousands of academic, student, and corporate colleagues who sparked our interest and contested our thinking at what has amounted to over 100 presentations given on this research in the last ten years. There are also the many individuals who helped with this work by simply answering our questions, being interviewed by us, and being involved in our experiments.

As will be evident, it is also the case that it is impossible to conduct the sort of research exhibited here without financial and other support. The project began with a small grant from the Research Grants Council of Hong Kong and City University, Hong Kong. Over the years we have received generous financial support from the Discovery program of the Australian Research Council, which funded the bulk of the work and continues to fund it today. In addition, the Australian Graduate School of Management and its Centre for Corporate Change provided infrastructure and people that allowed the projects to run smoothly. Timothy Devinney was also supported by the Alexander von Humboldt Foundation, which named him a Research Awardee in

2008 and allowed him to spend time in Germany at Humboldt University working on extensions of the project, and the Rockefeller Foundation, which gave him release to work on the early stages of the book and related projects at its Bellagio Center in Italy. He has special memories of his time there and the gracious care of Ms Pilar Palacia and her team.

Finally, our greatest thanks go to our families, without whom any such project is impossible and to whom we dedicate the volume.

Timothy M. Devinney, Sydney
Pat Auger, Melbourne
Giana M. Eckhardt, Boston

1 | *The appeal and reality of ethical consumerism*

What a man believes upon grossly insufficient evidence is an index into his desires – desires of which he himself is often unconscious. If a man is offered a fact which goes against his instincts, he will scrutinize it closely, and unless the evidence is overwhelming, he will refuse to believe it. If, on the other hand, he is offered something which affords a reason for acting in accordance to his instincts, he will accept it even on the slightest evidence. The origin of myths is explained in this way.

Bertrand Russell

The great enemy of the truth is very often not the lie – deliberate, contrived and dishonest – but the myth – persistent, persuasive and unrealistic.

John F. Kennedy

The ethical consumer and myth

The notion of ethical consumers has evolved over the last twenty-five or more years from an almost exclusive focus on environmental issues to a concept that incorporates matters of conscience more broadly, only to return to its "green" roots with the recent concerns about global climate change. During this same period we have witnessed a growing debate about the importance of ethical consumerism and, in particular, the impact that large-scale strategies have on consumer awareness and spending. Star-spangled initiatives such as Project Red – an initiative launched in 2006, spearheaded by U2's Bono and US politician Bobby Shriver, in which major brands such as Gap and Giorgio Armani sub-brand some of their products with the Red label and donate the proceeds to AIDS funds – are a direct assault on large companies' social responsibilities in manufacturing, retailing, and advertising and purport to satisfy a huge public desire for ethical products.

Such high-profile activities hide the effectiveness and limited uptake of products with ethical or social dimensions, leaving many company executives expressing private uncertainty about the financial efficacy of ethical consumerism and the role of their customers in sharing obligations to social ethics. Although corporations and policy makers are bombarded with international surveys purporting to show that average consumers do indeed demand ethical products, lingering doubts remain as survey radicals seem to turn into economic conservatives at the checkout. In the case of Project Red, Stephan Shakespeare, chief executive officer (CEO) of YouGov, a British market research firm, notes that "[w]hen we look at the impact of Project Red on these so-called superbrands . . . the scores are as flat as a pancake and the British public hasn't reacted in the manner that these companies, at least in private, would have hoped for. . . [There exists a level of consumer apathy] towards Project Red, which even Bono can't overcome." The reality is that initiatives such as Project Red are subject to higher failure rates than normal marketing activities, because they lack distinctive ownership that ensures that the campaign lasts beyond its initial hype.

Much of the difficulty in understanding the complexity of ethical consumerism resides in the failure to grasp more clearly and consistently what it is that motivates individuals socio-politically and how it is that the purchasing context operates to reveal or not reveal the wants, desires, values, constraints, beliefs, and mindset of the individual doing the purchasing. Although we know a considerable amount about political behavior in a voting or activist context, and consumer behavior in a functional or emotive product and service situation, how consumer behavior models operate in a socio-political environment embodied by notions of the ethical consumer is unclear and under-researched (Cotte, 2009). Although Harrison, Newholm, and Shaw's *The Ethical Consumer* (2005) focuses on small numbers of committed ethical consumers – outlining their behavior, discourses, and narratives so as to understand the effectiveness of their actions in the marketplace – their perspective is limited to "believers." Our concern is to make sense of a much wider range of consumers, some of whom act "ethically" while others do not.

Following on from this – and it certainly is an oversimplification – those interested in ethical consumerism put considerable faith in the belief that an individual's vaguely construed intentions say a lot about his/her specific actions and that broad generalizations can be made about specific versus general social stances. This belief is found in the quite considerable number of surveys professing to show that individuals will sacrifice themselves and their wallets to a higher cause and that individuals care about many complex social causes. What is surprising is that such a belief continues to be held quite passionately despite the continual failure of such surveys to predict behavior other than in the most isolated of circumstances. Despite the hype, the reality is that most "ethical" products have occupied niche market positions except in the few circumstances in which major multinational corporations have taken on the cause and marketed these products broadly and as replacements for conventional offerings, such as Unilever and Ben & Jerry's (Hays, 2000; Austin and Quinn, 2007) or Starbucks and Fairtrade coffee (Argenti, 2004).

An allied concern arises from the broad generalizations made on the basis of specific revealed behavior that represents a broad and complex set of motivations and causes. For example, the extent to which the Fair Trade movement is driven by consumer demand is unclear despite its specific successes. Beyond the United Kingdom, the movement is relatively limited except where it can generate corporate acquiescence. Hence, if Starbucks or Caribou Coffee switch to more Fairtrade sourcing, this does not imply anything about consumer desires, because the corporation is making the choice and not the individual (other than the consumer not revolting at the action). At the other extreme, it can be argued that the fact that shops do not promote labor-friendly athletic shoes does not imply that there is not a market for such products, just that the suppliers have made the choice not to promote such a product and the suppliers control the product offerings in the distribution chain.

A related issue is the degree to which one can generalize from a niche market to a mass market. For example, the Toyota Prius has been a successful engineering and marketing achievement, but it is hardly the most fuel-efficient or highest-quality hybrid automobile available. However, its first-to-market position has made it quite successful, with a niche willing to sacrifice design and performance for fuel efficiency. Its early adopters mainly switched from other small vehicles, not mass-market mid-size and large vehicles. However, its current model, which is now moving into the mass market, in which it must appeal to a broader demand segment, reveals compromises that are aimed at appealing to more median consumer desires: better build and design, a larger petrol engine, and more engine noise (which gives the sensation of performance). The reality now is that the "green" Prius is no more environmentally friendly than many small diesel offerings on the market.

It would be disingenuous simply to argue that ethical consumerism is an oxymoron motivated by belief and hope and antithetical to reality and experience; or that it is the purview of "do-gooders" attempting to get us to act as they wish, rather than as we are habitually programmed to behave. It is our argument, and the one that we hope to support through the research presented in this book, that the notion of the ethical consumer is little more than a myth that belies the reality of individual behavior, ethical and otherwise.

To appreciate our viewpoint it is important first to understand what we mean when we say that the ethical consumer is a myth. Mythologies permeate consumer culture, and are expropriated by both marketers and consumers to serve ideological purposes (Thompson, 2004). We can think of two definitions of a myth. Using Bascom's (1965) definition of myths as "tales believed as true, usually sacred, set in the distant past or other worlds or parts of the world, and with extra-human, inhuman, or heroic characters," we can argue that the ethical consumer is a "heroic" character operating in a reality that is not our own but one that is believed to be true. The ethical consumer is a myth in its form of a heroic but uniquely unattainable role model. Like many mythical heroes, the ethical consumer is perhaps doomed to fail despite the nobility of the cause. Radin's (1950) and Malinowski's (1992) more functional definition argues that myths serve as charters for social action and are there to encourage a specific *Weltanschauung* and proper activity within a society. According to this interpretation, the ethical consumer is a myth in that s/he is an idealization of what consumers should be doing to be proper members of society. Unlike the unattainable hero, this ethical consumer is the ideal to which we can aspire, and represents a level of behavior that we can achieve.

Second, it is also important to ask whether the notion of an "ethical" consumer is the correct specification for what we really mean when we talk about supposedly "ethical" purchasing behavior. The *Oxford English Dictionary* defines ethical as: (1) relating to moral principles; (2) morally correct. The problem with even referring to ethical consumerism is seen by perusing a few sites promoting such activity and seeing how many "ethical" consumer organizations address seemingly odd mixtures of activities under the rubric of correct behavior. For example, the site ethical.org.au considers purchasing "Made in China" products a reflection of negative corporate behavior (as well as donations to the US Republican Party) – a fact that can be construed as a value judgment as opposed to a well-defined, generally recognized moral principle. Linking consumerism to ethics, with its moral connotations of absolute right and wrong, is difficult to justify in today's world, where globalization implies natural conflicts between the standards of societies. Indeed, the ethnographic research we discuss in Chapter 5 revealed great diversity in terms of which consumption activities were considered ethical and which were not. Ambrose Bierce (1911) stated the conflict nicely in his definition of "moral" in *The Devil's Dictionary*:

Moral, adj. Conforming to a local and mutable standard of right. Having the quality of general expediency.

It is sayd there be a raunge of mountaynes in the Easte, on one syde of the which certayn conducts are immorall, yet on the other syde they are holden in good esteeme; wherebye the mountayneer is much conveenyenced, for it is given to him to goe downe eyther way and act as it shall suite his moode, withouten offence.

Gooke's Meditations

Hence, we follow Barthes' (1972) conceptualization of societal myths as existing to reproduce ideologies. The ethical consumer is a myth in three senses. First, it represents a role model that is fictional. Although the model represented may be noble, investment in its attainment is neither rational nor sensible on the part of a large segment of the society. It is by definition unique and, hence, uncommon. Second, and more positive in orientation, it is mythical in the sense that it represents idealizations that open to contestation the existing, flawed, behavior of members of the society. In this sense, it is the moral standard that creates the guilt surrounding our typical self-interested behavior. Third, it represents a role model wherein the morality of the model itself is subject to contestation. Ethical consumers stand as reminders to us of the short-sighted nature of our worship of the false gods created by multinational corporations. However, the traditionally anti-corporatist and fringe nature of many ethical consumer campaigns begs the question of whether society would accept the replacement of existing norms with those of groups at the extreme.

In the most general sense, we are putting onto the table the hypothesis that the ethical consumer is a myth in that it is a characterization that is false, despite the fact that it serves a communicative function for those that present it as a model of idealized behavior. In this sense, we are juxtaposing the "ethical" consumer as a myth that is believed as a constructivist epistemological phenomenon (and hence non-testable) against an ontological notion of whether such a creature as an "ethical" consumer exists (which is testable).

It should be clear from the positioning of our thesis that we view the notion of the "ethical" consumer with suspicion, and our research will reveal the evidence behind this skepticism. However, it would be wrong of us to argue that all consumers are little more than hedonistic automatons worshipping at the altar of the checkout line. If we are arguing that the traditional conceptualization of the ethical consumer is simplistic and flawed empirically, it would be foolish of us not to back up our statements empirically and to be clear as to the specific domain we are discussing. It is important therefore to understand what it is that we are saying and what it is that we are not saying.

First, we are not saying that individuals do not bring values and beliefs into the purchasing context. However, we will contend that these values and beliefs are not so immutable as to be more than one of many contributors to the individual's consumption decision. To see the logic of this one has only to look at what is known as the Good Samaritan Experiment (Darley and Batson, 1973). In this experiment, students studying to be priests at a theological seminary were asked to come to the university to give a lecture to students on the Parable of the Good Samaritan. When they arrived to give their lecture, the researcher indicated that the lecture had been moved to another building and that the theologians had either five minutes, fifteen minutes or thirty minutes to get to the new location. As each theologian entered the building to give his/her lecture an actor feigned illness and collapsed in the doorway. The research question was how many of the theologians on their way to give a lecture on the Good Samaritan stopped (and hence were a living example of the parable). The results were astonishing, in that the single biggest determinant of what the theologians did was how much time they had to get to the lecture. Their Samaritan-esque nature was driven not by their character, or beliefs, or values but by the simple fact of whether or not they faced time pressure. According to Darley and Batson (1973, p. 107):

A person not in a hurry may stop and offer help to a person in distress. A person in a hurry is likely to keep going. Ironically, he is likely to keep going even if he is hurrying to speak on the parable of the Good Samaritan, thus inadvertently confirming the point of the parable. Indeed, on several occasions, a seminary student ... literally stepped over the victim as he hurried on his way! It is hard to think of a context in which norms concerning helping those in distress are more salient than for a person thinking about the Good Samaritan, and yet it did not significantly increase helping behavior.

Second, we do not argue that there are individuals who behave according to their values and norms independently of the context in which they find themselves. The question is how pervasive this behavior is and whether it is representative of a unique type of individual – i.e. our mythical consumer hero. Again, we can look to classical psychological experiments to find an analogy. In the Stanford Prison Experiment, conducted in 1971 (Zimbardo, 2007), otherwise normal individuals were randomly assigned to the roles of guards or prisoners in an experimental prison in the basement of the Stanford University psychology department. Within a very short period of time the prisoners began acting submissively, while the guards began abusing prisoners both physically and psychologically. However, what Zimbardo and his team found was that approximately 10 percent of the prisoners and guards refused to play according to the assigned role (a number found in repeats of the experiment). In the guards' case, they failed to obey orders and treated the prisoners leniently and with respect despite being ostracized by their fellow guards. In the prisoners' case, they revolted both violently and non-violently (e.g. through hunger strikes), despite the punishment inflicted (such as solitary confinement or the removal of privileges for them and other inmates). Nothing predicted who these "rebels" would be, because the role assignments were totally random and all the subjects were screened to be "average" on standard batteries of psychological profiles.

Third, we argue (and show) that individuals exist who do take into account the social aspects of the products purchased but do so very specifically. This, too, is consistent with existing research in other areas, particularly in experimental economics, which shows that individuals act with aspects of social intent and take into account the welfare of others, even when there is no apparent return from that behavior (e.g. Levitt and List, 2007). However, we will show that the individuals we study make their choices in a manner that has little to do with general notions of ethical consumerism as espoused in normative academic research and the popular press, or research promoted by civil society organizations. Moreover, contrary to much research that has attempted to typecast the ethical consumer demographically, we find little difference between people who take into consideration social aspects of products and those who do not. Simplistic notions about gender, education, income, culture, domicile, and so on prove unfounded. Additionally, we show that individuals do not behave with general ethical intent but with very specific choices related to the products at hand. In other words, knowing that someone is sensitive to child labor does not provide evidence that s/he will care disproportionately about any other non-labor cause.

Fourth, these behaviors are only very weakly related to culture and domicile. It has commonly been assumed that Europeans, with more of a tradition of social democracy, are more socially aware. However, there is only weak support for this. Similarly, it is naturally assumed that individuals from emerging market countries are significantly less sensitive to social issues, being more concerned about economic development. Again, the reality is more complex. Our work reveals that the rationalization of behavior and an understanding of the phenomena being studied are quite culturally informed, but that the behavior is remarkably similar. The implication is that, although people seem to behave similarly, their understanding of their own behavior and their rationalization for inaction is quite culturally embedded.

Fifth, we show that a major issue with much of the research in this field is that it is either too general or too specific. In the first place, there is a tendency toward broad statements about behavior that belie the contingent decisions that consumers are making. As noted above, and is clear from much psychological research, the context is very important, if not overwhelming, in determining behavior. At the opposite extreme, and again a contingency argument, is the problem found in much social science: that studies of specific narrow phenomena are representative only of the circumstances examined. In the case of ethical consumerism, much of the problem arises in how one hides the subject of the investigation in a manner that does not lead to socially influenced responses. To address these two issues together we utilize a generalized experimental polling approach that allows us to get a snapshot of social preference orderings of large samples of individuals. What this reveals is the complexity of individual trade-offs of social causes. This is important when one considers the overgeneralization problem in a broader context. Individuals will care about many things that are part of the "ethical" agenda – Third World debt, child labor, pollution, animal welfare, and so on – but must also trade these off against more mundane issues that are generally more salient and immediate – children's schooling, healthcare, mortgages, interest rates, and so on. The question then becomes one of asking: "How important is the ethical issue when compared to other basic issues?" This answer is critical in a world where trade-offs are not free and social agendas are in competition.

Overall, these five points bring to the fore our concern with overly simplistic characterizations of human behavior in the context in which individuals' day-to-day purchasing behavior joins with the socio-political. We argue for, and support with research findings, the position that the ethical consumer is a myth, an idealized fiction supported by neither theory nor fact. However, our goal is not to destroy the myth as a myth but to bring science to bear on those parts of the myth that can be considered representative of a truth about human behavior, and, in so doing, guide corporate and public policy in an informed way.

Ethical consumerism versus consumer social responsibility

It is our contention that the notion of ethical consumerism is too broad in its definition, too loose in its operationalization, and too moralistic in its stance to be anything other than a myth. However, it should also be clear that we are not arguing that individuals will not, when facing contexts and prices, reveal social preferences through their consumption behavior – something that is fundamentally an empirical issue subject to scientific testing. Hence, from our perspective, the label "ethical" consumerism carries mythological baggage that needs to be discarded.

To distinguish clearly between our conception of socio-political purchasing and that applied more generally in the business ethics literature, we argue that the focus should not be on "ethical" consumerism but on "social" consumerism, or what we have coined in prior work as consumer social responsibility (C_NSR) (Devinney *et al.*, 2006). In its broadest form, C_NSR can be defined as the conscious and deliberate choice to make certain consumption choices based on personal and moral beliefs. It includes two basic components: (1) a "social" component, relating to the underlying importance of the non-traditional and social components of a company's products and business processes; and (2) a "consumerism" component, which implies that the preferences and desires of consumer segments are partially responsible for the increasing influence of social factors.

C_NSR shows up in three ways, the first two of which reflect the "social" while the last embodies the "consumerism."

(1) Expressed activity with respect to specific causes – such as donations or willingness to be involved in protests and boycotts. We call these revealed social preferences, as they relate to behavioral activities linked to values and beliefs.
(2) Expressed opinions in surveys or other forms of market research. We call these stated social preferences, as they may have no relationship to specific behavior.
(3) Expressed activity in terms of purchasing or non-purchasing behavior.

The relevance of (1) can be seen in highly publicized developments such as the increasing number of large-scale protests directed at multinational corporations and international organizations. In fact, demonstrators have often become the main focus of news reports during large-scale meetings, such as those of the World Trade Organization (WTO), World Bank, International Monetary Fund (IMF), G8, United Nations (UN), and World Economic Forum. The meeting of the World Bank in Hong Kong in December 2005 offers a perfect example. Most of the news reports did not focus on the substantive issues discussed at the meetings but on the frequent clashes between anti-globalization protesters and the Hong Kong police. Who can forget the sight of a large number of South Korean farmers jumping into the polluted waters of Hong Kong harbor in protest against globalization initiatives?

(2) is the most common, and perhaps the most dubious, means by which C_NSR is operationalized. If one is to believe studies of ethical consumerism based on opinion polls and surveys, consumers are giving increasing consideration to the ethical components of products and business processes, and these concerns have financial implications for the businesses involved. A 2005 Global Market Insite (GMI) poll across a wide range of countries, including the United States, United Kingdom, India, Australia, Canada, and countries throughout Europe, found that 54 percent of consumers would be prepared to pay more for organic, environmentally friendly or Fairtrade products. In each country, the majority were positive to ethical consumerism.[1] A large-scale survey by Market & Opinion Research International (MORI) found that over one-third of consumers in the United Kingdom were seriously concerned with ethical issues. The same survey also suggested that the potential for ethical products could be as high as 30 percent of UK consumer markets.[2]

(3) can be seen in the low levels of purchases of "ethical" goods, in contrast to the enthusiasm shown in (2). For example, although consumer activism and pressure from non-governmental organizations (NGOs) led to Starbucks prominently displaying and selling Fairtrade coffee, the sales levels have been much lower than expected and demand has remained relatively flat since its introduction in 2001. Indeed, our own casual empiricism at local coffee outlets indicated that not a single barista could recall a customer either asking for Fairtrade coffee or complaining that it was not available. Despite the enthusiasm shown for "Fairtrade activities," such products rarely account for anything but a minuscule percentage of the market, normally 1 percent to 2 percent, and when they do account for more market share it is generally due to the activities of retailers rather than consumers. Further lack of ethical behavior in the marketplace can also be seen by the increasingly high levels of counterfeit goods purchased around the world, whether they are pirated DVDs or fake Louis Vuitton handbags. For example, *The Economist* (2006) has reported that the sale of pirated DVDs in China deprived US filmmakers of approximately $2.7 billion in 2005, a massive amount compared to the $250 million or so taken in total box-office receipts in the country.

When C_NSR is measured by methods (1) and (2), a very positive picture of consumer involvement in ethical issues emerges. It is easy to envision noble protesters and up to a half of the general population as concerned and motivated consumers, ready to change behaviors and brands to support the causes they endorse. However, when C_NSR is measured using the metric of behavior, as in (3), a starkly different picture appears – one that suggests that consumers are not willing to put their money where their mouths are. As noted by one Australian in the ethnographic component of our research, "Morals stop at the pocketbook. People may say they care, but they will always buy the cheaper brand." A Spanish respondent in the same study echoed this assessment: "We comment when we see these programs on TV, we think what a shame, what are they doing, they're exploiting people. And we say we shouldn't buy them. And then we go and buy them anyway. It's really very sad."

Moving from ethical consumer to C_NSR

How can we make sense of this disconnect? We contend that, to understand this seemingly dissonant reaction, C_NSR must be understood as one component of the complex consumer decision-making process and an imperfect measurement process. Only in this way can we develop effective and meaningful approaches that engage the potentially social consumer.

This has a number of implications, which we will discuss, and provide supporting evidence for, throughout the book. First, the notion we are espousing of $C_N SR$ does not have a de facto moral or ethical component. By this we mean that $C_N SR$ allows for the fact that individuals account for non-functional aspects of products in their assessment of the value and satisfaction they receive from consumption, but that the moral or ethical components of this are neutral. In other words, the moral or ethical "value" aspects of the product are determined by individuals and their society and not by any larger "authority." For example, although we might personally believe that child labor or animal testing is bad, we do not make any statement about this in the characterization of "ethics." Our concern is whether (1) the individual makes such a stance and (2) whether s/he behaves in accordance with that stance when there is a price for doing so.

Second, although we agree that creating the mythical ethical consumer has value to those who promote the activities embodied by the "hero" (and do not begrudge the fact that it is so promoted), we are very much concerned with the degree to which the characterization has any basis in reality. At one level this is uncomfortably inductivist. However, our goal is to aid in the influencing of individual, corporate, political, and societal decision making via repeated scientific inquiry. Promoting a myth may further a cause, in much the same way that it created cohesion in ancient societies, but it can be dangerous and costly socially and economically through its erroneous use as a justification for strategy and policy.

Finally, our inquiries reveal that $C_N SR$ has characteristics that are unique and demand more rigorous empirical inquiry. In other words, many standard interview and survey approaches common in the commercial and academic literature appear to lose their validity when applied to the intersection of socio-political and individual consumption behavior. This arises not only because individuals respond in ways that are socially expected but also because the behavioral models being assumed by the investigators potentially underestimate the complexity of the decision-making process. By utilizing more incentive-compatible research instruments, plus accounting for the natural trade-offs that occur in the consumption context, we are – hopefully – better able to see and understand the consumer's logic and actual behavior.

In what follows we first walk through two conceptual anchors for thinking about ethical consumerism and social consumption behavior. In Chapter 2 we take a macro-perspective by focusing on the firm and asking how corporate social responsibility and consumer social responsibility sit within the context of the corporation. This is important, as most studies of ethical consumerism abstract from how it relates to the firm's incentives and the equilibrium characteristics of markets. In Chapter 3 we discuss the nature of individual and consumer decision making and behavior. This is a micro-perspective that is more in line with extant discussions of ethical consumption seen in the academic literature and the press, and one that allows us to begin to link the empirical work that follows to a general conceptual framework of decision making.

Chapters 4 and 5 bring the conceptual discussion of social consumption to life by summarizing a series of quantitative and qualitative studies conducted to answer two very basic questions. (1) To what extent do individuals take into account the social characteristics of products they purchase? (2) How do these individuals rationalize their consumption, particularly when it is at odds with their stated beliefs? Chapter 4, which covers the quantitative and experimental research, additionally examines: (3) the relationship between individuals' survey-based stated beliefs and intentions and their preferences as revealed through experiments; and (4) the degree to which a social consumption segment of consumers can be discovered and characterized. Chapter 5 discusses research based on video ethnography (the results of which can be seen in the documentary included with the book), and helps to address the degree to which we can enhance our understanding of the lack of social consumption behavior by looking more deeply at the individual in a more realistic setting. Together, these chapters present a holistic picture of the individual in the consumer persona.

Chapter 6 takes a mixture of macro and micro approaches to open a discussion on the role of the individual as both consumer and citizen. Discussions of ethical consumption invariably imply that the individual has a socio-political role to play when engaging in consumption yet few, if any, of these debates attempt to broaden the context of social consumption empirically by examining the wider range of concerns that impinge on the individual's daily life. In Chapter 6, we show that the results of Chapters 4 and 5 have something to say about a wider range of societal concerns and that, by broadening our focus, we can begin to understand some of the contradictions that have bedeviled the ethical consumerism literature. Indeed, we show that, rather than contradictions, we find a great degree of consistency between what individuals do as consumers and what they do as citizens.

Finally, in Chapter 7, we pull together the conceptual and empirical discussions to generate normative conclusions about what we can do to enhance social consumption in a meaningful and socially legitimate manner. The first step is recognizing the degree to which the "ethical" consumer is a mythological figure – one that does not, and cannot, exist in its idealized form but has enough human-like features for us to be deluded into believing that it is real because we need it for our salvation. The ethical consumer is a modern-day Prester John,[3] who, in speaking of his realm, notes: "With us, no one lies, for he who speaks a lie is thenceforth regarded as dead – he is no more thought of or honored by us. No vice is tolerated by us."

Our conclusion is a simple one. We can accept human intent and behavior for what it is but work to change it, or we can idealize intention and behavior and be bitterly disappointed when we and our peers do not live up to the espoused standards. We humans are, according to Triandis (2009), "cognitively simple self-deceivers . . . creatures of natural processes," who fail to take the perspective of science and are subject to collective and self-deception. In his case, deceptions are beliefs that have "no basis in reality, such as religions," and lead to coercion, conflicts, and aggression. Our argument is that collective and self-deception can include the noble, such as "we should all be considering our social footprint when consuming." Such deceptions are, moreover, dangerous despite their nobility, because they substitute faith and social acceptance for science, and are also based on coercion rather than reason and understanding in a democratic discourse. As noted by Triandis (2009, p. 207):

Missionaries . . . want to convert people with a different religion to their own religion. If they succeed they feel that their religion must be valid because others agree with it. This is a satisfying self-deception, but it creates unnecessary conflict, and merely involves switching systems of self-deception.

Our goal is not to destroy the nobility embodied in the myth of the ethical consumer but to replace the divisive anti-consumer, anti-corporatist rhetoric associated with the debate over social consumption with a sensible scientific understanding of consumption behavior in a social context. As noted by Richard Dawkins (1995), "Scientific beliefs are supported by evidence... Myths and faiths are not." Only through a deep and contested evaluation of the intersection of the economic, social and political aspects of consumption can we protect ourselves from blindly following the myth.

2 | *Social consumerism in the context of corporate responsibility*

Neither the entrepreneurs nor the farmers nor the capitalists determine what has to be produced. The consumers do that. If a businessman does not strictly obey the orders of the public as they are conveyed to him by the structure of market prices, he suffers losses, he goes bankrupt, and is thus removed from his eminent position at the helm. Other men who did better in satisfying the demand of the consumers replace him.

Ludwig von Mises

Since the governments are in the pockets of businesses, who's going to control this most powerful institution? Business is more powerful than politics, and it's more powerful than religion. So it's going to have to be the vigilante consumer.

Anita Roddick

Social consumerism and firm profitability

It is important to recognize, first and foremost, that social consumerism exists in conjunction with corporate activity; that corporate activity can provide consumers with the context in which they can reveal values, desires, and needs but can also restrict choice (either purposefully or otherwise) by putting products and services into the market that either possess specific social components or do not. In addition, it reflects whether the corporation is operating reactively and views consumers as motivators driving it to act, or whether it is the consumers who are acting reactively to the context that the corporation is creating.

One can get into a long discussion about what corporate social responsibility (CSR) is and what motivates corporations to act according to any specific or vague social goals. We will avoid this discussion and look simply at the major factors that play into the profit motive of the corporation. We recognize that many individuals and academics who argue for more corporate social responsibility will contest the role that profitability *should* play as the core operational criterion for firm performance. However, we leave this to one side, except to note that our concern is with the positive goal of understanding social consumption, not in generating normative reasons for why it should be promoted.

Our focus in what follows is compartmentalized around the simple, well-understood definition of economic profitability. We then discuss how the civil society components of purchasing can influence, and be incorporated into, this thinking. Not only does this discussion have broad repercussions for the practical image of "ethical" consumerism, it also has very direct and important implications for the empirical measurement of the extent to which individuals take into account social components of products and services.

Economic profit

If we accept the notion that firms are driven by an economic profit motive, whereby economic rents are generated from the resources under the firm's control and over which it has claims, and consumers seek to maximize the utility or satisfaction from their choices, it follows that two sorts of value are of relevance. There is, first, the *economic profit*, or *producer surplus*, accruing to the firm, which is the difference between the price paid by the customer and the next-best-use value of the resources necessary to produce the product:

$$\text{Economic profit}_{\text{Firm}}$$
$$= \text{Price} - \text{Cost of the resources in their next best use} \quad (2.1)$$

where the cost of the resources in their next best use accounts for the market for the resources (if one exists), or what those resources could command in another external or internal use.

There is, second, the *customer value*, or *consumer surplus*, that the individual receives from purchasing the product. This is represented by the demand, or the price the individual is willing to pay for each unit of the product, less the price s/he must pay to receive the product:

$$\text{Consumer surplus}_{\text{Individual}} = \text{Willingness to pay} - \text{Price} \quad (2.2)$$

In traditional economic models, the willingness to pay (WTP) represents the absolute value, from a utility standpoint expressed in dollar terms, that the individual gets from the having and/or using of the product or service. When one hears the term "customer or (consumer) value," it is normally the WTP to which the speaker is referring.

Willingness to pay and C_NSR

What is critical to understand at this juncture is that the economic model of value just given is one that implies separation of the generation of the producer surplus and the consumer surplus. In other words, total value to the society is simply the sum of the consumer and producer surpluses, and the factors that influence the creation of the product are not considered as part of the consumers' value determination process. However, this need not be the case, and work in the field of welfare economics focuses on the degree to which the distribution of value is (1) fair in a distributive sense (meaning that the right people get the right share of the value) and (2) that the prices received for the resources used in the production of the product or service are economically correct (meaning that all externalities are accounted for and the price truly reflects the next best use of the resources) (see, for example, Atkinson and Stiglitz, 1980, and Sen, 1997).

From our point of view, we are not concerned at this point about whether or not externalities exist, or that any specific set of claims by stakeholders or other third parties are dealt with fairly, but with whether or not individuals in their role as consumers are prepared to act upon this perceived unfairness or the externalities that exist, or are sufficiently willing to pay for production and other processes that meet their idealized notions of how their products are produced.

It is from this perspective that it becomes clear that social consumerism implies, by definition, that there is no such independence between the value received from the product or service and the means by which the product or service is produced. In other words, the process by which value is created is, by itself, a component of the individual's valuation equation. This has two components that are frequently muddled together: a *functional* component and a *true social value* component. The confounding of these two mechanisms leads to a significant overstatement of the extent and impact of social consumerism, and frustration on the part of those attempting to understand the phenomenon of C_NSR.

First, there is value that the consumer receives from the actual production process itself, which is independent of whether that production process is good or bad, but which reflects other functional components of value. In other words, the customer gets value from knowledge of the fact that the product is produced in a specific manner because this is related directly or indirectly to the functional components of the product or service that matter to him/her. This has two sub-components.

There is the *signal value* of the process used to create the product or service. In essence, knowledge of the process by which a product or service was created is not valuable in and of itself but because it serves as an indicator about a functional component of the product that the customer values. For example, in some of our own pilot research we discovered that many consumers believed that Fairtrade coffee was somehow of higher quality, despite the fact that this is not the case (it is simply sourced differently). Similarly, it is generally commonly held that organic food is "healthier" or "tastier," when the scientific evidence is decidedly mixed as to the veracity of these claims. In these cases there is no value in Fairtrade or organic claims except insofar as they provide information about something that the individual values – in this case the quality of the product being purchased. The same would be true of "handcrafted" watches, or "German-engineered" automobiles, or brand names.

There is, next, the *reputational or image signifier value* from the act of purchasing. For example, would we consider a Hollywood actor who purchases a Toyota Prius to drive to the Academy Awards ceremony as a socially responsible consumer? Our answer would be "No" (or, certainly, "Not necessarily"), as the Prius is being used to enhance and signal something that has functional value to the actor: his/her public image. The same would be the case for any status good for which there is positive value in being associated with the group that owns that specific product. For example, over 50 percent of Prius purchasers say that buying a hybrid says something about them. What is interesting is that this is a fact that is specific to the Prius and does not seem to spill over to other hybrid brands (a number of which have been discontinued due to slack demand). Hence, it is the buying of the Prius itself, and not a hybrid per se, that is the motivating factor – something that can call into question whether the motivator is purely value-driven, or driven largely by image. Indeed, this aspect of the Prius's reputation has been the subject of spoof and parody: the cartoon series *South Park* had an episode in which the purchasing of "Pious" automobiles caused an outbreak of "smug" that nearly destroyed South Park (Maynard, 2007).

What this highlights is how branding can have an image signifier value, since specific stereotypes exist that are used to characterize or vilify those who appear in public sporting the logo of their purchases. The personality of the individual and the personality of the brand can be thought of as coexisting (Aaker, 1997; Freling and Forbes, 2005). This can, of course, be related to a consumer's social credentials, but one must be careful: what might appear to be an obvious reflection of fundamental values might equally or more strongly be an expression of that person's ego and image in a more general social sense.

Second, there is the *pure social value* that the consumer gets because of the fact that s/he attaches worth to aspects of the production process independent of any signal or reputational value. This arises because the individual gets true utility or satisfaction from the specific aspects of production *independent of whether they make the product or service functionally better or reveal something the individual wants revealed to the public*. In other words, the pure social value has no direct functional or use value and is valued as a social, and not a product-related, outcome.

It is this aspect that is critical when we are discussing social consumerism, as value is being ascribed to what is obviously a non-functional aspect of the product or service. The value is absolutely and totally psychological and does not imply that any functional or social signaling aspects of the product come into play. Value is attributed only because the individual considers it "correct" or "good" to do so. In other words, would the Prius buyer buy a non-logoed version of the product or a version that is known to be eco-friendly only to the owner? One can think of the pure social value of a product or service in two ways.

First, it can be psychological but rational, in that the individual is acting according to a *thought-out* or habitual set of values and beliefs. It is this aspect that reflects "*core*" *social value*: something that is unlikely to vary dramatically from situation to situation, since the values and beliefs are well engrained in the individual's psyche. The fact that most households engage in the recycling of paper, plastic, and glass without the need for overt policing would be an example of a core social value.

However, there are also "*emotive*" *social values*, which are a response to an emotional appeal. They are more transitory, as they appear and disappear with the specific emotional appeal. An example of such emotive responses can be seen in the taboo experiments conducted by Tetlock *et al.* (2000). In these experiments, individuals were forced to make taboo trade-offs – in other words, sacrifice something that was sacred. The subjects were then given the opportunity to engage in "moral cleansing" by volunteering for a social cause. Those forced to make trade-offs on attributes they considered to be sacred were more likely to engage in moral cleansing by volunteering. As noted by Tetlock and his colleagues (p. 867): "People who function like intuitive scientists or economists in one setting can be quickly transformed into intuitive moralists-theologians when provoked by assaults on sacred values."

Žižek (2008) suggests that these types of emotive appeals are a part of the problem rather than the solution to social ills such as global poverty, increasing carbon footprints, and so on. By throwing a dollar in a collection box at Starbucks with a picture of a malnourished African child on it, or purchasing carbon offsets before taking a plane trip, consumers feel they have done their part toward helping social ills, and do not question their position in a global system that has led to systemic hunger in Africa or an excess of carbon emissions. In other words, by responding to emotive appeals that assuage socially induced guilt surrounding ethical issues consumers are supposed to care about, consumers are then less likely to engage in changing their behavior in meaningful ways that would have the potential to alter the global system that results in such imbalances. According to Žižek, emotive appeals are used by corporations so that they can continue their "complicity in economic exploitation."

This characterization has a number of rather profound implications for the whole notion of ethical consumerism. For example, it implies that the fact that consumers might purchase products that possess what ostensibly appear to be "green" or "ethical" characteristics is meaningless to the ethicality without further investigation as to the motives behind those purchases. The fact that an individual purchases items that save energy in the context of high energy prices can amount to nothing other than rational consumer choice that reflects realistic trade-offs. Someone who gives to a cause may be doing so because of an emotional appeal that has nothing at all to do with the veracity of the appeal to his/her fundamental values. The burden of proof as to the veracity of phenomena in the case of social consumerism is more onerous than with conventional consumption, since it must be shown that functional factors are not the true motivator for the supposed social influence on consumption. This is certainly no easy task given the complexity of

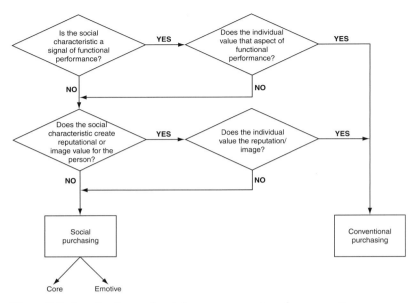

Figure 2.1 A stylized test of social versus conventional consumption

consumer decision making, but one that must be addressed (as we will do in Chapter 4).

What might a test of true social consumption be? Figure 2.1 provides a flow chart of an extreme test of whether consumption was truly representative of C_NSR or simply conventional consumption with a social veneer. By "extreme test" we are assuming that consumption is either social or conventional (which we are assuming, for the moment, is non-social). However, we are not distinguishing between whether social consumption is "core" or "emotive." There are two aspects to this test. First, does the consumption either imply a signal of functional value or represent the creation of functional value for the individual? If the answer is "Yes," then the second question is whether or not those aspects matter to that individual. In other words, unionization of the workforce might signal that the quality of work on some aspect of a product is better because standards of work are tighter. However, I may not care about that aspect of the product at all, and so the signal, while existing, has no value to me. I may "look for the union label," but doing so says nothing about my opinion about the ethics of unions.[1] Second, I might purchase a scooter or bicycle because I want to be able to travel to work and zip around town and in between cars quickly. My only concern is that I want to get from point A to point B as quickly as possible. However, people seeing me ride my bicycle or scooter immediately believe that I am concerned about the environment as I am using an "alternative" form of travel. Hence, although I might be perceived externally as a "green" commuter, this has no value to me, as I am concerned only with travel time.

This is, of course, an extreme test, as mentioned earlier, and one that belies the fact that purchasing may have both conventional and social components simultaneously. The reality, therefore, is that what we have is something akin to a funnel where the social component of any perceived consumption activity is left as all the more conventional aspects are winnowed out. In other words, what might be perceived naively to be a case of "ethical" consumerism will generally be much less so once the non-social aspects of the consumption are removed. This is particularly important when we get to the issue of empirical measurement. To ensure that the value of the social characteristics of products are correctly estimated, we must be careful to have removed as many as possible of the other confounding effects that could lead to the same behavior.

Economic profit in light of C_NSR

Returning to equations 2.1 and 2.2, we can now see the complexity that is added to the economic profitability when the social components of production are added. The consumer surplus received by the individual is now a function not only of the vector of functional attributes that make up the product or service $A = [a_1, a_2 \ldots a_N]$ but also of the vector of resources that make up the processes used to create the product or service $R = [r_1, r_2, \ldots r_M]$.[2,3] This is in addition to the fact that any product attribute mixture that is chosen by the firm will follow directly from the resources chosen for its production – that is, any product x with attribute mixture $A^x = [a_1^x, a_2^x, \ldots a_N^x]$ will imply a resource mix $R^x = [r_1^x, r_2^x, \ldots r_M^x]$. Hence, the WTP can now be considered as a function of A and R, WTP $= W(A, R)$, thereby expanding the demand curve outward or inward depending on the degree to which the production aspects engender a positive or negative utility on the part of the customer.

Taking a purely economic perspective, we can characterize the firm's choice as a maximization process in which it is choosing the mix of resources, $R^* = [r_1^*, r_2^*, \ldots r_M^*]$, and price (P^*) to generate a mixture of the levels of product attributes $A^* = [a_1^*, a_2^*, \ldots a_N^*]$ that maximizes its economic profit. The maximization also accounts for both the functional and non-functional aspects of demand:

$$\text{Max } [P - \text{Cost}(R = \{r_1, r_2, \ldots r_M\})] \qquad (2.3)$$
$$P^*, \ R^*$$

subject to

$$F(R^x = \{r_1^x, r_2^x, \ldots r_M^x\}) \Rightarrow A^x = \{a_1^x, a_2^x, \ldots a_N^x\} \qquad (2.4)$$
$$W(A^s, R^s) - P^s \geq 0 \qquad (2.5)$$

What all this means is that C_NSR will alter the firm's profitability equation, even when we are making rather limited assumptions about what C_NSR entails. In this case, we are assuming that consumers know what they want and that firms are reacting in a profit-maximizing way to the demands that they observe in the market.[4]

Firm and market reactions to social consumption

What is important about this prior discussion is that it allows us to address the question of what market reactions would be to the additional social components of demand and supply. We outline this in a stylized fashion in Figure 2.2.

Figure 2.2 shows four possible market scenarios. The first of these, panel (a), depicts the market with no social consumption at all and the independence of production and consumption. It serves as our baseline scenario. In this "neutral" market, demand is given by D_0, supply by S_0, and the equilibrium price and quantity by P_0 and Q_0. The producers' economic profit is PS_0, which is the area $P_0E_0T_0$. The consumers' surplus or value is CS_0, which is the area $P_0E_0V_0$.

Panel (b) presents a situation that is probably the most general case discussed in the popular and academic literature: negative social components of production (such as child labor or low wages) reduce demand (since consumers consider them "bad") and the alleviation of these negative social characteristics implies a higher cost of production. In this circumstance, demand shifts downward $(D_1 < D_0)$, as the quantity demanded at any price is lower, and supply shifts upward $(S_1 < S_0)$, as the price at which any quantity can be supplied is higher. We have

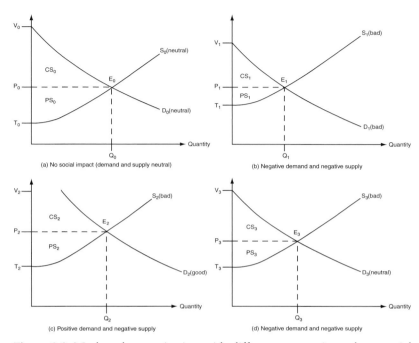

Figure 2.2 Market characterization with different assumptions about social consumption

stylistically structured panel (b) such that the price remains the same as in the neutral market case ($P_1 = P_0$). However, this is at the expense of a reduction in the quantity available ($Q_1 < Q_0$) and both the value received by consumers ($CS_1 < CS_0$) and the economic profits earned by the firms ($PS_1 < PS_0$).

At this point we have not said anything about the welfare of the individuals at the heart of the issue – e.g. the children or laborers. All our example shows is what the economic value potentially lost by the consumers and producers caused by taking into account the circumstances of these third parties amounts to $[(PS_0 + CS_0) - (PS_1 + CS_1)]$. This arises because consumers who value the social components will reduce their demand if those issues are not addressed (hence the $CS_0 - CS_1$ component), and producers would need to increase the costs to the tune of lost economic profits equal to ($PS_0 - PS_1$) to address the issue through the redistribution of value to the aggrieved third parties (such as through higher wages or social contributions). The implication is that social consumption reduces the size of the market, and the value derived therein, from circumstances in which producers and consumers remain blind to the social consequences of production.

Panel (b) is fairly representative of our mythical ethical consumer (who is sacrificing for the greater good) battling against corporations that must be coerced into putting social considerations above profits. From a consumer and producer perspective, it results in a lose-lose situation. However, the situation shown in panel (b) is unrealistic, as it is unlikely that both demand and supply would decline as dramatically as implied here. Producers would have an incentive to reduce their "bad" production activities, as this would mitigate the response of consumers to what they view as heinous behavior on the part of the corporation, freeing up value that can be capitalized as economic profit. Indeed, the increase in their costs would reflect this fact. Alternatively, it is also possible that consumers would view the new circumstance as one in which an additional positive attribute of the product was revealed, and this would enhance their willingness to pay. At the very least, the vast majority may not care at all and demand would be unaffected.

Panels (c) and (d) present examples of these more realistic states of affairs. In panel (c), consumer demand increases because consumers now ascribe value to the good social activities of the firms in the industry (hence $D_2 > D_0$). However, firms face an increase in their costs, because being more socially responsible is costly to them (hence $S_2 < S_0$). For simplicity, we have equated S_2 to S_1 and structured the demand increase such that the size of the market remains the same ($Q_2 = Q_0$). We immediately see one clear result: price increases to $P_2 > P_0$. However, there are two unclear results. There is no a priori expectation that consumer value and producer profit increased or decreased ($CS_2 <=> CS_0$, $PS_2 <=> PS_0$) and there is no conclusion as to the direction of total value. However, what is intriguing is that total value, and its consumer and firm components, can increase in this scenario, because the addition of the social attributes into the product mix reveals customer value that can now be capitalized in the price.

Panel (d) replicates the cost increase from panel (c) but looks at circumstances in which consumers place no value on the social aspects of production. This would be akin to a voluntary or involuntary regulatory solution whereby the removal of the offending production practices amounted to a tax on production, but consumers paid no attention and simply continued to purchase the product for its functional characteristics. What follows from this is also very clear: price increases ($P_3 > P_0$), quantity declines ($Q_3 < Q_0$), consumer value declines ($CS_3 < CS_0$), and producer profit declines ($PS_3 < PS_0$). As with a normal ad valorem tax, the tax receivers (in this case those affected by the prior "bad" production behavior) would benefit from a redistribution of value, and the costs would be borne directly by producers and consumers. Additionally, there would be a general deadweight loss associated with the reduction in the size of the market (also borne by consumers and producers, but indirectly).

We can take one very profound lesson from this technical analysis. If corporate social responsibility is imposed (either voluntarily or not), but there is no consumer social responsibility, in the sense that consumers ascribe value to the corporate actions, the idea of a win-win for consumers and producers is simply a non-starter. Obviously, the third parties who are exploited by the existing market circumstances would be made better off, but they would achieve this from a value-reducing redistribution rather than through the value created by revealing latent consumer preferences. Panels (b) and (d) show the implications of CSR without C_NSR, while panel (c) reveals how the willingness of consumers to assign value to the social components of products can release new value that can be capitalized and even lead to increased value for the society at large.

This is quite critical to the whole CSR debate and highlights the important and misunderstood role of the consumer. What we are saying is that CSR without C_NSR will imply redistribution of value but without the real possibility of the creation of new value! CSR without C_NSR will amount to little more than operational taxation and regulation. It will not fundamentally alter the nature of the value equation, as that equation will be driven, at its very core, by what consumers do and do not value.

Table 2.1 provides a summary of the value impact that also accounts for the aggrieved third parties – such as laborers, children, the environment, animals, and so on – that are the source of the social issue at hand. What can be seen is that even the impact on total social value can be considered to be suspect (although the distribution may no doubt be fairer socio-politically). If we define the third-party value as the value or utility of the aggrieved parties (or their representatives, as in the case of animals or children), we see three overall effects. First, in the neutral base case, the major issue is that third-party value is not capitalized and

Table 2.1 *Changes in value based on scenarios*

	Consumer value (CS)	Producer value (PS)	Third-party value (TPV)	Total societal value (TSV)
(a) Neutral base case	Capitalized $CS_0 \geq 0$	Capitalized $PS_0 \geq 0$	Not capitalized $TPV_0 <=> 0$	Partially capitalized $TSV_0 = CS_0 + PS_0 + TPV_0 <=> 0$
(b) Negative demand; negative supply	Value declines to $CS_1 < CS_0$	Value declines to $PS_1 < PS_0$	Value increases to $TPV_1 > TPV_0$	$TSV_1 <=> TSV_0$
(c) Positive demand; negative supply	Value most likely increases: $CS_2 \geq CS_0$	Value can increase or decrease: $PS_2 <=> PS_0$	Value increases to $TPV_2 > TPV_0$ with $TPV_2 > TPV_1$ likely	$TSV_2 <=> TSV_0$ with $TSV_2 > TSV_1$; $TSV_2 > TSV_0$ is also possible
(d) Neutral demand; negative supply	Value declines to $CS_3 < CS_0$	Value declines to $PS_3 < PS_0$	Value increases to $TPV_3 > TPV_0$	$TSV_3 <=> TSV_0$

hence not a complete part of the social value equation. There is, economically, a deadweight loss being imposed on the society for the failure to account for the production of value from a specific source. Second, once we begin to account for this value, its impact is quite complex. Only in one scenario (panel (c)) is there the possibility of value creation as well as value redistribution. Third, in all other cases, the welfare of the third parties is increased at the expense of consumers and producers.

Firms and the social consumption context

The next chapter focuses on the consumer decision-making aspects of social consumption, but it is important, before discussing this, to deal with the issue of the context created by corporations. Our technical discussion in the previous section of this chapter assumed that firms engaged in reactive behavior with respect to consumers. However, this is only a partially realistic assumption, and it would be naive to argue that the likes of Nestlé, Unilever, Sony, Toyota, Procter & Gamble, and Wal-Mart do little more than acquiesce to the will of the consumer, and that any specific percentage of consumer purchasing activity is rational in the purely economic sense. Indeed, the direct targeting of major corporations such as these by NGOs and social activists is done in the belief that corporations are a vector, if not the major vector, of social change (Vogel, 2005). Such actions would be rational only if these groups believed that corporations were in a position to dictate to, or influence, consumers.

For the purposes of our interest in social consumerism, we can look at two ways in which firms, both small and large, create a coevolving system of supply and demand. One of these, the degree to which firms innovate to satisfy needs, can be considered dominantly positive. The second, the extent to which firms manipulate the purchasing environment, has to be considered in a more negative and calculating light.

First, *firms engage in experimentation* for, and with, consumers. It is well understood that individual preferences are not predetermined phenomena that are immutable to both persuasion and opportunistic revelation, a fact that we address in some detail in the next chapter (see, for example, Aaker, 1999, Hodgson, 2003, and Gregg, Seibt, and Banaji, 2006). Experimentation aids in the revelation of consumer preferences to the firm and reveals to the consumer what is feasible in terms of product and service delivery. At the same time, weak or unknown preferences on the part of the consumer open them to being persuaded about what their preferences should be.

The *revelation of preferences* arises when individuals either do not know their preferences, or begin to form those preferences only in coevolution with the market and its products and services. An example of such coevolution can be seen in the cases of mobile phones, short message service (SMS), laptop PCs, and the portable music player (to name only a few). It is inconceivable to argue with any conviction that consumers had any conception of the technologies underlying these products or that they arose because consumers expressed a demand for them. The products arose because firms were willing to bet on technologies that solved real and latent problems, or could appeal to a functional need in a new way. Mobile phones' early penetration was through the high-end corporate market, but fed into the basic human need for communication. SMS was an afterthought that allowed for cheap and cheerful communication, first exploited by the young and then captured for other corporate purposes. Consumers learned by interacting with the products and services, while firms adapted the products and services in line with evolving consumer tastes.

Persuasion arises when individuals respond to the positive or negative affect associated with specific social occasions. Product advertising persuades by linking a specific image that the consumer likes, and wants associated with his/her self-image or ego, to the brand (e.g. *The Economist*'s "Free enterprise with every issue"; MTV's "I want my MTV!"; Vogue's "If it wasn't in VOGUE it wasn't in vogue"), through the purchasing context (e.g. Harrod's "Enter a different world"; McDonald's "Good time, great taste, that's why this is my place"; David Jones' [Australia's oldest department store] "There's no other store like David Jones"), and via generating an emotional response (AT&T's "Reach out and touch someone"; Calvin Klein's "Between love and madness lies Obsession"). Logos and brand images that can be observed publicly possess value to consumers only to the extent that others can see them and those others reveal the positive affect back onto the consumer. Indeed, the phenomenon of counterfeiting brand logos and styles would lose its reason for existence without this fundamental linkage. Those concerned with social causes reverse this, linking negative images to the brand and attempting to counter the positive self-image with one that the consumer would rather not reveal. For example, People for the Ethical Treatment of Animals' (PETA's) "Murder King: you'll get it our way" was a direct parody of Burger King's "Have it your way" slogan. "Sla✓ery" was a parody of the Nike swoosh and was associated with many organizations promoting boycotts of Nike.

Social persuasion arises when "in-group" pressures create an incentive to align with the thinking of the "tribe." A classic example of this was seen in the Robbers Cave experiments conducted in Connecticut and Oklahoma in the 1950s (Sherif *et al.*, 1961; Berreby, 2005). In these experiments, groups of youths were shown to align their beliefs and actions around those of their assigned in-group (which was random). What was astounding about these experiments was not that they showed the prevalence of such group influences but that they were able to undo and then redo the influence by moving the children around, suggesting the fundamental malleability of attitudes and beliefs and the degree to which they emerge from group social interaction. Similar effects are evidenced in purchasing, where group effects lead to similar behavior and reference group effects can have profound influences on preferences. In the case of social activism, a large body of literature exists (e.g. Drakeford, 1997; Klandermans, 1997) that highlights the social nature of protest and activist movements.

Second, *firms attempt to manipulate the shopping experience* in a way that creates constrained preferences for their products. This arises in two ways: (1) playing to the habitual nature of human behavior (e.g. Martin, 2008); and (2) creating limited contexts in which purchasing occurs (e.g. Callebaut, Hendrickx, and Janssens, 2003). Constrained preferences are those that may not be optimal in a purely economic sense but are "best" given the limitations faced by the consumer in a natural purchasing context (such as "I prefer Pepsi, but the restaurant only serves Coke").

Because individuals possess limited cognitive processing power, it is entirely rational that they engage in heuristic-based decision making, which leads to rules and habits that are not necessarily optimal or economically rational on a case-by-case basis. Similarly, because information gathering is cognitively expensive, consumers rely on signals, reference points (e.g. word-of-mouth communication, recommendations, clubs, social networks, etc.), and other information aggregation techniques (e.g. websites, specialist publications, etc.) to make what they perceive to be better decisions. By controlling these reference points, and hence what information is obtainable and what signals are flowing to the consumer, firms can influence purchasing behavior in subtle and not so subtle ways. For example, catalogs will present more expensive merchandise early on since this creates an anchoring point around high-price products, allowing them to charge higher average prices for the items in the remainder of the catalog (Nagle and Holden, 2001). Marketers engage in viral or influence marketing, "seeding" campaigns with lead consumers in situations in which social network effects are significant. In the product context, this was exemplified by Nokia's effective promotion of its multimedia GPS car kit via a game in which the user rescues a seductive French female. In the social space, Greenpeace was a Webby People's Voice winner with its "Send a whale to Japan" campaign against whaling by the Japanese (www.send-a-whale.com), which attracted more than 100,000 visitors.

Firms can, to a limited extent, control the purchasing environment directly through the control of the channels of distribution and the mixture of products on offer. For example, although mass retailers such as Wal-Mart, Target, Kroger, and Best Buy in America and Saturn, MediaMarkt, Carrefour, and Tesco in Europe have an incentive to offer the most appropriate mixture of products in their stores, they have a great degree of latitude in terms of which products, made by which manufacturers, make it onto their shelves. Increasingly, a major determinant of which products are in the stores is not just customer preferences but the ability to link into the retailers' supply chain systems, to engage in large-scale joint marketing activities, and to provide a range of products across hundreds of stores.

The implications of all of this is that in a world where the consumer is neither completely purposeful nor a blank slate there is a constant to and fro between actual and latent consumer preferences and their manifestation in the marketplace. In many cases, the outcomes from this are benign, in the sense that the fact that Tesco stocks one set of brands and Sainsbury's another can be immaterial. Consumers who do not have strong preferences simply purchase what is available wherever they are shopping, while those with stronger preferences reveal them by going out of their way to seek the desired product from the location stocking it. Sophisticated consumers learn quite quickly which emotional appeals to tune out and which to listen to.

However, in the case of social consumerism, the implications can be profound. If we believe that consumers are social radicals in surveys and economic conservatives at the checkout line, then there is no reason for rational corporations even to bother considering adding a social dimension to the product mix from a consumer demand perspective. Indeed, independent of their own profit motive, many corporations pushed back against activists in the full belief that what was being asked of them was not in the best interests of the stakeholders that they cared about – i.e. owners, employees, *and* consumers.

If under threat from activists and NGOs, firms might choose to offer more "ethical" products, but then they have to figure out what the distribution of costs will be from doing so. If you are a Wal-Mart, with vast control over a significant proportion of the buying public, it is not inconceivable that your "Everyday low prices" are not going to be quite as low as they could be, and the consumer ends up bearing the brunt of the price of social consciousness. Indeed, it is not hard to imagine that a rational course of action on the part of social activists would be to go after the larger and more oligopolistic firms, as these are the ones with the greatest ability to transfer the costs onto either consumers or others in the supply chain. Consumers become "ethical" consumers not because they are disposed to do it but because the activists have convinced or prodded major suppliers into shifting more of their product mix to the products and product types they are promoting.

Similarly, if those with a social conscience in purchasing are a minority of the public, it is also rational for large corporations and large retailers merely to allow this niche to operate at the fringes (e.g. the Oxfam Shop), since it would be more costly to accommodate than ignore it. Alternatively, corporations can simply compartmentalize the consumption into a component of the business without altering their base demand (or the nature of their other operations). For example, Unilever's purchase of Ben & Jerry's allowed for the expansion of the Ben & Jerry's franchise, but it is clear that Unilever's strategy was less "ethical" or social than instrumental; Ben & Jerry's stands as one of Unilever's premium offerings amongst its many ice cream brands. Indeed, although it keeps a bit of its social positioning in the United States, this is all but absent in other parts of the world, where Ben & Jerry's history is completely unknown and, very probably, culturally irrelevant.

The evolution of preferences and the role of the firm

What does this discussion imply for CSR generally and C_NSR more specifically?

First, following on from Hart and Milstein (2003), it can be argued that CSR is not just a redistributive exercise but also an innovation exercise. Based on this thinking, CSR is about a new way of organizing economic activity and value delivery. In this sense, the fact that firms are engaging in experimenting upon, and influencing the formation of, customer preferences means that C_NSR, at this point in time, may be an emergent, rather than fully formed, phenomenon. The issue of whether today's consumers are willing to pay for social goods therefore needs to be phrased more broadly: might tomorrow's consumers be willing to pay for social goods?

Second, if consumer preferences evolve to the point at which value is ascribed to the social aspects of consumption, then the case outlined in Figure 2.2 panel (c) becomes a real possibility and a much stronger case can be made for value-creating CSR and C_NSR. The possibility of that win-win option becomes less of a mythical Holy Grail. As value ultimately arises in economic markets because customers reveal a willingness to pay, the ultimate test of CSR will be whether or not $C_N SR$ can be fostered. However, $C_N SR$ is not a foregone conclusion even when large, powerful corporations promote it. For example, Wal-Mart actively promoted organic cotton products and other organic products in its stores as part of CEO Lee Scott's sustainability strategy. In the end, consumers reacted in a lukewarm manner and the initiative was scaled back after only a year. Scott "concede[d] that the company has struggled to persuade customers that Wal-Mart can mean high quality, rather than simply low price. 'I think we went too far too fast'" (Gogoi, 2006, 2007).

Third, these points open up the possibility of value-creating CSR and $C_N SR$, but they do not necessarily imply that such value is easily discovered and capitalized, or that it is ethically correct to do so. For example, it may be that the only way in which preferences can be influenced is to subject them to collective or group pressure or to restrict the right of choice. Even Wal-Mart found that its market power could not turn its consumers into mass consumers of organic products. This raises the question of the extent to which it is ethically justifiable for a corporation or government to restrict choice that does not necessarily lead to collective harm but to what a small group in the society perceives to be a harm (such as the case with extremist animal rights groups). Although elected representatives are elected and paid to make these choices, there is no indication that society is better served by turning over the right to make those decisions to corporations and activists, none of whom are elected or subject to the transparency demanded of democratically elected representatives (Devinney, 2009).

Finally, although corporations may be able to influence and reveal customer value, there is no indication that they would, based on their own market interests, allow that value to accrue to the customer. Going back to the Wal-Mart and Unilever examples again, it is clear that the motives for their actions were not societal. It is also clear that neither of these decisions had anything to do with the corporations being more ethical or wanting to be in line with consumers' moral values. If that had been the case, Wal-Mart would not have scaled back its organics campaign, since in doing so it revealed its willingness to pay for its professed sustainability. If it were the right thing to do and not the profitable thing to do, the program would have been continued. For

Wal-Mart, organics was a way to move up the chain of value and earn higher profits. Similarly, Ben & Jerry's under Unilever is significantly less politically active, since such activism – a positive point in the ethos of Ben and Jerry's – is antithetical to Unilever's code of conduct, which forbids making controversial public political stands. Ben & Jerry's was purchased specifically to fill out Unilever's brand portfolio.

The ethical consumer and CSR

Our conception of social consumerism is one that is embodied within and embodies general notions of corporate *and* consumer behavior coevolving to create, characterize, and police a marketplace. As we will discuss shortly, such coevolution can have profound consequences for the question of what values and beliefs are, and the degree to which they influence decisions and choices. This puts the ethical consumer in yet more of a mythical position, since it implies that social consumption is not something driven by the fundamental beliefs of consumers but something that is a reaction to corporate actions; and that corporations in turn respond to customers' reactions.

No doubt activists, politicians, and other opinion leaders play a role, but they do so in the sense that they can provoke a change in context. For example, Al Gore's winning of the Nobel Peace Prize – or the Nobel Film Prize, as one right-wing commentator joked – did not change facts, or even serve to convince individuals to act more nobly, as much as it motivated governments and corporations to act on carbon trading schemes (which put a price on a previously underpriced externality). Gore's achievement was not in convincing you and me but in convincing legislators, presidents, and prime ministers. As noted by a UK Whitehall insider (Leake, 2009):

We are aiming to cut emissions by a third in the next 10 years and then by 80 per cent in the next four decades. These things are not happening because the population has had a green psychological transformation. If that were true, we'd never get anywhere, we'd never have got rid of slavery or brought in seatbelts or abolished hanging. No social change is force-driven by mass psychological change. It is about government leading and people changing accordingly.

Unlike ethical consumerism, our notion of $C_N SR$, is one that implies evolution. Indeed, we would argue that it is likely that the development of C_NSR is not dissimilar to the evolution of the acceptance of many technologies. Activists can be considered as akin to the "techies" who built their own computers (and the more radical activists as hackers), or the Ralph Naders promoting regulatory changes to product safety. Indeed, Nader can be considered as the embodiment of a mythical hero, all the way down to the tragic, self-destructive fall in the 2000 US presidential election.

We also know that many feasible technologies fail to gain traction and that many technologies that are inferior come to dominate. Just because a technology is better it does not mean that it will be successful. Just because social consumerism is "good" it does not mean that it is an inevitability. Evolution is known for both stunning successes and a significant number of dead ends and extinctions. What determines successful technology is not simply its feasibility but also its ability to integrate into existing modes of behavior, customs, and thinking. For C_NSR to survive and not just be a passing fad it must integrate well with existing market forces and present a durable proposition to those who take on its traits. In this sense we agree with Žižek (2008), that if "ethical" consumption is dominantly an emotive appeal it will fail. It is only when social value becomes core that it becomes relevant and has the potential to make macro-level changes in society.

Mythological heroes are known to be toys of the gods. Odysseus (he of the Odyssey) and Perseus (he of the Gorgon Medusa) were frequently influenced and manipulated by the likes of Athena and Zeus, although both believed they had control over their actions and the consequences (and bemoaned the interference of the gods). So, too, ethical consumers believe that they are controllers of their behaviors, doing good by purchasing correctly. However, there is an Olympus of firms and markets that create the contexts in which behavior occurs, giving an illusion of free will that is only partially free, and free in ways that are obscure. Athena could not get Perseus to act, but could create the circumstances in which that action was inevitable. So it is with Wal-Mart, Tesco, Kroger, Carrefour, Starbucks, and Ikea.

3 | *Are we what we choose?*
Or is what we choose what we are?

You have brains in your head. You have feet in your shoes. You can steer yourself any direction you choose.

Dr. Seuss

For the myth is the foundation of life; it is the timeless schema, the pious formula into which life flows when it reproduces its traits out of the unconscious.

Thomas Mann

I would never die for my beliefs because I might be wrong.

Bertrand Russell

Radical attitudes, conservative behaviors

In March 2007 the website of SustainableBusiness.com heralded the findings of a survey from Tanberg Research: "Consumers ready to reward pro-environmental corporate brands at the checkout line."[1]

More than half of global consumers (53 percent/representing 1.1 billion people) prefer to purchase products and services from a company with a strong environmental reputation.

Digging further into this survey of over 16,000 consumers in fifteen countries, one sees not only that people are saying that they will pay more as consumers to save the environment, but that 80 percent want to work for environmentally friendly companies and nearly 60 percent have done "something" to reduce the impact of climate change. The most environmentally aware individuals are not the Germans (fifteenth out of fifteen) or Dutch (tenth of fifteen) but the Chinese (first) and Australians (second)!

An even more interesting finding is that from the National Geographic. According to their Greendex,[2] Brazilians, Indians, Chinese, and Mexicans are the most "green" consumers while Americans, Canadians, French, and Japanese are the worst – a result influenced by the simple fact that the more sustainable consumers were those with the least capacity to purchase. The Chinese were lauded for the fact that they walked and bicycled. However, anyone with experience of walking the streets of Beijing, Shanghai, Chongqing, Delhi, Mumbai, Mexico City, or São Paulo would find these results somewhat suspect, and their health potentially impaired.

It is easy to pick out one or two surveys to critique but there are literally hundreds of such surveys appearing every year – many honest attempts to get a picture of public opinion – which provide confusing and conflicting results. For example, a Datamonitor (2005) survey of consumers found that "67% of consumers in the US and Europe claim to have boycotted a food, drinks or personal care company's goods on ethical grounds," yet a 1999 global survey found that only 40 percent had boycotted or "would consider boycotting a product." The Australian consumer group Choice pegs the number at 30 percent. In the United Kingdom, a 2006 Ipsos MORI poll found that only 16 percent of UK consumers engaged in boycotts, yet a 1995 survey found that 60 percent of consumers said they would do so (but apparently had had no reason to act on their intent in the intervening eleven years).[3]

Moreover, these surveys and polls range across the "ethical" spectrum. Seventy-one percent of French consumers said they would choose child-labor-free products even if the prices were higher (Garone, 1999). Seventy-five percent of European consumers indicated that they would alter their consumption behavior to aid social causes (Capron and Quairel-Lanoizelee, 2004). According to IrishHealth, 48 percent of those surveyed were against animal testing for medical research,[4] while Opinion Research Business found that 86 percent of the British public would support their local grocery store if it introduced a range of household products not tested on animals.[5] In the United States, a Gallup survey showed that Americans were considerably less animal-friendly, with 61 percent supporting the wearing of fur and 57 percent supporting animal testing for medicine.[6] If we are to believe the Ethical Consumer Research Association, "20 per cent of consumers buy ethically *all of the time* [emphasis added] with up to 70 per cent of consumers reacting to things they don't like. In the past, price and quality have been the only issues but ethics is now a firm third."[7]

However, despite the apparent wave of evidence seeming to indicate a veritable tsunami of consumer activism, the degree to which survey activists become consumer radicals appears to be overestimated significantly. As noted by O'Rourke (2004, p. 23):

Evidence from approximately 20 years of "green consumer" campaigns indicates that people do think and care about ethical, social, environmental, and health concerns. Again, roughly three-quarters of people polled in OECD [Organisation for Economic Co-operation and Development] countries call themselves environmentalists and report that they would purchase a green product over an environmentally problematic product. However, again only 10–12 percent of consumers actually go out of their way to purchase environmentally sound products. Debates continue on explaining this divide between stated preferences and actions.

We can question the scientific quality of much of this work and the fact that a significant majority of it is influenced by the intent of the surveying organization, be it an NGO or activist organization or consultants and pollsters creating a market for service and information. For example, most information about animal welfare comes from work commissioned by groups such as the Humane Society and the British Union for the Abolition of Vivisection (which sponsored the research mentioned earlier), and much of the general work on ethical consumerism is related to organizations such as the Ethical Consumer or the UK Co-operative Group. These groups are hardly unbiased (nor should they be), and they are certainly unlikely to commission work that is going to reveal that their raison d'être is suspect. Similarly, pollsters such as Ipsos MORI and Globescan are not likely to continue investing in surveys that do not resonate with purchasers. If their work continually showed that consumers did not care about the issues being investigated, it is doubtful whether they could sell follow-on services or that there would be much interest in hearing that nothing had changed from year to year.

However, the importance of the above confusion is that it hints at a deeper concern for us. If, as noted by Vogel (2005, pp. 48–9), "consumers will only buy an [ethical] product [if] it doesn't cost more, comes from a brand they know and trust, can be purchased at stores where they already shop, doesn't require a significant change in habits to use, and has the same level of quality, performance, and endurance as the less [social] alternative," then much of our discussion of consumer social responsibility becomes little more than consumption as usual, and the consumer most likely falls out of the CSR equation. It also hints that the positioning of the ethical consumer revealed by the likes of the above surveys is truly mythical, in the sense that it is not only false but, even as a role model, appears to be unattainable and contrary to the natural tendencies of human behavior.

Understanding the nature of consumer choice

It is our thesis that social consumption and $C_N SR$ are best understood as manifestations of consumption more generally. However, as will be discussed, there are distinct aspects of social consumption that suggest that standard models of consumption, and standard approaches to understanding beliefs and behavior, need to be modified, or that different components of these models and research approaches need to be emphasized. For example, one of the roles of qualitative market research techniques is to probe individuals for the rationales underlying their decisions. Similarly, survey techniques rely on the surveyed to be both knowledgeable and truthful. However, when the moral and ethical mix with personal self-interest in a public forum, very serious issues of respondent bias arise. For example, few people publicly reveal their racial preferences, but all societies possess well-ingrained racial prejudices that influence private behavior and private opinion. This is potentially compounded by the circumstances in which individuals lack knowledge and may be more susceptible to pressure to give socially acceptable responses. In standard product and service research, customers have a strong incentive to reveal their preferences, since not doing so can lead to inefficient products and services being developed. In social consumption this fact may also be true, but it is confounded with a well-understood tendency to want to reveal a socially "correct" public position – a fact revealed by the very large percentage of consumers who profess a social conscience, as opposed to the few who appear to consume actively based on that consciousness (see, for example, Cotte, 2009).

In what follows we, first, stand aside from the issue of social consumption and focus on consumer behavior more generally. In doing so we are setting both a context for our arguments and proposing a general perspective on consumption behavior that will motivate a large portion of our empirical analysis. Our purpose is not to come up with a unique singular model of social consumption, as we believe no such thing exists. Our goal is to point out how social consumption fits into our general understanding of consumption behavior, and the implications that this has for the veracity of the empirical approaches used. One of the true weaknesses in the field of "ethical" consumerism is the failure to recognize that different empirical approaches are embedded within different models of behavior – something understood more generally with respect to ethical decision making (Tenbrunsel and Smith-Crow, 2008). If those models of behavior are invalid, or flawed in any degree, the empirical approach will be suspect, the data derived from such research questionable, and any interpretation of it open to criticism. By utilizing multiple methods across multiple contexts, we provide a more forceful and valid picture of social consumption behavior.

Archetypes of consumer behavior

Let us begin by giving a general picture of the individual as consumer. For simplicity, we portray consumer behavior as falling onto a combination of four stylized dimensions, based upon the assumptions that we have about how consumers operate.

Consumers as rational informed processors

This approach views the consumer as engaged in an investigation of the product and service landscape in search of those products and services that best meet his/her needs at the price s/he is willing to pay. Although the consumer is rational, in the sense of possessing information and having knowledge of his/her own values, beliefs, needs, and wants, the rational model does not rule out the possibility of consumers facing limitations in terms of search costs or other market impediments. What it does imply is that consumers are engaging in an optimization based on their own utility or value, subject to market constraints. The rational perspective is a proactive viewpoint of the consumer that implies that corporations focus on predicting consumer needs and fitting into them appropriately.

Consumers as quasi-rational reactive purchasers

This approach views consumers as engaged in grazing the product and service landscape in search of products and services that they believe, at the moment, satisfy their needs and desires at a price they are willing to pay. This viewpoint of the consumer is based on many factors that impact a momentary desire to purchase, which can also be influenced by the context in which the consumer is operating. Unlike the rational model, this approach is "quasi-rational," in that it allows for the evolution of needs and wants based on emotional appeals and the consumer's mood, and assumes that the consumer is not knowledgeable about the total market landscape. Consumers are potentially ill- or under-informed and can be subject to momentary and long-term biases. Additionally, it does not imply that consumers engage in strict optimization but can be satisficing (Simon, 1957), seeking other intermediate goals (such as the minimization of loss), or using other decision-making models, such as prospect theory (Kahneman and Tversky, 1979), or heuristics such as lexicographic ordering (Bettman, Johnson, and Payne, 1991). In this situation, the corporation can influence the consumer by altering the environment in which purchasing is occurring and work to influence the evolution of needs, wants, and desires, as well as, potentially, values and beliefs.

Consumers as quasi-rational co-producers of value

This approach views the consumer as engaged in the production of value by combining a complex mixture of activities, of which product and service purchasing is a component (Vargo and Lusch 2004; Etgar, 2008; Payne, Storbacka, and Frow, 2008). This viewpoint sees consumers as very actively creating a lifestyle that reveals to others who they are and what they represent. However, it says nothing about whether the individual is optimizing or satisficing, or whether or not s/he is engaged in individual or group co-production. In this situation, the corporation must invest actively both to influence and to react to what consumers are attempting to do.

Consumers as actors for the adaptive unconscious

This viewpoint holds that consumers do not know themselves the motivations for their behaviors because they are predominantly caused by the unconscious mind (Hauser, 2007; O'Shaughnessy and O'Shaughnessy, 2008). The adaptive unconscious embodies the here and now and represents the opposite of longer-term, deliberative decision making. In this situation, thought is the manifestation of the complex interaction of modules in the unconscious that have been built up over a long period of time (Fodor, 1983). The model of the adaptive unconscious is best summarized by Hauser's distinction (pp. 24, 26) between Kantian and Humean creatures:

Kantian creatures think you need good reasons for making a particular judgment. When a Humean creature is asked for justification, all she can do is shrug and say "it feels right"... [The Humean creature has] an innate moral sense that provides the engine for reasoned judgments without conscious reasoning.

In this situation, the corporation must seek to create an emotional response that engenders a reaction that is then rationalized as thought processes kick in.

These four stylized archetypes have different implications for consumption in general, and "ethical" and social consumption in particular. For example, the rational and quasi-rational models imply conscious action. The decisions made may be inefficient and biased, but they are "reasoned" out by the consumer. In the case of the adaptive unconscious, reasoned action is *ex post*. In addition, individuals can normally walk an observer through the logic of the analysis that led to their decision. In the case of the adaptive unconscious, the process is not observable directly and not even known by the individual him- or herself. Instead, the analysis of unconscious decision making relies heavily on physiological responses (such as brain scans), experiments that create emotive reactions, and inferences from related behaviors. The rational models are not only more amenable to theoretical understanding, with clearer and more measureable causes and effects, but also more consistent with the philosophical precepts of free will.

For social consumption, all this is of paramount importance. It has implications for not only how we read the data but also what we might consider to be the normative response to that data. For example, the conscious and rational models (within which we include the quasi-rational model for the moment) imply that the voice of the consumer is meaningful. The unconscious mind model implies that the consumer does not so much have a "voice" as *ex post* rationalizations to unconscious responses. This leads to two extreme viewpoints on the consumer: one that views the consumer as the sacred arbiter of value and another that views the consumer as a tool of biological evolution.

The consumer as vox populi

The rational and quasi-rational models of behavior give credence to the consumer-as-voter model of social consumption (Smith, 1990; Dickinson and Carsky, 2005). The logic here is simple. First, consumers are the ultimate determinant of value, both social and economic. As noted by Adam Smith (2000 [1776], p. 625):

Consumption is the sole end and purpose of all production; and the interest of the producer ought to be attended to, only so far as it may be necessary for promoting that of the consumer.

Second, individuals, not others, are the determinants of their own value. To quote John Stuart Mill (2002 [1859], p. 10):

The principle [liberty] requires the liberty of tastes and pursuits, of framing the plan for our life to suit our own character, of doing as we like, subject to such consequences as may follow; without impediments from our fellow creatures, so long as we do not harm them even though they should see our conduct as foolish, perverse or wrong.

Third, markets are one reflection of the collective value of individuals acting in their own interests. As articulated by Thomas Murphy, chairman of General Motors, in the 1970s (Smith, 1990, p. 29):

This sensitive tailoring of productive resources to the complex and diverse preferences of people, expressed through free markets is a fundamental though often under-appreciated characteristic of our system. Each consumer, given his free choice, can purchase those products which he feels most suit his own special needs and resources. Unlike the political system, every person can win in an economic "election."

The power of this argument can be seen in the value of economic exchanges when used as prediction markets. Exchanges such as the University of Iowa's Iowa Electronic Market, Betfair, or the Hollywood Stock Exchange allow individuals to invest in specific events (e.g. awards, elections), individuals (e.g. candidates, actors), or entities (e.g. political parties, movies), receiving a payout when the event is realized. Their investments amount to weighted bets on outcomes in which individuals with more and better information can capitalize that information by investing based on their knowledge. Such markets prove remarkably accurate in predicting events, and are superior to standard polls in circumstances when investors are broadly representative of the holders of knowledge (Wolfers and Zitzewitz, 2004; Erikson and Wlezien, 2008).

The consumer-as-voter model has a serious philosophical limitation, in that it weighs the importance of an individual by his/her purchasing power, effectively disenfranchising significant and important constituencies who are not "in the market." When social aspects of economic markets are of less relevance this criticism is less worrisome, but still germane. For example, it raises the simple economic question of whether only those "in the market" should possess rights to determine how the market operates – a common refrain heard from anti-globalization activists. However, from our perspective, even if this issue were ignored there are other conceptual and practical drawbacks to the economic voter logic that implies that it is, at best, only an imperfect approximation of the public voice, or even the consumer's voice, at large.

First, it is not clear that consumers possess the information necessary to make the decisions on which they are voting. Indeed, this is a critical problem with all opinion elicitation approaches, and the consumer-as-voter model is just preference elicitation by other means. It is well understood that polls and surveys can lead to nonsense in circumstances when individuals are being asked to reveal something they know nothing about. Furthermore, there are certainly circumstances in which consumers purchase products about which they know nothing except that they are satisfied by the acts of purchasing and consuming. Similarly, the argument that consumers have "skin in the game" because they are spending their own money assumes that they view the money expended as sufficiently significant to invest in knowledge acquisition. For low-involvement products, and even high-involvement products that are inexpensive, such an investment may not be worthwhile. As will be seen in later chapters, very few of the consumers we studied had knowledge of the social components of the products they purchased, and our ethnographic work revealed that few were interested in investing in such information.

Second, voting assumes that all the ballots contain all the candidates on which the voter can legally vote. However, markets are not flat, and consumers will be presented with limited and different ballots. For example, the consumer shopping in San Francisco at Safeway or Ralph's will have a different ballot from the consumer shopping in Kroger or Giant Eagle in Toledo, or at Aldi or Edeka in Berlin. The more varied the cultures, the potentially more varied the consumers' ballot will be. However, a more problematic issue for the economic voter model is that none of the ballots may have the candidates of interest. For example, as few product packages contain information about the labor practices used in the making of the product, it is difficult to argue that a market full of ill-informed consumers can act as effective policers of labor practices through their purchasing behavior. This is the case even if we have the mythical ethical consumer wanting to "make a difference" through his/her everyday purchasing. As an average grocery store would have as many as 15,000 different products, it is unlikely that any group of consumers, no matter how committed, would be willing to invest in an information search for all but a trivial handful of critical products. This fact helps explain the very limited success of boycotts and why they are targeted at the corporate owner and not the individual product (Ettenson and Klein, 2005; Chavis and Leslie, 2009).

When preference inferences are being made from observing consumption, there is an explicit model about what consumers are doing mentally when purchasing. The data is not "speaking" but being interpreted, and such interpretation can be biased. Hence, all that can be said is that the economic voter model of consumption has validity to the extent that one understands that it is a constrained revelation of preferences. It is valid to the extent that, if a product or service is offered into a marketplace with informed consumers and succeeds/fails, one can be reasonably assured that it was satisfactory/unsatisfactory on *enough* critical dimensions when compared to *the other alternatives available.* However, product complexity implies that success or failure does not necessarily amount to a vote for or against any one of those dimensions alone. Nor does success say anything about general opinion. Consumer economic voting is a case of approval voting with minimal proportionality, with each market determining the minimal share of approval that is necessary for the product/service to survive. As noted by Fine (2006, p. 305):

There is much more to the politics of consumption than the participation as consumer, just as there is more to politics than just voting. Arguably, much more goes on behind the scenes of electioneering and shopping than is revealed by them.

The consumer as evolved ape

The adaptive unconscious model presents at one and the same time a simple and complex model of behavior. It puts considerable emphasis on an evolutionary analysis of human behavior, continually pointing out that our evolution was based on simple instinctual rules of survival rather than on complex rational thought, and that the conscious mind is a recent addition to a history that was ruled primarily by the unconscious mind. Because it puts emphasis on habitual learned and evolutionary responses, as opposed to informed and knowledgeable action, the adaptive unconscious model is one in which social pressures battle against millennia of biological adaptation. Such behavior makes us self-interested yet loyal and protective of our genetic tribe, aggressive and warlike yet caring and altruistic, sly and cheating yet honest, while at the same time open to, and thriving from, social interaction, because historically a lone individual was unlikely to survive. The internal conflict is summarized by James Kirk in, "A taste of Armageddon," in the original *Star Trek* series, when speaking of human savagery:

[War] is instinctive. But the instinct can be fought. We're human beings with the blood of a million savage years on our hands! But we can stop it. We can admit that we're killers ... but we're not going to kill ... today. That's all it takes! Knowing that we're not going to kill ... today!

The adaptive unconscious model also helps to explain why, despite complete knowledge of the impact of specific foods, a significant number of the people in developed countries are obese and seem unable to do little to control their own caloric intake (Friedman, 2003). It also helps us understand why women and children are more effective beggars than adult males (Adriaenssens and Hendrickx, 2008) and why we are more likely to save animal species that are more attractive (Gunnthorsdottir, 2001).

Unlike the rational approach, the unconscious model flips the nature of causality around, and also hints at why campaigns targeting changes in behavior face difficulty when they are contrary to engrained sociobiological imperatives. As noted by Hauser (2007, pp. 419–20):

There is reason to believe that there are universal properties of the human mind that constrain the range of cultural variation. Our expressed languages differ, but we generate each one on the basis of a universal set of principles. [...] When we judge an action as morally right or wrong, we do so instinctively, tapping a system of unconsciously operative and inaccessible moral knowledge.

Not only is this "grammar" deeply buried, it is quick in response. A number of studies have found that brain activity precedes awareness. According to one study, "the outcome of a decision can be encoded in the brain activity of prefrontal and parietal cortex up to 10 seconds before it enters awareness. This delay presumably reflects the operation of a network of high-level control areas that begin to prepare an upcoming decision long before it enters awareness" (Soon *et al.*, 2008).

The evolutionary, biological view of the consumer is almost completely unemphasized by those concerned with ethical consumerism and social consumption. It is not clear why this is the case, but what is true is that evolutionary biological models raise uncomfortable truths, one of which is that appeals to rationality can be in direct conflict with the subtle behavioral motivators that drive a very significant proportion of human behavior. In addition, it opens up quite serious questions as to the nature and interpretation of empirical measurement. As we will see shortly, ethical consumerism is based on a model in which values are revealed through behavior. Perhaps such a model presents an overly naive picture of what it is that consumers are truly revealing by consumption. Let us turn to this.

Two meta-models of social consumer behavior

Hopefully, what the prior discussion demonstrates is that the process that drives individual human behavior is not just complex but also subject to potentially conflicting rational and non-rational motivations. Taken onto the consumption stage, we can see that the decision-making process that culminates in purchasing is affected by experience, information, emotion, social norms, and opportunity.

There are many different models of consumer behavior that we could bring to bear on the argument at this point. However, two simple meta-models of consumer decision making are enough to present a general view of social consumption. For simplicity, we will refer to them as the linear and recursive models. Neither is meant to provide a definitive model of social consumption decision making, but together they help us highlight the differences in the logic premises and empirical implications that follow from these very different theoretical conceptions of what consumers are doing when making purchasing decisions. The linear model is the dominant one seen in models of ethical consumption, while the recursive model is more in line with extant theories of consumer behavior (as in Solomon, 2009) and general ethical decision making (as in Tenbrunsel and Smith-Crowe, 2008).

A *linear model of social consumption*

Figure 3.1 presents a very simple example of a linear model of social action, of which consumption is one manifestation. According to this structure, a fundamental set of values influences beliefs and attitudes,

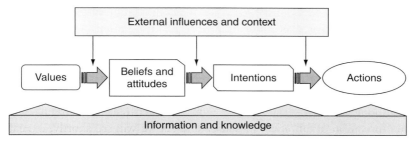

Figure 3.1 A linear model of social action

which in turn impact on intentions, which ultimately turn into actions. All the various components of the model are influenced by the information and knowledge of the individual actor, while the various stages of the process are moderated by external factors and the context in which the decision to act is being made.

Although it is a very simple representation of behavior, the linear model, or minor variants thereof, is at the heart of the vast majority of theoretical and empirical models of ethical consumption found in the management and business ethics literature. This has implications for the meaning of these models and how it is that they are validated empirically.

First, the model implies that there is a beginning and an end; and at the beginning are values and at the end are actions. Values are generalized characterizations of the individual's ethical and moral self. Although they are at the core of behavior, nothing internal to the model explains how those values form. They are assumed to exist and possess a degree of stability. From our perspective, the philosophic notions of intrinsic and extrinsic values are less relevant than the psychological search for universal values. Schwartz and Blisky (1987, p. 553) define a value as "an individual's concept of a [tran-]situational goal that expresses interests concerned with a motivational domain and evaluated on a range of importance as a guiding principle in his/her life." Empirically, Schwartz and his colleagues characterize values on ten dimensions that they believe are present in all cultures in some mixture: power, achievement, hedonism, stimulation, self-direction, universalism, benevolence, tradition, conformity, and security.

Second, beliefs and attitudes flow from values and relate to opinions about specific circumstances, dilemmas, or contexts (e.g. animal welfare, abortion, Third World debt, and so on). In this sense, beliefs and attitudes can be considered as a manifestation of a combination of the values and the circumstances that are being probed or investigated. Although they are treated as separate constructs by psychologists and philosophers, we have chosen to simplify the presentation by tying them together, since they are typically measured contemporaneously. Beliefs can be considered as the mental representations that contain core and dispositional components. They serve as a common-sense articulation of values (see, for example, Baker, 1989). Attitudes are "a predisposition to respond cognitively, emotionally [affectively], or behaviorally to a particular object in a particular way" (Rajecki, 1982). They are influenced by the target (e.g. abortion, animal welfare), the source of the origin of the trigger (e.g. a survey on abortion or a statement by a politician), and the context in which the attitude is revealed (e.g. a family gathering, a public forum, or a five-point Likert scale). Unlike values, which are assumed to be "cognitive representations of three types of universal human requirements: biologically based needs, social interactional requirements for interpersonal coordination, and social institutional demands for group welfare and survival" (Schwartz and Blisky, 1987, p. 551), and are influenced only slowly by information and knowledge, beliefs and attitudes can be influenced more directly by providing supporting or counterfactual information that moderates the translation of values into beliefs and attitudes, or contexts that can spur an emotive reaction. Figure 3.2 shows a schematic of the logic of this thinking.

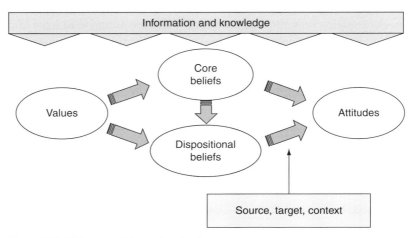

Figure 3.2 Values, beliefs, and attitudes

Intentions are the stated willingness to act in a specific manner (such as the answer to a survey question about whether or not you would purchase a product made by child labor). Like attitudes and beliefs, intentions are subject to moderation by the circumstances, and can be influenced by external information and knowledge. Note that intention does not imply a true assessment of what will occur, but a statement by the individual that gives his/her revealed stated reaction to something in such-and-such circumstances. Unlike values, beliefs, and attitudes, it is a prediction the individual makes about his/her own behavior that s/he is willing to reveal to whomever is asking and in the form they are requesting the information.

Finally, the action is the actual behavior that follows from the intent, such as showing up at the protest march or failing to purchase the organically grown, Fairtrade coffee. The path from intent to action is, again, moderated by situational factors that enhance or limit the individual's ability to act as s/he intended.

A recursive model of social consumption

The linear model represents one extreme theoretical specification for social consumption. The model given in Figure 3.3 presents an example of a recursive model of social action that is meant to account for aspects of the unconscious adaptive mind model of behavior.

Unlike a linear model, a recursive model has no distinct beginning or end. It should also be obvious that the type of model given here has an

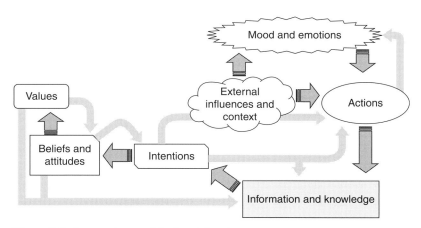

Figure 3.3 A recursive model of social action

enormous number of variants (and can incorporate the linear model with simplifying assumptions). In the one example shown, the flow is from the external environment, through action and back to intentions, beliefs, and values. Hence, we can see a logic that has two parts. The first is a primary path on which the individual finds him-/herself in a context that elicits an emotional response that leads to an unconscious choice being made. The action leads to a search for information to reconcile the unconscious decision of the actor to the external circumstances and internal cognitive states. This leads to the quasi-rational formulation of an intent, which influences beliefs and triggers a set of values consistent with the belief. Over time, as more decisions are made, the distinction between the initial response and future rationalizations and behaviors becomes muddied by feedback loops (the less shaded arrows in Figure 3.3) that attempt to maintain continuity between the individual's internal states (values, beliefs and attitudes, intentions), his/her emotional state, and his/her external state (actions). As in self-perception theory, individuals infer their values, attitudes, and beliefs from their actions (see, for example, Bem, 1972).

The recursive model opens up avenues for more complex interactions between the precursors to behavior. Unlike the linear model, it can incorporate more intricate psychological theories, such as affective events theory, which accounts for the circular path between context, actions, and attitudes (Weiss and Beal, 2005), or the elaboration likelihood model of persuasion, which highlights the difference between the central and peripheral routes for engendering a change of beliefs and attitudes (Petty and Cacioppo, 1986). In the case of the latter theory, the central route represents the more cognitive effort and will entail more long-term change, while the peripheral route, which is more reliant on quick heuristics, will lead to, at best, temporary acquiescence to the attempt to persuade.

One can question the specific model given by Figure 3.3, but the main point it raises is that the direction of causality is not necessarily apparent (or logical). In the linear model there is a clear progression, as in a funnel. If there were no contingencies impeding the path from values to behavior, then behavior would be a direct manifestation of values. Values *cause* behavior (or behavior occurs because of values). Although no scientist would argue for a strong causal model, the linear model implies a progression that puts certain factors in core positions. In the recursive model there is no such logic. Values are as likely to lead to a behavioral manifestation as behavior is to lead to a value manifestation. The same is true of beliefs and intentions, which can be construed as a symptom of choice as well as a determinant of choice.

Implications of the models

These two different types of models imply differences in what is emphasized theoretically and practically, and how one approaches measurement.

In the linear model, emphasis is put on values, beliefs, attitudes, intentions, and behavior as direct or nested effects, and external influences as moderators of these effects. Each can be measured independently as they are effectively stand-alone constructs. One need not worry about how values, beliefs, and intentions are formed, but simply that they can be characterized. The more the contingencies are accounted for, the more likely it is that the relationship between values, beliefs, and intentions will relate to behavior. The implication is that differences are scientifically meaningful because they matter to predictions of behavior; if they did not they would simply be meaningless pieces of information of no particular value. Hence, studies that examine differences in value or belief structures between different cultures or segments of individuals achieve their scientific validity via the assumption that such measured values are meaningful precisely because they are precursors to higher-order constructs that do matter. If the causal chain is value → beliefs → intentions → behavior, then values are a window on beliefs, which are a window on intentions, which are a window on behavior.

Indeed, this is the logic found in a priori segmentation based upon surveys of the values, beliefs, and intentions of consumers – something that dominates quantitative research on ethical consumerism. For example, Al-Khatib, Stanton, and Rawwas's (2005) categorization of consumers into "principled purchasers," "suspicious shoppers," and "corrupt consumers" is based entirely on psychological belief and attitude scales. Its normative marketing recommendations assume that such beliefs and attitudes translate into behavior in at least a reasonable number of cases. Moreover, their work is not an isolated case, either in academia or the commercial domain. The Institute of Grocery Distribution's (IGD's) (2008) survey of grocery consumers in the United Kingdom is just one of hundreds of examples: they categorize shoppers as "ethical evangelists (15 percent)," "focused followers (27 percent)," "aspiring activists

(21 percent)," "blinkered believers (16 percent)," and "conscious casuals (21 percent)," with only the latter being completely non-ethical. As noted by Cotte's (2009) review of the ethical consumer literature, over 45 percent of academic research in the field used this logic, accounting for nearly 90 percent of all the empirical research to date.

Ignoring for the moment issues of measurement bias, the linear model implies that surveys and polls asking consumers their intentions should be meaningful measures of social consumption as they are part of the chain leading to behavior. Similarly, the search for the "ethical" consumer would be relatively easy, since all one would need to know was the structure of values and beliefs. As noted, characterizing the "ethical" segment via standard market segmentation techniques should prove fruitful, and corporate and NGO strategies based on information and knowledge would be logical and effective since, the more informed people are, the more they can make a reasoned choice that is consistent with their underlying values. The utility value one gets from the act of consumption is, basically, a reflection of one's underlying values conditioned on the environment in which that purchasing is occurring.

With a recursive model, the lack of clear exogenous and endogenous influences makes empirical characterization difficult. Simple surveys and polls are fairly meaningless in the case of a recursive model because they fail to tell us anything about the linkages between the components. Additionally, it brings into question the degree to which data from the "real" world represents a sufficiently robust natural experiment to reveal the nature of what is actually happening. One can speculate that individuals work to create consistency between values, beliefs, intentions, and behavior, but, as everything that can be observed is malleable, the direction of causality can be the opposite of what appears to be logical and rational (or at least in accordance with our notions of human free will). For example, the fact that intentions and beliefs are correlated would not reveal the directionality of any effect in the recursive model.

For those believing in the recursive model, the context matters, as do the decision models that individuals are using, how they use information, and where inconsistencies and rationales come into play. Consumption also plays an ego role, in the sense of co-production whereby the consumer creates value through the evolution of an identity. For recursive quasi-rationalists, those who believe that behavior is still dominantly amenable to (quasi-)rational action, experimentation would be the analytic mode of choice, as it allows specific components of decision making to be captured and estimated. For recursive non-rationalists, a hermeneutic approach would be the method of choice. As Chapters 4, 5, and 6 reveal, it is our contention that both approaches are necessary even to begin to understand the nature of social consumption.

The linear model implies that if you want to influence behavior you have to give people information, or work to change their values and beliefs. In the recursive world, the appropriate strategy might be to ignore values and information and to alter context, then let the individuals recalibrate their own internal state to align with their actions and external signals. Those believing in a linear model would, for example, attempt to reduce smoking by pointing out the harm that it is doing to the smoker and those around him/her. Similarly, they would approach environmental problems in the manner of Al Gore, by telling people that unless they act something disastrous is going to occur. Those believing in a recursive model would be considerably more eclectic. While acknowledging that information campaigns can be useful, they would work first on altering the context in which behavior is manifest. Smokers would be discouraged not by moralizing but by making it difficult and more expensive to smoke and by creating a social context in which smoking was not supported positively. In the latter case, individuals "freely" choose not to smoke. Similarly, in the case of environmental initiatives, appeals would be made to other aspects of choice, such as their children's health, the cost of energy, and the opportunities for "green jobs" in an economic downturn.

What this discussion highlights is that underlying the search for the "ethical" consumer are explicit models of what motivates behavior. Hidden in the surveys and polls is a quite explicit model of how people do behave and should behave. Activists believe that either (1) individuals have a natural tendency to "do good" that is being thwarted by the actions of corporations and governments or (2) that individuals are acting habitually because they do not understand or know that their behavior is contrary to what their values should be. An example of (1) is seen in the formation of the International Right to Know campaign – a coalition of more than 200 NGOs that have joined together to support international right-to-know legislation – and, more directly, in this letter in the *Corporate Crime Reporter* (1999):

Monsanto as a corporation has fought tooth and nail to oppose consumer right to know whether milk or crops are produced through genetic engineering processes. It has won overwhelmingly in the US, thanks primarily to its current or former friends and employees in the Clinton/Gore administration. Thanks especially to Al Gore and his gang at FDA [the US Food and Drug Administration], the agency has acted consistently and repeatedly in Monsanto's interests to thwart consumer right to know.

Point (1) assumes that individuals would "do the right thing" if they had the chance. Point (2) has more negative connotations, which imply that pressure would need to be put onto consumers to alter their values and beliefs so as to change behavior.

The attitude–behavior gap and its implication for measurement

As we noted earlier, estimates of the importance of ethical issues in consumer purchasing decisions vary significantly depending on the methodology used and/or the source of the analysis. One constant seen in this research is the gap between what individuals say they will do and what they actually end up doing. This phenomenon has been euphemistically coined the "attitude–behavior gap," and it is something of a trademark for the lack of validity of research in this field (see, for example, Boulstridge and Carrigan, 2000, and Carrigan and Attalla, 2001). Traditionally, attempts to address the attitude–behavior gap have relied on using modifications of existing theories to delve deeper into attitudes, and attempts to find those mediators – for example, market and environmental, personal or informational – that limit how and when attitudes will be revealed in behavior (Newholm and Shaw, 2007). However, the above discussion hints that this is not just a case of theoretical respecification or methodological failure, but is fundamentally related to the meta-model of behavior that the investigator assumes and the fact that theory and measurement are integrally linked.

Let us turn now to the methodological limitations and failings of much of the public work on social consumption.

The four methodological flaws: incentive compatibility, comparability, inference, and context

It is well understood that research instruments with simple ratings scales (e.g. Likert-type scales used in surveys) or "semi-structured" group responses (e.g. focus groups or case studies) will overstate the importance of factors for which there are socially acceptable responses, as there is no incentive to answer the questions truthfully. As noted by Schwarz (1999, p. 97), individuals "may want to edit their private judgment before they report it to the researcher, due to reasons of social desirability and self-presentation." This is fundamentally an *incentive compatibility* issue: to what extent does the structure of the research method allow (or force) respondents to reveal their "true" underlying behavior, preference, or attitude? This is a very serious issue in CSR and C_NSR research, given the sensitivity of the issues under investigation, the lack of any penalty for not revealing the "truth," and the obviousness of the research's intention (to tap ethical attitudes and behavior).

A stark example of the degree of "social desirability" bias can be seen in the annual sexual well-being survey sponsored by the condom manufacturer Durex, involving over 300,000 respondents. Every year the survey reports a discrepancy between the number of sexual partners that men (thirteen) and women (seven) have had over their lifetime; and significantly more "one-night stands" for men than women. However, excluding homosexual behavior, it is impossible for both these claims to be true. The number of average partners women have cannot be different from the number that men have, nor can the number of one-night stands. The problem is either that people do not remember with whom they had sexual relations (possible but unlikely, as you normally notice what is going on), that they are deliberately confused (e.g. Bill Clinton's definition of what "sex" is, or a difference in what "one-night stand" means), or that they are lying or being purposefully manipulative. What is intriguing is that, despite this fatal methodological flaw, the Durex survey is repeated every year and receives press in thousands of newspapers and websites.

A second issue is the language and informational content of the method itself. There are two parts to this. The first sub-issue is fairly obvious. The wording used in rating scales is critical, and vague wording can lead to erroneous conclusions (Schwarz, Grayson, and Knäuper, 1998). For example, Uusitalo and Oksanen (2004) report that 70 percent of their survey respondents stated that a firm's business ethics had "some influence" on their purchase behavior. This relatively vague label begs for more information: how much "influence" is "some influence," and is one person's "some influence" equivalent to another person's "some influence"? This is not just a problem of the meaning of the scale. In our discussion of boycotts, it is not clear that every individual faced with the question "Have you ever boycotted a product because. . .?" would define "boycotted" in the same way. Does a boycott mean never, ever buying the product again, or is it sufficient not to buy it the next time to have engaged in a boycott? Does a boycott have to be organized around a social or political cause, or can it simply be an action based on an individual's personal negative reaction to a product/ service experience? What we see here is fundamentally a *comparability problem* that arises when the focal measure (the scale) or construct is being calibrated internally and individually in real time.

A second sub-issue is related to the informational content of the method itself, and is much less obvious. Questions (and, more generally, questionnaires, but also semi-structured interview protocols) are often an important source of information for participants in a research study. Participants draw on the information embedded in surveys or questions to arrive at an "answer" (Schwarz, 1999). Essentially, the subject makes *inferences of importance* from the context of the investigation. Research also shows that respondents utilize this information more heavily when the behavior is poorly represented in memory and/or when the behavior is ill-defined. The impact of this bias can be seen in Hartley's (1946) classic study on prejudice, in which individuals were asked their opinion of various social groups, including the fictitious Wallonians, Danerins, and Perenians. Subjects liked the latter two but not the Wallonians! Bishop *et al.* (1980) find that about one-third of individuals surveyed gave responses concerning their opinions of fictitious laws (what are known as pseudo-opinions). More interesting was that this effect had more general ramifications (p. 202; emphasis in original):

Of greater significance to many researchers is the question of whether respondents who offer opinions on the [US] Public Affairs Act will do the same on topics that are real but not especially salient in their daily lives. The [results] tell us that such people were indeed more likely to express an opinion on *all other issues* we investigated. This was particularly true ... for the more abstract matters of policy, such as resumption of arms shipments to Turkey and the SALT negotiations. [. . .] [A]pparently the more remote the topic becomes from day-to-day concerns, the greater is the effect of this predisposition.

A third issue is the *abstract nature of the context* in which the research is being conducted. For example, when prostitute patronage in an AIDS-ravaged region of northern Thailand was examined, it was found that young Thai men were quite aware of the risks as well as the precautionary safeguards. In fact, before patronizing local brothels these men often bought alcohol and condoms with the intention of using both. Inevitably, they used the alcohol first and then forgot about the condoms. Surveys showed that the men were significantly likely to use a condom when having sex. However, reality proved otherwise, and the alcohol provided a convenient excuse when they claimed in the morning that they had been drunk and therefore could not be held responsible for having had unprotected sex (Belk, Østergaard, and Groves, 1998).

These four issues – incentive compatibility, comparability, inference, and context – reveal a need (1) to use caution when addressing socially laden issues and (2) to build methodological approaches that (a) recognize the link between theory and method and (b) interrogate the phenomena of interest with different lenses.

Increasing the predictive validity of intentions

Incentive compatibility, comparability, inference, and context are predominant concerns when the social nature of consumption is under the microscope. However, there are also general concerns about the ability of stated intentions to predict actual action when investigating any area of consumption. Although this is a quite general issue, it, too, comes to the fore in the case of social consumption, and it is important that we note it at this point. According to Morwitz, Steckel, and Gupta (2007), intentions are more correlated with purchases when:

(1) they are for existing products;
(2) they are more for durable goods than for non-durable goods;
(3) they are for short, rather than for long, time horizons;
(4) respondents are asked to provide intentions to purchase specific brands or models, rather than to provide intentions to buy at the product category level;
(5) purchases are measured in terms of trial rates, rather than being measured in terms of total market sales; and
(6) purchase intentions are collected in a comparative mode, rather than being collected monadically.

The importance of these six points can be seen by noting a few things about social consumption at this juncture. First, many "ethical" products are speculations about changes to existing products, or new products that have yet to be put in the market. Hence, point (1) implies a potential for overestimation of the actual likelihood of purchase. Second, based on point (2), the intention to purchase social capital goods (such as cars or energy-saving appliances) is more likely to be believed than that relating to infrequently purchased consumables (such as organic cotton clothing). Third, based on point (3), questions about immediate purchase are clearer than those for vague future purchases. However, given that most ethical products do not present such an opportunity, we would, again, expect that purchase likelihood would be overestimated. Fourth, point (4) implies that general questions, such as "To what extent does seeing the Fairtrade Certified label affect your perception of a brand?," is a less valid question than asking the same question with respect to a specific brand. Hence, research on existing brands for which labels have credibility and salience is most likely more accurate. Fifth, the measurement of who is likely to try a product is more valid than trying to measure the likelihood of a repeat purchase after they have tried the product. Hence, point (5) implies that intention does not imply satisfaction, simply a willingness to consider a product for evaluation. Finally, point (6) implies that asking for choice in a trade-off format is more relevant than simply asking "Would you consider a product that . . .?". As the latter format is common in surveys, we are less likely to get a valid response than we will when using the approaches to be discussed in Chapter 4.

The myth of ethical consumption; the reality of social consumption

Chapter 2 put social consumption in the context of the firm and asked the question "Where is the benefit to the firm from encouraging or accommodating social consumption?". We saw that in specific circumstances there is a tight link between our notion of $C_N SR$ and CSR. Without $C_N SR$, the value-creating potential of CSR is dramatically limited, if not negated in total. However, the positive social aspect of this is that there is an economic rationale for firms in a market to accommodate and develop the social dimension of consumption. This is simply one necessary, but not sufficient, condition for social consumption to exist and thrive, though.

This chapter has focused on two topics. First, there are the logical models of consumption that follow from work in psychology, economics, marketing, and evolutionary biology and that underpin our intellectual hypotheses about how consumption decisions are made. Second, there are the empirical approaches related to these models that provide us with information about consumption and its potentially related components and give credence to specific hypotheses. The two are inextricably linked.

As noted before, without consumers releasing value through their choices, the notion of social responsibility at any level is moot. Understanding the nature of social consumption is therefore critical: C_NSR is a necessary and sufficient condition for there even to be the potential for value creation in social consumption, and that potential will be realized only when corporations are convinced of its veracity. Hence, valid measurement becomes the binding joint between the corporate and consumer sides of the equation. In the words of Bachelard (1984 [1934], pp. 3–4):

Any work of science, no matter what its point of departure, cannot become fully convincing until it crosses the boundary between the theoretical and the experimental: experimentation must give way to argument, and argument must have recourse to experimentation.

As in Chapter 2, we need to re-emphasize that C_NSR requires the coevolution of corporate and individual interests. Corporations must realistically expect that some consumers will incorporate relevant aspects of production and product and service process when making pragmatic choices in the market. Only with that expectation would firms work to accommodate the consumers' now broadened decision-making processes into their product development and marketing activities. It is only with this symbiosis that the necessary and sufficient conditions align, creating a market in which social consumption does not just exist but thrives as well.

What should be obvious from our discussion is how little we have made of abstract notions of morals or ethics. Our approach to "ethical" consumption is, rather ironically, entirely atheistic. It is also apolitical. Social consumption decisions are no more or less ethical or moral than any other decisions, nor are they arrived at in a unique manner. Some choices are made purely for logical reasons; others are not, being based on habit or whim. Some are individual, taking into account only the value created for us; others are collective, being made for friends, relatives, or the family pet. Some are private; others public, presenting our consumption as a window the world can see. It is our argument that recourse to models that emphasize the uniqueness of the ethical or moral nature of consumption are inappropriate precisely because they stand outside the realm of the sort of day-to-day decision making that is required to make social consumption a boring everyday reality. Watson (2007), uniquely, recognizes this. He argues that most of the social facets of products, such as Fairtrade or labor aspects, are very much at a distance from the consumer, which implies that the consumer's focus is predominantly on the commodity aspects of consumption. Hence, the moral aspect is distinctly removed by the very fact of market transactions (p. 271):

The non-sentient characteristics of a product mean that it can never be the object of mutual sympathy. [...] The consumer can only activate this imaginative faculty when understanding themselves to be interacting, not with the product per se, but with the producer of that product. If a producer-oriented cognitive frame can be made to replace that of the conventional commodity fetish, then the consumer may well recognize the legitimate moral status of the producer and accept that the producer is consequently worthy of ethical treatment.

We are not saying that individual notions of what is right or wrong, good or bad, tasty or nasty, blue or green do not influence choice. Our contention is that the mechanisms by which these factors become incorporated into a consumption decision are not unique because of what they are. A truly effective and robust model of C_NSR is one that fits seamlessly with consumption in general. In this sense, we align well with Barnett, Cafaro, and Newholm (2005, pp. 19–21):

This ... underscores the importance of taking account of the concerns that motivate ordinary consumption. [...] Social science research on consumption has found that much ordinary consumption is suffused with moral rhetoric and ethical concern. [...] [c]onsumption, therefore, cannot be divided simply into "good" and "bad" or condemned and extricated from our cultures to leave some untainted good society.

Our goal, to paraphrase Carl Sagan (1995), is to "grasp the [phenomenon] as it really is [rather] than to persist in delusion, however satisfying and reassuring." In the next three chapters, we bring to bear evidence that reveals a complex picture of individual choice and social consumption. It is certainly not a complete picture but, unlike much work in this field, it is not one based on a single a priori model of consumer behavior with a single methodological slant. By looking at social consumption from alternative angles with alternative tools, we subject the idealized behavior of the ethical consumer to contestation. We take to heart Feyerabend's (1975, p. 46) statement that "variety of opinion is necessary for objective knowledge. And a method that encourages variety is also the only method that is comparable with a humanitarian outlook." In doing so, we are seeking a realistic and valid picture of the individual as a consumer who takes into account the social facets of his/her consumption; not one who is ethical or unethical, moral or immoral, but one who is simply a human being making choices with consequences. In doing so, we create an unvarnished picture of consumers as both social and commercial animals. However, to mis-quote Ralph Waldo Emerson, our "picture[s] must not be too pictur-esque," otherwise we, too, descend into myth.

4 | *Ethical consumers or social consumers? Measurement and reality*

What would I give if I could live out of these waters? What would I pay to spend a day warm on the sand?

Ariel, in The Little Mermaid

There are no solutions, only trade-offs.

Thomas Sowell

The importance of the consumer

As noted in the prior chapters, the degree to which individuals overstate their willingness to engage in "ethical" consumption behavior is indeed extraordinary. If it were simply a matter of yet another poll revealing a meaningless factoid that filled a column in a local newspaper, this would not be an issue worthy of substantive discussion. However, the failure to come to grips with the gap between beliefs and attitudes and the claimed behavior of consumers and the reality of their market activity has important economic, social, and political implications.

First, if consumers are to play a role in social change then the impression that they are little more than fickle "survey radicals" does harm to their potential impact. Firms attempting to engage in proactive, socially oriented product development will find themselves at a disadvantage as their target market proves significantly smaller than predicted by their focus groups and surveys, or their costs of providing social product features are not covered by the price consumers are willing to pay. A good example of this is the case of dolphin-safe tuna. Starkist found that making its tuna "dolphin-safe" allowed it to increase its market share but at what effectively amounted to a price reduction for consumers, as it could not command a higher price in the competitive grocery market (Reich, 2008). Those looking at evidence such as this and wanting to engage in cynical commentary might say that concerns about climate change, child labor, Third World debt, and poverty are really best left to politicians and activists, as "ordinary people" just want to get on with their lives and not be bothered with issues that really do not impact what they need or do on a daily basis.

Anecdotally, we found that many corporate executives have succumbed to what appears to be "ethical" consumer and CSR fatigue – the result of disappointment in the uptake of initiatives aimed to enhance the firm's position with key constituencies and the general public. This also has policy implications with direct public costs. For example, in 2007 Australia received considerable positive press for being the first country to ban incandescent light bulbs.[1] What was not said was that, one year beforehand, the Australian state of New South Wales (where Sydney is located) had pulled the plug on a light bulb giveaway scheme (Warren, 2006). The scheme involved giving households 10 million energy-saving light bulbs, at significant cost to the taxpayers. Unfortunately, even at a zero price it was discovered that fewer than half the free bulbs were ever used. On the one hand, the incandescent light bulb ban was a savvy stroke of political leadership (and theater) by the environment minister. On the other hand, it was a reflection of the failure of the public to react positively to the energy-saving light bulbs even when they were free.

Second, firms will react not to potential demand but to social activist pressure. This, in and of itself, may not be socially inefficient as long as the activists are themselves representative of a broader public. By "representative" we do not mean just that they reflect the voice of the public – which they do not do in any general sense, since they reflect the voices of specific constituencies – but that they represent a position to which some significant portion of the population would acquiesce. For example, Agnone (2007) argues, with some convincing empirical findings, that environmentalism in the United States was predominantly driven by activists who directly influenced political change. It was that political change that influenced the public opinion of the US population with respect to the need for environmental regulation. In other words, public opinion lagged political change. The public, in a general sense, agreed with the activist agenda and aided it not with support but by simply not pushing back against the legislative outcomes. However, if the socio-political position of the activists is not in line with any specific opinion, then there is no a priori reason to believe that it will lead to a socially or economically efficient outcome. For example, PETA put pressure on the Australian wool industry not just through an attempt to influence public opinion but also via a direct threat to their business via retailers.[2] PETA took issue with practices on Australian sheep farms and pre-invested in a television advertising campaign aimed at major multinational retailers – such as Abercrombie & Fitch and J. Crew – that used Australian wool. The organization's threat was that, if the retailers did not switch from using Australian wool, it would air the ads, thereby destroying a significant amount of the retailers' brand capital. The retailers, unsurprisingly, caved into what was obviously a very credible threat. Ultimately, the Australian wool industry came to an agreement whereby PETA would act within the law and the industry would drop its lawsuit against the organization.[3]

Third, and most importantly for what follows in this chapter, is the value that is left on the table (and lost to consumers) by firms failing to develop socially responsible products and services that succeed in the marketplace. This arises not because of a lack of desire on the part of the corporations and their managers, but from the failure of the firms to get an accurate picture of their customers' reaction to the social positioning of their potential products. This failure to create products and services that appeal to individual social proclivities and wants effectively represents a significant missed opportunity for value creation, for producers and consumers alike. In other words, rather than a win-win situation for consumers and firms, inaccurate information and politically enthusiastic but predictively inaccurate market research leads to a lose-lose outcome. Firms abandon social product development and positioning, losing the potential market, while those consumers willing to pay for products and services that add more value to their lives are left wanting. The potential for C_NSR is lost because of faith in the myth of the ethical consumer.

In this chapter, we present a series of experiment-based studies that examine four facets of consumer social consumption. First, using a sample that is purposely skewed to find individuals whom one would expect and individuals whom one would not expect to have a proclivity toward social consumption, we seek to find whether such individuals do indeed exist. Second, following on from this, and using the same sample, we attempt to determine whether or not there is a relationship between what consumers say they would do in an unconstrained poll and what they would be willing to pay for when faced with a more realistic trade-off situation. Third, we seek to address the issue of whether or not functionality would be sacrificed for ethics by putting people in circumstances in which there is an ethical functionality dilemma. Fourth, using a sample from six countries, we expand out from the first question and attempt to get a picture of the degree to which social consumption spans product categories and countries. Finally, in conjunction with the fourth point, we investigate the segment characteristics of social consumption more generally.

The experimental approaches that we use allow us to avoid many of the pitfalls of prior research, and to link this work more firmly to research in economics and psychology that has examined how individual choice varies when there is a price for specific behaviors.[4]

Experimentation and consumer social behavior

Perhaps the Holy Grail of ethical consumerism is the question of whether or not people would be willing to pay for good social features in products and services. Although not often pointed out, the parallel to this is the degree to which consumers would require a discount from a producer using less than stellar production practices. Most studies that have attempted to address this question have involved simple questions, such as "'Yes' or 'No': would you be willing to pay more for that [insert your favorite social cause here]?" or "How much would you be willing to pay for a product that [insert the issue]?," with a series of prices or percentage changes. The limitations of these approaches have been discussed extensively in prior chapters.

However, in some limited cases there are examples in which more complex and robust approaches have been used to try to get a picture of this issue, both in the specific case of "ethical" consumerism and, more generally, societal altruism and socio-economic behavior. Together, this work reveals a complex combination of rational and subconscious processes that influence how we conduct ourselves within our society (Wilson, Near, and Miller, 1996).

Many experimental economics studies have revealed a willingness on the part of individuals to sacrifice narrow self-interest for group outcomes, or to engage in blind altruism or positive reciprocity. For example, Fehr and Gächter (2000) show that individuals behave in less than completely rational, self-interested ways when it comes to altruistic opportunities, such as those in a trust game, in which subjects can choose to leave money for others in the hope that they will reciprocate. Fehr and Camerer (2004) show that this seems to be a general phenomenon and that it is influenced by cultural norms: more collective societies engage in more altruism in economic games.

However, the generalizability of findings such as these has been subject to contrary evidence and considerable contestation. For example, Laury and Taylor (2008) argue that the extent of such altruistic behavior may be an artifact of the experimental approach, which has tended to be context-neutral and cannot be extrapolated to more specific circumstances. In their experiments, individuals who were altruistic or non-altruistic in the experiments were only weakly altruistic or non-altruistic in a real-world setting in which they gave money to a charity. Levitt and List (2007), in a comprehensive review of the literature, argue that laboratory experiments are influenced by five factors: (1) moral and ethical considerations; (2) scrutiny of one's actions by others; (3) the context in which the decision is made; (4) the individuals making the decisions; and (5) the monetary and non-monetary stakes in the game. It is the degree to which these five factors match with reality outside the laboratory that has an influence on the ability to extrapolate real behavior from experimentally studied behavior. Overall, they argue (pp. 160–1) that there is

weak evidence of cross-situational consistency of behavior... [I]t means either that (a) there is not a general cross-situational trait called "social preferences", and/or (b) the subjects view one situation as relevant to social preferences and the other as irrelevant.

In the more narrow confines of consumer behavior, several studies stand out. Prasad *et al.* (2004) and Hiscox and Smyth (2008) use market-based experiments to examine the effect of labor standards labeling. Anderson and Hansen (2004) do the same for eco-labeled forest products. In Anderson and Hansen's study, consumers were offered a choice between virtually identical eco-labeled and unlabeled plywood products at two Home Depot stores in Oregon. When the two products were offered at the same price, sales increased with the eco-label. However, when the certified plywood was priced at a 2 percent premium, its sales fell. Nonetheless, 37 percent of consumers purchased the pricier product, hinting at some degree of social sensitivity to the environment in this context. The problem is that we do not know, based on the design of their study, what the price fall would have been from a 2 percent increase without any labeling.

The approaches used in the Prasad *et al.* (2004) and Hiscox and Smyth (2008) studies were similar. Prasad *et al.* (2004) investigated the demand for athletic socks that were on a rack with a sign indicating they were made under "good working conditions" (GWC), meaning that such conditions involved no child labor or unsafe working conditions. The socks on that rack were also labeled "GWC." Next to this rack was another rack of socks, identical in every respect to the first except that neither the rack nor the socks carried the GWC label. Over five months they increased the price differential between the two racks of socks from 0 to 40 percent. At a zero price difference, 49 percent of consumers purchased the GWC-labeled socks. This declined to 28 percent when the price differential was 40 percent. As with Anderson and Hansen's study, these results hint that a niche of labor-sensitive consumers exists, but, again, we do not have an effective base for comparison since we do not know what would have happened to the demand for non-labeled socks in the face of the higher prices.

Hiscox and Smyth (2008) labeled two products in a store in New York with a "Fair and Square" label that was defined on the rack: "These [towels/candles] have been made under fair labor conditions, in a safe and healthy working environment which is free of discrimination, and where management has committed to respecting the rights and dignity of workers." Unlike Prasad *et al.* (2004) they used existing branded products and did so in a store that included many other products advertised as "cause"-related. According to the authors, and contrary to Prasad *et al.* (2004, p. 2), to whom they make comparisons, "Sales rose for items labeled as being made under good labor standards, and demand for the labeled products actually rose with price increases of 10–20% above pre-test (unlabeled) levels." Hiscox and Smyth therefore appear to confirm that people are not only socially sensitive, but that they defy the law of demand.

These last two studies seem to contradict one another, but in reality they confirm each other in revealing a lack of basic demand for the labeling. Prasad *et al.* show clearly that some people will continue to pay, but that the number of those people is significantly below the levels revealed in surveys. Demand, so to say, still declines. However, one can read Hiscox and Smyth's data differently from how it at first appears, and the two studies then align. First, when the label is applied to towels, and no price change occurs, there is no change in the sales of the cheaper brand (which is labeled) and the more expensive brand (which is not). It is only when the price increases that the labeling appears to matter, but we do not know whether the increased price was taken by consumers as a signal that the quality difference in the towels was comparable. In other words, quality inferences are not controlled for in the experiment. When the more expensive towels are labeled we see an impact as well; but the authors do not change price, so we have no idea what the real impact would be. None of this is surprising given the effect associated with the impact of display changes independent of what the display indicates (see, for example, Inman, McAlister, and Hoyer, 1990, and Chandon *et al.*, 2008). In the case of their second product, candles, the labeling appears to have an immediate impact with no price change and with an increase in price of 10 percent. However, when price is increased 20 percent the opposite occurs and sales are equivalent to the baseline. Hence, in one of the two price change conditions there is no impact.

Mather, Knight, and Holdsworth (2005), in the most sophisticated study in this genre, set up a stall in New Zealand selling a locally grown premium cherry variety which they labeled as (1) "organic biogrow certified," (2) "low-residue Cromwell cherries," and (3) "100 percent spray-free genetically engineered cherries." All the cherries were, in fact, identical but the prices were varied using an experimental design with nine different price conditions, ensuring that the prices across the categories were balanced as equal, above, or below the other categories. Their results showed that organic labeling made little difference but there was sensitivity to the genetically modified (GM) food variety to the extent that it implied latitude for a price premium. Mather *et al.* (2007) repeated this experiment in five other countries – Sweden, Germany, France, Belgium, and the United Kingdom – where anti-GM feelings were considered quite strong. They find that these consumers were less sensitive to GM produce than New Zealanders, with a potential market share of approximately 20 percent.

Rode, Hogarth, and Le Menestrel (2008) applied a different approach more in line with experimental economics. In their experiments, individuals acted as traders in a market trading game with three producers, in which producers could sell an ethical product but only at a higher cost. In the case in which traders knew the cost associated with producing the ethical product, they were willing to pay a premium in recognition of the higher cost. The premium remained when the cost was unknown to the traders, but the willingness to compensate the producer was significantly less. The experiments also showed that, when the non-ethical price level is close to marginal cost, the ethical producer can gain considerably by charging a high premium but to a select, small niche. When this is not the case, and hence the general price is in line with the high price, the ethical producer is better off charging no effective premium and going for high market share. These authors also discovered considerable heterogeneity in their experimental subjects, in that different participants reacted to the game in very different ways. We show shortly that the finding of similar heterogeneity in our work reveals a much more complex view of social consumption than models of ethical consumerism imply.

These few studies hint at two critical factors for C_NSR. First, the magnitude of social consumption practice is limited, but there are some consumers who will purchase products with social attributes. In the market experiments, attributing intentionality to purchasing is unjustified without more information. As noted before, market sales can be biased by the fact that some consumers may simply be purchasing at random and it is the availability that is driving the sales. The results reveal that social consumption is not without some possible street credibility, but we need to know more. Second, there is the potential of profit from these activities. In the case of Prasad *et al.* (2004), the price elasticity is such that GWC labeling would reduce profits for almost all price increases. However, the findings of Rode, Hogarth, and Le Menestrel (2008), Mather, Knight, and Holdsworth (2005), and Mather *et al.* (2007) reveal that some price combinations, in conjunction with competitor reactions, can imply significant market share and profits for the social products.

Although these studies possess a degree of realism, none of them deal with several critical issues that we address in what follows. First, none of the studies deal with the issue of functional feature versus social product feature trade-offs. For example, the labeling experiments did not have "bad" products, just products on which no information was given. Second, they did not link their findings directly to unconstrained choice. While most noted that they had significantly smaller groups of social consumers, none attempted to address within their samples what the relationship was between "saying" and "paying." Finally, only one of the studies (that of Mather *et al.*, 2007) examined social consumption in a cross-cultural context. Although they find a remarkable degree of consistency in terms of the magnitude of the importance of the social issues in consumption, this might be attributable to the fact that they examined only developed countries. In what follows we will address each of these issues in turn.

Are we willing to put our money where our conscience is?

Our first group of experimental studies (which we denote as study no. 1) examined three extreme groups: (1) revealed supporters of a social cause (members of Amnesty International [AI] in Australia); (2) young Hong Kong undergraduate students; and (3) full-time and part-time Master of Business Administration (MBA) students at an Australian University. The sample is described in detail in Appendix 1, but a few words are important in setting the context. The sample lacks representativeness but has the characteristic of quite disparate individuals both culturally – Hong Kong versus Australia – and in terms of hedonistic orientation. By looking at these samples we are able to address whether individuals exist who will make substantive trade-offs between functional and social features of products and whether these extremities reveal something about where areas of segmentation can be made. Our intent is not to make statements about representativeness, but simply to see whether we can discover the degree to which individuals who have a specific orientation reveal this through a variety of means – in this case, surveys and experiments.

Two product categories were studied. The first was athletic shoes, for which the social focus is on labor issues. The second was bath soaps, for which there are embedded environmental issues. We examined the individual's choices for alternatives in one or the other product category.

The approach used was a combination of (1) a discrete choice experiment, (2) an ethical personality inventory, and (3) an unconstrained survey on ethical consumption of the type popularly used by practitioners and market research organizations. The structure of the experiment is shown in Figure 4.1. Below we describe each component in detail and then move on to a series of implications from specific analyses based on the data generated from the sample.

Discrete choice experimentation

Discrete choice experimentation (DCE) allows for the modeling of the decision process of an individual or group of individuals in a particular context via the comparison of trade-offs between the discrete components underlying the choice. In the case of consumer choice we can characterize the decision as involving the evaluation of a hypothetical product or service that is made up of a bundle of attributes (or features)

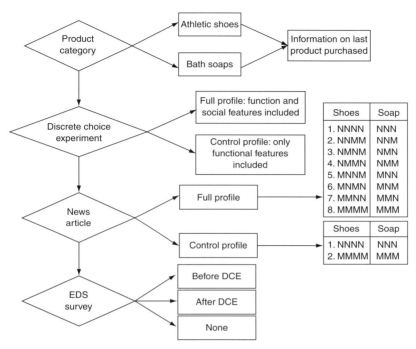

Notes: N = Ethical feature is not mentioned in the article and M = ethical feature is mentioned in the article.

Order of ethical features (e.g. MMMM implies that all ethical features are mentioned in the article):
shoes – (1) child labor, (2) workers paid minimum wage, (3) working conditions, and (4) living conditions;
soap – (1) biodegradable formulation, (2) animal testing, and (3) animal by-products used as ingredients.

Figure 4.1 Structure of study no. 1

that can each vary across a range of levels (Louviere, Hensher, and Swait, 2000). The variation of the attribute levels is controlled via an experimental design that ensures that the maximum information about the decision model is extracted from the minimum number of hypothetical choices (see, for example, Street, Burgess, and Louviere, 2005, and Street and Burgess, 2007). The dependent variable is the probability that a product or service made up of a specific mixture of attribute levels is chosen in the specific context by individuals of specific types. Hence, we are interested in discovering whether or not there exists a group of individuals – socially responsible consumers – who will be more likely to purchase products with specific social features – such as good labor practices – when faced with a price for doing so.

DCE is especially effective in the situation examined here because it allows for more realistic comparisons of potential products, particularly those that currently do not exist in the marketplace, such as products with specific labor practice attributes. List, Sinha, and Taylor (2006, p. 24) find evidence that

the choice-based approach performs well for both private and public goods: in both the purchase and intra-buy decision hypothetical and real values are similar, and in all cases hypothetical choices . . . are statistically indistinguishable from actual responses. This evidence suggests that the choice experimental approach might provide a valuable avenue to credibly estimate use and passive use values of non-market goods and services.

DCE also has distinct advantages over other sorts of self-report measures, such as survey-based rating scales. First, there is greater realism, in three respects: (1) greater task realism, as the situation is closer to the actual choices being made in a market; (2) greater product realism, as the hypothetical products are based on a mixture of different features involving trade-offs normally made by consumers; and (3) greater competitive realism, in that individuals are comparing between brands and features that are in competition in the marketplace. Second, the discrete choice nature of the decision – the individual is simply choosing or not choosing to consider or buy the product – alleviates most concerns about experimental task bias described in Chapter 3, in that (1) DCE reduces the incentive for respondents to behave strategically, as there is no socially acceptable answer possible; (2) as trade-offs must be made across the attributes, individuals are forced to differentiate between products possessing different attribute levels (not everything can be "good"); (3) as there is only the choice of choosing or not there is no question of inequivalence between individuals (i.e. a "No" is a "No" for everyone); and (4) aggregation of choices is now possible, since the operative dependent variable is the probability of choosing a product with a specific configuration of attribute levels.

The components of study no. 1

The experimental component of study no. 1 had three parts.

Part 1 Individuals were first assigned (50:50) into a product category and received the materials pertaining to either athletic shoes or bath soaps. They were then asked about their last purchase in the focal product category as a means of gathering product recall information on the product attributes used in the experiment.

Part 2 Participants then received a mocked-up newspaper article that included information about the functional and social features of the product category in question. This newspaper article had a core paragraph that always mentioned the functional attributes of the product but varied as to whether or not one or any or all of the social attributes were mentioned. There were eight combinations in which the information was mentioned or not, as specified in Figure 4.1. In the control condition, either all the social issues were mentioned (e.g. MMMM) or none were mentioned (e.g. NNNN). This allowed us to examine whether providing information influenced the magnitude of the impact of the social issues. Figure 4.2 provides an example of the article profile used for athletic shoes.

Part 3 Finally, the participants evaluated whether or not they would "consider" or "purchase" each of thirty-two experimentally varied, hypothetical products. "Considering" meant that "the athletic shoes described [were] attractive enough for [the consumer] to consider them (i.e. include them in [their] list of possible choices) or if they are simply not worth considering." This is equivalent to the asking of a trial question (Morwitz, Steckel, and Gupta, 2007). "Purchasing" indicated that the consumer would "buy the athletic shoes *instead of or in addition to* [their] current athletic shoes the next time [they] purchased athletic shoes. That is, [they] would be willing to buy the athletic shoes described to replace or to complement [their] current athletic shoes."

Ten percent of individuals received a control profile that included the newspaper article but did not include the social product features in the product presented. Hence, 90 percent of the subjects made choices between products that included social attributes.

Note that the order of parts of the experiment given in the flow diagram of Figure 4.1 is not the order discussed above. For example, the newspaper article conditions are influenced by whether or not the individual receives the full or control profile. However, Figure 4.1 does show how different versions of the total survey were put together.

Table 4.1 provides information on the social and product features (attributes) for each of the products, along with the levels used in the experimental design. Individuals saw thirty-two different products, with the levels of the features varied based on an experimental design, and made a consideration and purchase decision about each. Figure 4.3

A sneaker by any other name

By Sandra Brandt

The product choice available to today's athlete – professional, amateur, or casual – is truly amazing. Also, what was once a product for use only by the athletically inclined has become an everyday fashion item. The humble sneaker has come of age.

Today's sophisticated athletic shoes are made for many different people and purposes. They differ not only in terms of comfort and cushioning but have many additional specialized characteristics as well. Shoes vary based on their ability to ventilate your feet, whether they support your ankles, their weight, and the durability of the soles. Reflective athletic shoes protect the nighttime athlete by increasing his/her visibility. Shoes are available in a variety of synthetic and natural materials.

Most athletic shoes are made in developing nations, where labor rates are lower and production less costly. This has raised a dilemma for shoe manufacturers since the labor standards in these countries can be quite lax. It is not uncommon to find that products coming from these countries have been manufactured using child labor *or produced in substandard manufacturing facilities. Additional complaints are that many workers work for less than the legally mandated minimum wage and their employers do not provide adequate living conditions at the factory.*

It was once the case that when you purchased a running shoe or basketball shoe your choice was limited to a few standard options. However, the variety available to today's consumer is a blistering array that is meant to satisfy almost any consumer's athletic requirements.

Notes: **Bold** shows information that is used whenever any of the social issues are mentioned in the paragraph. The underlined information is added when child labor is mentioned. The *underlined italicized* information is added when unsafe working conditions are mentioned. The ***bold italicized*** information is added when minimum wages are mentioned. The *italicized* information is added when adequate living conditions are mentioned. All the other information always remains, independent of whether or not any social issues are mentioned.

Source: GlobeNet News Service

Figure 4.2 Mocked-up news article for athletic shoes

gives a screenshot of what the individual saw in the experiment when making his/her choice.

There were two non-experimental components to the study: an ethical disposition survey and the replication of a poll used by the MORI organization, along with a series of standard demographics.

Ethical disposition inventory

We created an ethical disposition survey (EDS) that included two items that commonly appear in the literature. Both are presented in full in Appendix 2.

The first is the well-known Machiavellianism scale developed by Christie and Geis (1970). We use the MACH IV variant.

Table 4.1 *Product features and social attributes used in study no. 1*

Athletic shoes	Bath soap
Basic product features	
Shock absorption/cushioning (LOW or **HIGH**)	Shape (ROUNDED or **SQUARE**)
Weight (**LIGHTER** or HEAVIER)	Natural ingredients (NO or **YES**)
Ankle support (LOW-CUT or **HIGH-CUT**)	Scented (**NO** or YES)
Sole durability (SHORT or **LONG**)	Artificial colors (**NO** or YES)
Breathability/ventilation (LOW or **HIGH**)	Moisturizer (NO or **YES**)
Fabrication materials (SYNTHETIC or **LEATHER**)	Antibacterial protection (NO or **YES**)
Reflectivity at night (NO or **YES**)	Will it clog your pores? (**NO** or YES)
Comfort/fit (LOW or **HIGH**)	Will it worsen your acne? (**NO** or YES)
Brand of shoe (Nike, Adidas, Reebok, New Balance, Converse, Brooks, Fila, Puma, Etonic, Asics, Saucony)	Brand name (MAJOR MULTINATIONAL or LOCAL BRAND)
Price ($40, $70, $100, $130) – in Australia	Price ($2.25, $1.65, $1.05, $0.45) – in Australia
Price ($300, $550, $800, $1,050) – in Hong Kong	Price ($6, $9, $12, $15) – in Hong Kong
Social features	
Is child labor used in making the product? (**NO** or YES)	Biodegradable formulation? (NO or **YES**)
Are workers paid above minimum wage? (NO or **YES**)	Tested on animals? (**NO** or YES)
Are workers' working conditions dangerous? (**NO** or YES)	Animal by-products used as ingredients? (**NO** or YES)
Are workers' living conditions at the factory acceptable? (NO or **YES**)	

Note: All the "good" attributes are represented in **bold**; the "bad" attributes are non-bold.

Machiavellianism represents the tendency of individuals to be manipulative and deceptive. The scale is calibrated so that the population median is a score of 100. A low Machiavellianism score (<100) has been shown to be correlated with greater cooperation in a prisoners' dilemma game (see, for example, Lyons and Aitken, 2008) and more

Features of the shoe	Features of shoe X
Shock absorption/cushioning	High
Weight	Heavier
Ankle support	Low-cut
Sole durability	Short
Breathability/ventilation	High
Fabrication materials	Leather
Reflectivity at night	Yes
Comfort/fit	High
Is child labor used in making the product?	No
Are workers paid above minimum wage?	No
Are workers' working conditions dangerous?	No
Are workers' living conditions at the factory acceptable?	Yes
Brand of Shoe	Adidas
Price	$40
1. If the shoes described above were available in your local shops now, would you consider trying it (Tick ONE box only)? ☐ No ☐ Yes	
2. If the shoes described above were available in your local shops now, would you buy it instead of or in addition to your current shoes next time you shop for shoes (Tick ONE box only)? ☐ No ☐ Yes	

Figure 4.3 Example of the choice task for athletic shoes

reciprocity in economic trust games (Gunnthorsdottir, McCabe, and Smith, 2002), as well as a tendency toward more altruism (Wilson and Csikszentmihalyi, 2007). Wilson, Near, and Miller (1996) argue that Machiavellianism reflects one of many evolved social conduct strategies.

The second scale is Forsyth's (1980) ethics position questionnaire (EPQ), which measures moral relativism and ethical idealism. It is one of the most frequently used scales in the business ethics literature. For example, since 2004 more than thirty-five articles in the *Journal of Business Ethics* alone have used this scale, or a variant of it, to assess moral positioning, typically in a cross-cultural context. The EPQ operationalizes Forsyth's thesis that moral judgment and behavior can be hypothesized to exist on two dimensions: that which emphasizes the importance of universal ethical rules versus a posture of relativism, and that which emphasizes humanitarian ideals, or no harm, versus one that involves basic trade-offs for the greater good. The scale variant used here ranges from low (1) to high (5).

The MORI poll

We also utilized a heavily referenced survey conducted by MORI for the Catholic Agency for Overseas Development (CAFOD) and Christian Aid Abroad in the United Kingdom as a way of calibrating our findings with those normally seen in the popular press. This survey questions individuals about why they purchase and whether or not they would purchase products made under specific circumstances. The MORI poll is presented in full in Appendix 2. The poll was first conducted in 1997 and has been repeated in various forms ever since. It is uniformly quoted as an indicative source on the tidal wave of support from average consumers for ethical products, labor practices, and ethical sourcing (see, for example, Crew, 2004, Nicholls and Opal, 2005, and Low and Davenport, 2006).

The study sample

Table 4.2 presents the demographics of the sample along with some basic information about the respondents. The AI supporters are older, with greater family income, and are more likely to be married, more likely to have children, and more likely to be white. More tellingly for the subject of ethics, they are less Machiavellian, more likely to be moral absolutists (the Australian MBAs are the most morally relative), and strong ethical idealists (the Hong Kong students are the least idealistic). These last facts are all quite consistent with a stereotypical view of a human rights group supporter.

Willingness to consider/purchase; willingness to pay

The most critical question is the first: to what extent do social product features influence product choice? If consumers do not substantively change behavior to accommodate the social features of the products and services they buy, all other questions relating to ethical consumption and C_NSR become somewhat moot. To investigate this we use two measures. The first is the probability that an individual will choose a product based on whether or not a specific social feature is embedded in

Table 4.2 *Sample characteristics for study no. 1*

	Hong Kong university	Australia MBA	AI supporter
Male (percentage)	46.40	60.40	29.30
Age (percentages)			
≤ 19	0.60	0.62	1.70
20–29	93.80	61.11	16.90
30–39	5.40	31.48	22.00
40–49	0.00	3.70	25.30
50 +	0.00	1.23	31.90
Education (highest degree)			
High school	1.40	17.80	10.10
Attended university	58.30	26.70	15.30
University degree	36.80	46.50	52.90
Postgraduate degree	0.00	4.00	17.40
Family income (inc. parents)			
≤ $20,999	35.60	13.90	13.10
$21,000–$35,999	33.70	53.50	18.50
$36,000–$61,999	12.90	0.00	28.10
$62,000–$77,999	5.00	25.70	6.70
≥ $78,000	10.90	0.00	28.60
Lifestyle			
Single (inc. divorced)	93.10	60.10	38.90
Married or cohabiting	5.00	34.7	50.50
Children (percentage with)	1.70	14.29	48.00
Ethnicity			
White (European/American)	0.00	46.30	83.60
Chinese	98.20	19.75	0.00
Other Asian	0.00	16.82	15.90
Ethical disposition survey			
Ethical idealism	3.26	3.57	3.63
Moral relativism	3.08	3.39	2.75
Machiavellianism	96.05	96.66	91.95
N =	111	162	172

Notes: At the time of the surveys A $1.00 = US $0.63 and US $1.00 = HK $7.73.
Numbers may not sum to 100 percent because of missing data or the exclusion of an
"Other" category. The Hong Kong university students were questioned about their
parents' income. The Australian MBA students include part-time students, for whom a
university degree is not a requirement for admission.

the product, every other feature – social and functional and price – held constant. The second is the willingness to pay, or the marginal dollar value of the social attribute(s). In what follows we concentrate on the "consider" choice and exclude discussion of the "buy" choice. However, the results of both are consistent and there is no loss of generality. Auger *et al.* (2003, 2008) and Auger and Devinney (2007) provide detail about other aspects of the data examined here.

Table 4.3 presents the raw choice probabilities based on whether or not a specific social product feature was present along with the influence of price. Two probabilities are presented: the simple unconditional probability that a product possessing the focal feature is chosen; and the percentage of purchases that includes a product possessing the focal feature. In other words, the first probability is the likelihood of choosing one of the thirty-two hypothetical products conditional on the feature being identified as part of the product; the second includes only those products that the participant says s/he would consider. One example illustrates how to read these results. For an AI supporter, the probability of considering any athletic shoe that was manufactured without child labor was 0.11. In other words, if the absence of child labor was a feature that appeared in the product offered, all other features held constant, an AI supporter indicated that s/he would consider it in 11 percent of cases. This represents the unconditional probability of consideration (or purchase trial). This 11 percent of cases accounted for 82 percent of total choices of athletic shoes for that sample of respondents. So, on average an AI supporter chooses 4.3 of the thirty-two products s/he sees and, of those 4.3 products, 3.5 are child-labor-free. The implication of this finding is that child labor was potentially a significant factor affecting choice for that group of consumers.

At this point, we should not read too much into these probabilities as they ignore the marginal influence of other features and individual differences. However, we can see a few important results that stand out and require further examination. First, the AI participants are much more likely to be influenced by the social features, particularly conditionally. They say they will consider fewer of the products, and when they do reveal a purchase intention it is for products that are more likely to possess a "good" social feature. Second, the Australian and Hong Kong samples are not very different in terms of the likelihood of choice of product based on the social features. Third, the big, differentiating issues are child labor and working conditions (in the case of athletic shoes) and animal testing (in the case of the bath soaps). Fourth, in all cases there are clear and strong price effects. As the price rises the

Table 4.3 *Probability of considering a product based on social product features (percentage of total choices in parentheses)*

		Athletic shoes				Bath soap		
		Child labor	Minimum wage	Working conditions	Living conditions	Biodegradable	Animal testing	Animal by-products
Sample								
Hong Kong university		0.16 (60%)	0.14 (55%)	0.15 (56%)	0.13 (50%)	0.21 (52%)	0.23 (58%)	0.21 (54%)
Australia MBA		0.20 (51%)	0.21 (54%)	0.21 (54%)	0.19 (48%)	0.20 (50%)	0.22 (55%)	0.20 (51%)
AI supporter		0.11 (82%)	0.08 (58%)	0.10 (75%)	0.09 (66%)	0.16 (65%)	0.20 (85%)	0.16 (61%)
Price								
Shoes	Soap							
$40	$0.45	0.20 (57%)	0.16 (45%)	0.19 (55%)	0.21 (61%)	0.25 (57%)	0.27 (61%)	0.17 (39%)
$70	$1.05	0.19 (65%)	0.19 (64%)	0.19 (64%)	0.13 (42%)	0.25 (61%)	0.28 (67%)	0.28 (67%)
$100	$1.65	0.12 (58%)	0.13 (64%)	0.13 (64%)	0.09 (43%)	0.16 (53%)	0.23 (75%)	0.23 (75%)
$130	$2.25	0.09 (65%)	0.07 (48%)	0.07 (53%)	0.09 (63%)	0.08 (48%)	0.11 (63%)	0.07 (37%)

likelihood of purchasing declines, and there is no pattern to the trade-off between price and the social features. Essentially, we do not see, at lower or higher prices, a tendency to shun or prefer products possessing the social features. Overall, this information suggests that some individuals will account for social features in making differential purchasing choices.

The discrete choice approach allows us to convert the probability of purchase directly into conditional dollar equivalents. By comparing the dollar value of specific bundles of product features, we can estimate the dollar equivalent of the utility that a consumer derives from the presence/absence of specific product features. Details of how to calculate WTP for product features are discussed in Louviere, Hensher, and Swait (2000). Briefly, the desired quantity is simply the price-sensitivity-adjusted difference in the expected maximum utilities of the different product mixes. We can characterize a product or service as a bundle of N product features, with the levels of these features given by j_i. For example, j_2 might be "safe working conditions," where j_2 can take on one of the two levels {YES, NO}. Hence, the product or service can be represented by vector $J = [j_1, j_2, \ldots, j_N]$. We can define J_k as representing J with one product feature (k) changed – e.g. two products are identical in every way except that one includes child labor. The dollar value difference between J and J_k will be $[1/-\beta_{price}](EU(J_k) - EU(J))$, where $EU(\bullet)$ is the expected value of the maximum utility of a set of product features and $-\beta_{price}$ is the price coefficient from the binary or multinomial logit model. In this study the expected utilities are estimated using a binary logit.

Table 4.4 provides the details of the WTP estimates for the individual social features, and the aggregate for the functional features along with the price elasticity. Detailed estimates can be found in Auger *et al.* (2003) and Auger, Devinney, and Louviere (2007b). We see the same sort of pattern as in Table 4.3, but the WTP estimate reveals more since it is based on the marginal value of the alternatives chosen and not chosen. On average, the AI supporters are willing to pay the most for social features, both in total dollar terms and as a percentage of the feature value. The feature value is the sum of the WTPs for all the features examined, excluding the price. Note that the feature value is considerably less than the average experimental price paid in the case of athletic shoes ($85.00) and considerably more than the average experimental price paid for bath soaps ($1.35). On average, the features of the athletic shoes examined were worth approximately 40 percent of the average price to the consumer (the range is 13 percent for Hong Kong students to 62 percent for

Table 4.4 *Willingness to pay for social product features (percentage of feature value in parentheses)*

	Athletic shoes				Bath soap		
	Child Labor	Minimum wage	Working Conditions	Living conditions	Biodegradable	Animal testing	Animal by-products
Sample							
Hong Kong university	$0.15 (1.28%)	$0.67 (5.73%)	$0.58 (4.96%)	$0.42 (3.59%)	$0.04 (0.56%)	$0.43 (6.02%)	$0.11 (1.54%)
Australia MBA	$4.68 (12.52%)	$2.21 (5.91%)	$2.70 (7.22%)	$0.17 (0.45%)	$0.08 (3.02%)	$0.33 (12.45%)	$0.15 (5.66%)
AI supporter	$13.03 (24.88%)	$5.19 (9.91%)	$10.84 (20.69%)	$6.55 (12.50%)	$0.69 (10.30%)	$2.26 (33.73%)	$0.67 (10.00%)
Functional features							
Hong Kong university	$8.52 (72.88%)				$6.56 (91.88%)		
Australia MBA	$24.94 (66.70%)				$2.09 (78.87%)		
AI supporter	$16.70 (31.8%)				$3.08 (45.97%)		
Brand (Nike and Reebok)							
Hong Kong university	$1.35 (11.55%)						
Australia MBA	$2.69 (7.19%)						
AI supporter	$0.07 (0.13%)						
Price elasticity							
Hong Kong university	−1.28				−1.18		
Australia MBA	−1.09				−1.07		
AI supporter	−1.07				−1.10		

AI supporters), meaning that more value is being ascribed to something other than the functional features. For bath soaps, the value ascribed is 400 percent, meaning that the average price is much lower than what it could be with the features embedded (the range is 196 percent for Australian MBAs to 529 percent for Hong Kong students).

Overall, the AI supporters reveal that they will overwhelmingly take into account the social features; indeed, it is a greater percentage of total feature value than the functional features (approximately 78 percent in the case of athletic shoes and 56 percent in the case of bath soap). The MBA students and Hong Kong undergraduates are approximately similar in the percentage of feature value that they give to the social features of athletic shoes, but the Australian MBAs value the features much more and are significantly less price-sensitive. The Hong Kong students are much more price-sensitive on average, but will pay considerably for two features in bath soaps, the avoidance of pore clogging and acne relief, which explains most of their $6.56 value for functional features.

We can read the numbers in Table 4.4 in several ways. First, as expected, we see heterogeneity in the degree to which social features matter. Those with a self-professed social orientation seem to be willing to pay more to align their product preferences with their conscience. However, this heterogeneity is also seen between the Hong Kong student and Australian MBA samples, even when there is no expectation as to the directionality of the effect. Second, the degree to which social features compete from a value perspective is impressive. Although we expect that these estimates are no doubt high (as we made no effort to hide the salience of the social features in the experiments), we still find that individuals will respond to their existence in what amounts to a material manner. Taken as a percentage of the paid price, rather than the total feature value, we find an average WTP of around 18.5 percent for athletic shoes (with a low of 2 percent for Hong Kong students and a high of 42 percent for AI supporters). In the case of bath soaps, because the feature value is considerably above the actual price, the percentages of purchase price are even higher, at approximately 117 percent (with a low of 42 percent for both Hong Kong students and Australian MBAs and a high of 268 percent for AI supporters).

More conservatively, we need to recognize that the sample used was purely a convenience and in no way can be subject to generalization – although many reporting on our work have done just that. In addition, the estimates of WTP assume that all other factors are optimal and that the features are simply being added to what are already desirable products. We address this issue shortly by looking at how choice changes when functionality is in doubt.

What is perhaps more interesting is the fact that virtually none of the individual level factors we examined appeared to have any predictive validity in terms of differentiating between those consumers who are more or less sensitive to the inclusion of social features. Survey-based work (such as that by Al-Khatib, Vittel, and Rawwas, 1997, and Al-Khatib, Stanton, and Rawwas, 2005) continuously indicates that there is predictive validity arising from demographic variables – gender, education, income, etc. – and ethical scales, such as Forsyth's EPQ and the Machiavellianism scale (see, for example, Davis, Anderson, and Curtis, 2001, and Donelson, O'Boyle, and McDaniel, 2008). In our case, as reported in detail in Auger *et al.* (2003, 2008) and Auger, Devinney, and Louviese (2007a), we find absolutely no influence of any demographics. Women versus men, older versus younger, those from wealthier families, and so on, do not seem to be any more or less sensitive to the inclusion of social features in product offerings. Although the Forsyth EPQ provides little information, Machiavellianism is slightly related to social issue sensitivity, as one would expect, since the AI supporters differ on this scale quite significantly.

How valuable is providing information?

Another component of study no. 1 was the examination of whether the provision of information played any role in choice. This was done by including in the estimation whether or not a specific feature was mentioned and how that influenced the degree to which individuals reacted to social features. The more sophisticated analysis can be simplified by looking at whether simply mentioning the social features influences the likelihood of choosing a product possessing either that feature or any other feature. This is done in Table 4.5, which effectively replicates Table 4.3. What we see is that mentioning or not mentioning the focal feature (which is the first feature) has no discernible impact on whether or not a product is chosen. The conclusion is that increasing the salience by providing information does not disproportionately influence choice, nor does providing additional information about the meaning of the social features.

Table 4.5 *Probability of buying a product based on whether or not social product features are mentioned in the news article (percentage of total purchases in parentheses)*

	Social features			
Athletic shoes	Child labor	Minimum wage	Working conditions	Living conditions
No features mentioned	0.12 (70%)	0.09 (50%)	0.12 (70%)	0.10 (55%)
1–2 features mentioned*	0.16 (60%)	0.14 (56%)	0.15 (57%)	0.13 (52%)
3–4 features mentioned	0.13 (60%)	0.12 (54%)	0.18 (83%)	0.12 (54%)
Bath soap	Biodegradable	Animal testing	Animal by-products	
No features mentioned	0.22 (57%)	0.23 (60%)	0.19 (51%)	
1 feature mentioned*	0.18 (57%)	0.22 (70%)	0.18 (57%)	
2 features mentioned	0.18 (53%)	0.22 (66%)	0.19 (56%)	
3 features mentioned	0.17 (61%)	0.22 (73%)	0.16 (59%)	

Note: * = including the focal feature.

Can we believe what consumers say when not constrained? The link between surveys and experiments

We have been critical of the claim that unconstrained survey responses reveal anything about true preferences. Study no. 1 allows us to examine this question by examining the degree to which popular unconstrained survey instruments reveal information about individuals' constrained preferences. To address this question, we used the quite well cited MORI poll developed for CAFOD. The instrument has been described earlier and is given in full in Appendix 2.

Table 4.6 presents the mean responses for all MORI poll questions for the three samples, as well as the aggregate means for all respondents. As would be expected, the AI supporters showed greater concern about

Table 4.6 *MORI poll responses by sample and in total*

	Sample			
	Hong Kong university	Australia MBA	AI supporter	Total
Which, if any, of the following would you take into consideration when you were buying it?	Percentage indicating that it would matter			
1. Appearance/style	82.5	79.8	67.7	74.0
2. Availability	5.3	40.3	35.9	32.8
3. Brand	45.6	51.2	16.7	32.6
4. Quality	12.3	97.7	86.9	79.4
5. People paid enough to live on	3.5	24.8	77.3	48.7
6. Little damage to environment	28.1	31.0	76.3	53.9
7. Work environment healthy	12.3	24.8	74.2	48.4
8. No animal testing	21.1	15.5	61.6	40.1
9. Human rights record of country	0.0	19.4	58.1	36.5
10. Need for the product	93.0	87.6	81.3	85.2
Which, if any, of the following things about the people who made the product would affect your decision to buy it?	Mean, on four-point scale (1) would still buy it, (2) would still consider buying it, (3) would make no difference, (4) would definitely not buy it			
11. Forced to work overtime	2.43	1.74	2.87	2.56
12. Did not earn enough wages to live off	2.48	2.18	3.62	3.19
13. Had no job security	2.68	2.81	2.84	2.56
14. Could be sacked if they became pregnant	2.86	2.13	3.81	3.53
15. Found their health to be in danger	2.88	3.38	3.90	3.58
16. Had no holidays or days off	2.69	3.37	3.65	3.23
17. Were not allowed to join a union	2.67	2.82	3.45	2.94
18. Had no right to sick pay	2.56	2.32	3.52	3.08
19. Were subject to discrimination or harassment	3.28	2.66	3.82	3.54
20. Were under the legal minimum age to work	2.87	3.21	3.74	3.49

social and ethical issues than the Hong Kong students and Australian MBAs. The Hong Kong students showed the least concern for most social and ethical issues while the Australian MBAs took the middle ground on most issues.

More interesting results can be observed from a correlation matrix of all the items in the MORI poll. Table 4.7 provides a summary, and the full correlation matrix is given in Appendix 2. Table 4.7 shows the average correlations within and between groups of items (the numbers correspond to the questions shown in Table 4.6). What is apparent immediately is that the social questions elicit significant correlations. The social questions in section 1 – "Which, if any, of the following would you take into consideration when you were buying it?" (questions 5–9) – are all enormously highly correlated: on average, 0.52. The same is true of all the answers to section 2 – "Which, if any, of the following things about the people who made the product would affect your decision to buy it?" (questions 11–20) – with the same average correlation of 0.52. The average correlation between questions 5–9 and 11–20 is 0.34 – again, quite a large significant correlation. Indeed, what is even more astounding is the fact that only one of the fifty pairs of correlation coefficients between items 5–9 and 11–20 is below 0.20 (between items 6 and 14), and that every social question in section 1 is significantly correlated (ten out of ten), as are those in section 2 (forty-five out of forty-five).

These results can be interpreted in three overlapping ways. First, the results demonstrate relatively high levels of consistency in the way respondents answered the different questions about ethical issues in the MORI poll. Second, the results also indicate that respondents do not engage in much differentiation between the issues. That is, respondents tended to have (or answer the questions as if they have) similar opinions on the ethical issues irrespective of the nature of the issue. Third, it may be that respondents simply want to appear to be socially responsible and the responses are nothing more than a socially influenced artifact. The implication of this is that either people do indeed care about "everything" (or nothing) or that such patterns are a result of their desire to answer the questions in an "acceptable" manner. As the same pattern is not observed with respect to the non-social features, this is not something related to the instrument itself but the nature of the questions asked.

What we see, therefore, is a picture that reveals some differences across samples (based on mean differences), particularly at the

Table 4.7 *Correlation matrix of MORI poll responses (all respondents)*

		Which, if any, of the following . . .					
		would you take into consideration when you were buying it?				things about the people who made the product would affect your decision to buy it?
Question		1–2	3 (Brand)	4 (Quality)	5–9 (Social)	10 (Need)	11–20 (Social)
Average	1–2	**0.33**					
	3	**0.24**	1.00				
	4	**0.30**	0.15				
	5–9	−0.02	**−0.25**	−0.09	***0.52***		
	10	0.19	0.07	0.15	−0.10	1.00	
	11–20	−0.02	**−0.23**	0.12	**0.34**	−0.04	***0.52***
Significant correlations/total correlations	1–2	1/1					
	3	2/2					
	4	2/2	0/1				
	5–9	0/10	4/5	0/5	10/10		
	10	0/2	0/1	0/1	0/10		
	11–20	0/20	8/10	1/10	49/50	0/10	45/45

Notes: |Correlations| ≥ 0.20 are shown in **bold**. Those |correlations| ≥ 0.50 are shown in ***bold italics.***

extremes, but little differentiation between the issues (as represented by the correlations). To get at this further, multivariate analysis techniques were applied to cluster individuals into more homogeneous groups. The approach is typical of much of the segmentation-based research in both academic and commercial operations, in which the goal is to generate clusters of individuals with different ethical proclivities. What we want to know here is whether there is much validity in this approach.

Details of the full analysis are given in Auger and Devinney (2007). Based on the sample from study no. 1, they find six clusters of individuals, who can be characterized on their responses to the MORI poll questionnaire on four dimensions: (1) their concern for labor/workplace issues (high on questions 11–13 and 16–18); (2) their concern over health and harassment issues (high on questions 14, 15, 19, and 20); (3) their concern for general rights issues (high on questions 5–9); and (4) their concern for product functionality (high on questions 1–4). To keep the discussion simple, we focus on the two extreme clusters. The results for the other clusters have similar implications but do not present quite so stark a contrast. For simplicity, we will call these extreme groups the "Utilitarians" and the "Anti-utilitarians." The Utilitarians rate product characteristics highly and generally seem unconcerned about any of the social issues. The Anti-utilitarians look down on product characteristics and indicate strong concern across the range of social issues. The Anti-utilitarians would be the ethical warriors.

Table 4.8 provides a comparison between these two extreme groups in terms of demographics, their responses to the various ethical questionnaires, and their willingness to pay for social product features as a ratio to their willingness to pay for functional features. What we see is that the clusters appear remarkably logical. The Utilitarians are younger, more educated, less likely to be Amnesty International supporters, and more likely to be MBA students. They also are more Machiavellian and more morally relative. In terms of the MORI poll questions, they are more concerned about the product and unconcerned about the social issues. The Anti-utilitarians are less morally relativist (based on Forsyth's scale) and more likely to be male, older and wealthier. In fact, at this stage, most analyses would stop, as it is clear that we have a characterization of the "ethical" consumer that is logical and consistent with most of our a priori suppositions about what such a person should look like – until, that is, we look at the WTP estimates. It

Table 4.8 *MORI poll responses by extreme segments*

	Utilitarian	Anti-utilitarian
Male (percentage)	46.40	60.40
Age (years)	25.99	39.88
Education (percentage with university degree)	90.00	76.50
Family income (inc. parents)	$35,806	$50,247
Lifestyle (percentage single)	93.30	58.82
AI supporter (percentage)	8.39	36.60
MBA student (percentage)	11.38	3.40
Ethical disposition survey		
Ethical idealism (five-point scale)	3.56	3.49
Moral relativism (four-point scale)	3.28	2.70
Machiavellianism	98.17	91.76

MORI poll responses	Percentage indicating that it would matter	
Which, if any, of the following would you take into consideration when you were buying it?		
1. Appearance/style	75.6	53.6
2. Availability	0.0	0.0
3. Brand	51.1	10.7
4. Quality	46.3	76.8
5. People paid enough to live on	2.4	96.4
6. Little damage to environment	22.0	98.2
7. Work environment healthy	2.4	96.4
8. No animal testing	12.2	78.6
9. Human rights record of country	7.3	66.1
10. Need for the product	100.0	69.6

Which, if any, of the following things about the people who made the product would affect your decision to buy it?	Mean, on four-point scale (1) would still buy it, (2) would still consider buying it, (3) would make no difference, (4) would definitely not buy it	
11. Forced to work overtime	2.58	3.05
12. Did not earn enough wages to live off	2.56	3.72
13. Had no job security	2.71	2.84
14. Could be sacked if they became pregnant	2.59	4.00
15. Found their health to be in danger	2.42	4.00
16. Had no holidays or days off	2.76	3.78

Table 4.8 (*cont.*)

	Utilitarian	Anti-utilitarian
17. Were not allowed to join a union	2.78	3.52
18. Had no right to sick pay	2.61	3.74
19. Were subject to discrimination or harassment	2.95	3.82
20. Were under the legal minimum age to work	2.93	3.91
Willingness to pay	Percentage price premium	
Athletic shoes		
Child labor	12%	16%
Dangerous work conditions	12%	9%
Minimum wages	12%	13%
Safe living condition	12%	14%
Bath soap		
Animal testing	12%	13%
Biodegradability	9%	8%
Animal by-products	10%	10%

is at this point that we see that there is very little – indeed, what amounts to an insignificant – difference in the willingness to pay for the social features. Although the Anti-utilitarians are slightly more likely to pay for most labor-related features – their price premium is on average 13 percent as compared to 12 percent for the Utilitarians – the difference is trivial and statistically insignificant. In the case of bath soaps, the average premium is identical, at 10.33 percent. What is more revealing is how big the differences are in the survey responses, yet how small the differences are when it comes to the price premium.

The problem seen here is common: unconstrained survey responses do not translate effectively into a means of predicting constrained choice. The question is, why is this the case? The answer is clear and is a function of two phenomena. First, it is not that consumers who have a proclivity to pay for social features are not saying that they would do so in surveys. The problem resides with those individuals with no such proclivity who answer in socially acceptable ways. They create statistical noise that drowns out the information about those who are truly revealing their preferences and intentions. Second, even those individuals with a true proclivity to pay for social causes will overstate the degree of their concern. For example, it is absolutely inconceivable that

96 percent of even the Anti-utilitarians would actually not purchase a product because people were not "paid enough to live on" or that 66 percent would not purchase a product based on the human rights record of the country of production. If that were the case, nearly two-thirds of these individuals would never purchase products made in Third World countries (which would probably make their life come to a grinding halt), or put fuel in their cars because the oil came from a totalitarian Middle Eastern dictatorship.

Will consumers sacrifice functionality?

To this point we have an image of consumers as multifaceted, complex individuals who present a picture that at one and the same time supports and refutes a social conscience. This is what we expected, given the extreme samples that we deliberately chose to study. However, the DCE approach we used has a limitation, in that we varied all the social and functional features in a way that forced marginal trade-offs, which may overstate the importance of individual social features. In other words, our approach has a bit of a "one improvement at a time" characteristic, which is fine for assessing a single feature but does not get at a big overhanging question commonly brought up in the ethical consumer literature: to what extent will individuals sacrifice functionality to get good ethics? This is an important question for two reasons. First, it gets at another side of the value equation, which is the sacrifice in terms of functional usage people are willing to tolerate. Second, it is rare for products to have bad functional features that can be traded off against social features. It is more realistic to consider products as meeting consumers' requirements, and then examining the degree to which the social features impact the total product package.

In study no. 1+, we varied only whether or not the functional features of the product in question were "good" or "bad," and whether or not the social features were "good" or "bad." In other words, a product can be characterized as all good or all bad, socially and functionally. Figure 4.4 shows the four cells being investigated for each product category. The functional and social features, as well as the base prices, were identical to the ones used in study no. 1, and the presentation was also identical. The "good" levels of the attributes are those shown in Table 4.1 in bold. The brands were those showing identical effects in study no. 1 – Reebok and Adidas in the case of athletic shoes, and

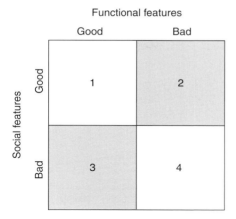

Figure 4.4 Design of social and function product feature mix in study no. 1+

international and local in the case of bar soap. We then selected three levels of prices, corresponding to the two extreme price levels ($40 and $130 in the case of the athletic shoes) and the average of the price levels in study no. 1 ($85 for athletic shoes). We next chose three markup percentages that would apply when all social features are "good," and crossed them with the three price levels to make nine price combinations (10 percent, 25 percent, and 50 percent). Following this process, we created twelve price levels in total. One of the most important features of study no. 1+ is that the product profiles containing the "good" social features are always priced more highly than product profiles with "bad" social features. For athletic shoes, the twelve price levels were $40, $44, $50, $60, $85, $93.50, $106.25, $127.50, $130, $143, $162.50, and $195. For bath soaps, the twelve price levels were $0.45, $0.50, $0.56, $0.68, $1.35, $1.49, $1.69, $2.03, $2.25, $2.48, $2.81, and $3.38. Such a design forces the subject to trade off social features, functionality, and price.

The experiment included nine sets of two product profiles. This was done for both shoes and soap. For each of the nine profiles, respondents were asked two questions: (1) to select between three options – product A, product B, or neither product; and (2) to select between product A and product B. Hence, each respondent made a total of eighteen choices (nine for shoes and nine for soap) for each question. The pairs were constructed as shown in Figure 4.4. This implies four possible pairs: some that required choices with no dilemma – both the social features

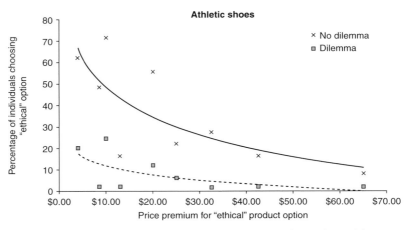

Figure 4.5 Pseudo-demand curves for athletic shoes with good social features

and the functional features were the same (cells 1 and 4) – and some that required a trade-off between the functional and social features (cells 2 and 3).

One hundred and twenty-two subjects completed the experiment (see Appendix 1). Demographically, they did not differ from the first sample of Australian MBA students, although they represented a different school and a different year of intake. Hence, they can be considered as a middle group relative to the two extremes seen in study no. 1. We also varied whether or not the subject received the same "professionally designed news article" as in study no. 1, in this case either describing all or none of the social features. This, again, did not matter materially to individual choice.

The point of study no. 1+ was to generate the equivalent of demand curves for the social features based on the price premium demanded for receiving a "good" social product. Figures 4.5 and 4.6 show these "pseudo-"demand curves. The price axis is the premium associated with receiving the product with "good" social features, and the quantity axis is the probability that the respondent chose the product with the good social features.

These pseudo-demand curves reveal very starkly that individuals will choose the product with positive social features when there is no sacrificing of functionality (the "no dilemma" case) but that any hint of poor functionality will cause demand to collapse. On average, and over the

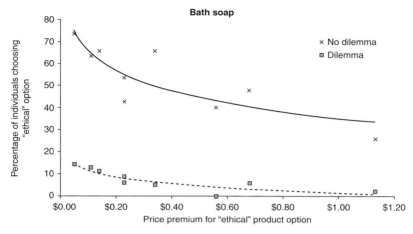

Figure 4.6 Pseudo-demand curves for bath soap with good social features

entire price range, the good social products were chosen 36 percent of the time in the "no dilemma" case, but only in 8 percent of the cases when there was a dilemma and functionality was compromised. In the case of bath soap, these numbers were 53 percent and 8 percent, respectively. Figures 4.5 and 4.6 also show that the more expensive product, athletic shoes, is significantly more price-sensitive than bath soaps in the "no dilemma" case. When there is essentially no price premium for the better social product, between 60 and 80 percent of the potential products are chosen. However, when the premium approaches 100 percent of the average price, this number drops to fewer than 10 percent for athletic shoes, but approximately 30 percent for the bath soaps.

An additional question is: what do people do when faced with the dilemma of bad functionality for good ethics? The answer is that it depends. If individuals are forced to make a choice, they will choose the product with good functional features and bad social features over the one with good social features and bad functional features at a ratio of approximately two or three to one (roughly 75 percent of the time across the two product categories). If they are given the option of not making a choice, they will choose to do so in nearly 60 percent of the cases for athletic shoes and 40 percent of the cases for bath soap. However, of those making a choice, even with the opt-out 70 percent will choose the product with good functional features.

Global segments of social consumers

Our second group of studies extended study no. 1 by investigating the preference structures of consumers in six different countries – Germany, Spain, the United States, Turkey, India, and South Korea. The choice of the consumers examined, and the logic of the country choices, are given in Appendix 1. Again, a short comment on this choice is worthwhile. These countries represent a broad range of economic development, religious and political history, and cultural orientation. Although the samples in each country are not necessarily representative of the population in total, they are indicative of consumers who can, and do, purchase the products under investigation.

Our purpose in study no. 2 is to get a picture of three phenomena. First, we are interested in whether cultural/country variation matters for the structure of social preferences. In other words, is social concern and the willingness to pay something that is the purview of Western, developed countries? Second, because our six country samples are better matched than those used in study no. 1, for which they were chosen to be extreme, we are better able to get a picture of the segmentation characteristics of individuals in study no. 2. Finally, rather than investigating one product at a time, individuals in this study examined two products, allowing us to compare their social preferences in different product contexts.

The structure of study no. 2

Study no. 2 followed the form of study no. 1, with several exceptions. First, we once more focused on two products, but in this case athletic shoes and a four-pack of AA batteries. This allowed us to achieve a number of aims. By using athletic shoes we were able to maintain product category continuity with study no. 1. Additionally, by keeping to the labor (athletic shoes) and environment (AA batteries) theme we were able to maintain social issue continuity with study no. 1. Second, unlike study no. 1, all the individuals evaluated the athletic shoes and a sample of half the remainder also evaluated the AA batteries, thereby allowing us to look at social preferences across product categories for the same individuals. Third, because we found little value from the EDS and information manipulation in study no. 1, we excluded the EDS and engaged only in minor information manipulation, in which a control condition excluded information about the social attributes. Once again, this had no impact and will not be discussed.

The sample
The demographics of the sample used are shown in Table 4.9. The sample was generated using market research agencies in the selected countries, and the procedure is outlined in Appendix 1. Generally speaking, the sample is meant to be representative of individuals who have the purchasing power to buy the most expensive product studied (athletic shoes) and who would have purchased in the product categories recently. There is significant variation across the samples, but this is related mainly to purchasing power. When the data is mean-adjusted for the country, there is considerably less variation. As we will see shortly, there is considerably less variation in preferences than might otherwise be expected from the differences in the demographics.

Product features and structure of the experiments
Table 4.10 presents the information on the product features examined. Those wanting to compare the differences between studies no. 1 and no. 2 can examine Table 4.1.

In the case of athletic shoes, there were three changes made to the features examined in study no. 1. First, there was an additional social attribute: "Are workers allowed to unionize?" Second, there was the addition of the country of production: Poland, China, Vietnam, and domestic (which was replaced with the country in which the sample was being drawn). Third, the number of brands was reduced to three: Nike, Reebok, and Adidas, plus an "All other brands" group. All the other social and functional features remained the same, including the price, which was converted directly from Australian dollars.

In the case of AA batteries, there were six functional features: useful life, storage life, rechargeable versus single-use, the availability of a money-back guarantee on quality, an on-battery or on-package tester, and whether or not the expected spoilage date was on the battery. These were decided upon after extensive in-store and online research. Again, the country of production was varied – Poland, China, Japan, and domestic (which was replaced with the country from which the sample was being drawn). The brands were varied such that two global brands were always present – Energizer and Duracell – plus two others, which included the dominant local brand. There were five social features:

Table 4.9 *Sample characteristics for study no. 2*

	Germany	Spain	United States	Turkey	India	South Korea	Total sample
Age (median grouping)	30–39	30–39	30–39	30–39	30–39	30–39	30–39
Age (percentage < 19)	6.00	17.00	9.10	16.20	17.00	2.00	11.33
Age (percentage > 50)	17.00	32.10	29.33	14.10	11.00	22.00	21.00
Gender (percentage female)	52.5	59.4	60.6	50.5	49.0	70.0	57.0
Income (median grouping, $ thousand)	25–40	15–25	25–40	15–25	15–25	15–25	15–25
Income (percentage < $15,000)	26.10	15.70	7.20	54.63	27.80	5.00	22.70
Income (percentage > $40,000)	28.40	19.10	51.47	11.30	3.10	7.00	19.90
Education (percentage university educated)	8.90	22.60	20.70	62.70	60.80	39.00	35.70
Marital status (percentage married)	33.33	50.90	39.80	31.33	50.00	66.00	45.30
Number of participants (shoes/batteries)	100/50	106/51	99/48	100/50	100/50	100/50	605/299

whether the battery was mercury-/cadmium-free, whether the battery was made from recyclable materials, whether the packaging was made from recyclable materials, whether hazardous waste was created from the production process, and whether safe battery disposal information was provided on or in the package. All the social and functional features were explained and defined in a glossary given to the participants. The price range was (in Australian dollar equivalents) $1.30, $3.30, $5.30, and $7.30. This was based on the median price for a package of four batteries of $4.30 across the countries studied. Unlike athletic shoes, the

Table 4.10 *Product features and social attributes used in study no. 2*

Athletic shoes	AA batteries (pack of four)
Basic product features	
Shock absorption/cushioning (LOW or **HIGH**)	Useful life (15 HOURS or **30 HOURS**)
Weight (**LIGHTER** or HEAVIER)	Storage life (3 YEARS or **5 YEARS**)
Ankle support (LOW-CUT or **HIGH-CUT**)	Rechargeable (NO or **YES**)
Sole durability (SHORT or **LONG**)	Money-back guarantee (NO or **YES**)
Breathability/ventilation (LOW or **HIGH**)	On-battery or on-package tester (NO or **YES**)
Fabrication materials (SYNTHETIC or **LEATHER**)	
Reflectivity at night (NO or **YES**)	Is the expected spoilage date on the battery? (NO or **YES**)
Comfort/fit (LOW or **HIGH**)	
Country of production (Poland, China, Vietnam, domestic)	Country of production (Poland, China, Japan, domestic)
Brand of shoe (Nike, Adidas, Reebok, others)	Brand of battery (Energizer, Duracell, plus two that varied per country) Germany: Sony, Varta Spain: Varta, Cegesa United States: Eveready, Maxell Turkey: Varta, Philips India: Eveready, Excel South Korea: Panasonic, Rocky
Price in A$ ($40, $70, $100, $130)	Price in A$ ($1.30, $3.30, $5.30, $7.30)
Social features	
Is child labor used in making the product? (**NO** or YES)	Is the battery mercury-/cadmium-free? (NO or **YES**)
Are workers paid above minimum wage? (NO or **YES**)	Is the battery made from recyclable materials? (NO or **YES**)
Are workers' working conditions dangerous? (**NO** or YES)	Is the package made from recyclable materials? (NO or **YES**)
Are workers' living conditions at the factory acceptable? (NO or **YES**)	Was hazardous waste created from the production process? (**NO** or YES)
Are workers allowed to unionize? (NO or **YES**)	Is safe battery disposal information contained on or in the package? (NO or **YES**)

Note: All the "good" attributes are represented in **bold**; the "bad" attributes are non-bold.

actual price range for batteries is quite stable and very tight around the median.

Because of time limitations, individuals were given only eight products in each category to evaluate. The product features were varied using an orthogonal design, and the order of the product categories was randomized (some saw the athletic shoe alternatives first, others saw them second). As in study no. 1, a professionally designed news article and a query about the individual's last purchase in the product category preceded the product evaluations. The questions asked – "Would you consider?" and "Would you purchase?" – were identical to those in study no. 1, and the format was identical to the one given in Figure 4.3. In addition to the product evaluations, the subjects were given a further task, which will be described in Chapter 6.

Global segments

Two analyses are possible with the data from study no. 2. One is to examine the data country by country and make comparisons. Auger *et al.* (2010) do this, and find that there are relatively insignificant differences between the models estimated for each country sample. We therefore move on to a more sophisticated type of regression analysis, referred to as latent class (or finite mixture) regression analysis (LCRA), which allows for the classification of individuals into segments (often called classes) and develops models for each of the segments simultaneously. LCRA is described in some detail in Appendix 3. The beauty of LCRA is that segment formation does not depend on a group of pre-specified clustering variables. Instead, the latent segments are formed with discrete unobserved variables, improving the ability of researchers to identify meaningful segments in circumstances in which observed variables (e.g. socio-demographics) have proven to be ineffective. LCRA simultaneously finds the optimal number of models and the forms of those models given the data. Detailed results from this analysis can be found in Auger, Devinney, and Louviere (2009).[5] We focus here on the implications and summary of this analysis.

Our results show that respondents for both product categories can be divided into three distinct segments, which possess very similar structures. Hence, we were able to label them with the same descriptors, namely "brand," "price," and "social." These descriptors were selected by examining the dominant set(s) of features (i.e. the attributes with the

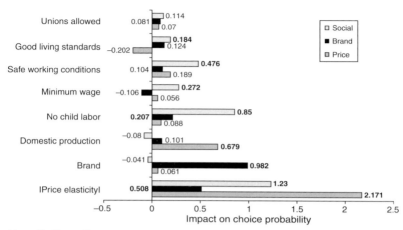

Notes: Significant effects are shown in **bold**. The price elasticity is in absolute value.

Figure 4.7 Impact on choice by athletic shoe segment

most significant coefficients) within each segment. Figures 4.7 and 4.8 provide information about the relative impact of the social attributes and location of production on the probability of choosing a product, along with the magnitude of the price elasticity for both product categories. For simplicity, we have excluded the results for the functional features. The numbers are the adjusted coefficients from the binomial latent class regression. Their magnitude can be compared across the segments within product category, but should not be compared across product categories.

Respondents in the "brand" segment placed greater importance on brand (either positively or negatively) than respondents in the other two segments. This is especially apparent for athletic shoes, for which respondents in the "brand" segment valued the Nike and Adidas brands highly. Respondents in the "brand" segment also displayed relatively low price sensitivity (especially for shoes), which is consistent with a brand-conscious consumer who is willing to pay a premium for his/her preferred brand. In the AA battery category, they also showed considerable domestic production bias, particularly when compared to production from China and Japan (which were strongly negatively associated with choice).

On the other hand, and hardly surprisingly, respondents in the "price" segment demonstrated very high sensitivity to price. This is

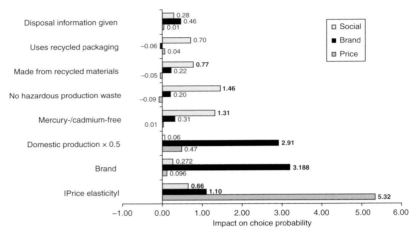

Notes: Significant effects are shown in **bold**. The domestic production coefficient is divided by two to align it to the scale. The price elasticity is in absolute value.

Figure 4.8 Impact on choice by AA battery segment

especially true for batteries, for which the price elasticity in the "price" segment is several orders of magnitude greater than for the other two segments. Respondents in the athletic shoe category of this segment also placed a much greater level of importance on the country of origin of the products. Specifically, these individuals demonstrated a high level of domestic country bias, favoring products that are manufactured in their home country, with a slight but significant bias against production in Vietnam and China.

The most relevant segment for our discussion is the "social" segment. A number of results emerge from a closer examination of the "social" segment for each product. Clearly, the most important is the existence of the "social" segments. People in the two "social" segments placed much greater importance on the social attributes than respondents in the other two segments. Our second important finding is that, for the two "social" segments, all the coefficients for the social attributes are in the expected direction, indicating that these respondents favored products that were more "socially desirable" overall. Third, individuals in the "social" segment are not simply purchasing on social issues alone. They are similar to the other segments in that functional attributes matter (which we do not show here but which can be seen in Auger, Devinney, and Louviere, 2009). It is just that, rather than brand and price, it is the social components of the products that are the differentiator. Finally, there is no country of production effect. In other words, once we account for the social aspects of the products, there seem to be no additional inferences being drawn about the products with respect to where they were produced.

Our results reveal that not all social attributes have an equal effect on consumer purchase decisions. This is something of an obvious result, but one that has significant implications for managers designing $C_N SR$ strategies, and policy makers attempting to understand the social aspects of production. It suggests two conclusions. First, it is critical for decision makers to understand the social issues that are especially important for their customers and constituencies. Second, it is important to avoid strategies that are too broad or that try to cover too many issues. These conclusions are equally relevant to NGOs and their membership. "Issue proliferation," the belief that alignment with multiple issues is necessary to establish oneself as a socially responsible organization, may be a negative in the minds of ordinary consumers, who seem to concentrate on relevance and specificity. What our respondents demonstrated is that there are indeed socially conscious consumers, but that they do not value equally all social issues associated with a particular product. As such, our results would argue strongly for "focused" CSR strategies in place of those that attempt to appeal to a broad social consciousness, or that do not address the more salient social issues relevant to the context of the individual's decision at the time.

Our results also reveal that the functional attributes, including brand and price, are not irrelevant to respondents in the "social" segments. For example, respondents in the athletic shoe "social" segment still react to price as expected, and to a much greater extent than respondents in the "brand" segment. It also turns out that they have a preference for alternative brands versus more well-known brands, such as Nike and Adidas. Similarly, respondents in the battery "social" segment have a clear brand preference for Energizer and tend to value the functional attributes (as a group) as highly as the respondents in the "brand" segment (and much more highly than respondents in the "price" segment). What this implies is that managers cannot simply ignore the core functional attributes of their products to create more socially acceptable ones. In other words, it is once again shown that consumers do not appear willing to sacrifice functionality for social desirability. What these consumers are telling us is that they purchase products to fill a certain basic set of needs and that no amount of social desirability is likely to compensate for a failure to meet these basic needs.

Demographics again

As in study no. 1, study no. 2 controlled for the degree that socio-demographic covariates – gender, age, income, lifestyle, status, education, the number of children, etc. – related to product choice and segment membership. Without belaboring results that are complex, we find once again that socio-demographics play no significant or predictable part in either the choice of product or the degree to which social features matter. This is independent of whether the estimation is done directly on a country-by-country basis (as is the case in Auger *et al.*, 2010) or whether it is based on the segment profiles (as is the case in Auger, Devinney, and Louviere, 2009). Because study no. 2 examined two products in six separate samples, there are many more possibilities whereby the socio-demographic covariates can influence the results, and there are isolated cases in which a coefficient is significant. However, what is important is that there is no pattern, meaning that the effects that are seen are basically just accounting for random heterogeneity in the decisions being made by respondents. In Auger, Devinney, and Louviere (2009) we find that eleven of seventy-two possible effects are significant; not much different from what one would expect randomly (15 percent), and a number of which went in the opposite direction to casual explanation.

Hence, as in study no. 1, the lesson is that the sensitivity to social features is not a priori predictable simply by knowing age, gender, income, education, lifestyle, and so on. The important heterogeneity is buried deeper in the individual, and is not obvious based on a naive observation of things such as gender or income.

Does "social" segment position exist independent of product context?

One of the nice characteristics of LCRA is that it allows us to categorize individuals based on their segment membership. Hence, in the case of the two product categories, we can easily ask the question: do people in the "social" segment for athletic shoes also belong to the "social" segment for batteries? This question goes a long way to proving the mythical nature of ethical consumerism, as the operative model of ethical purchasing is that individuals can be grouped into categories

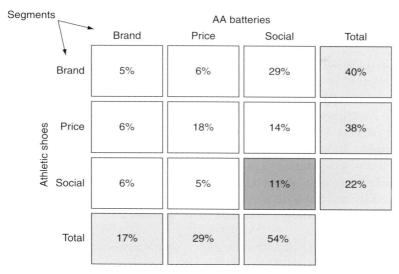

Figure 4.9 Overlap of segments for the product categories

that apply generally. Otherwise, what would be the purpose of general ethical disposition surveys, if they applied only conditionally? The basic mythical model is one in which individuals cannot be schizophrenic: they cannot be ethical consumers in one realm and evil Utilitarians in another. Unfortunately, this is exactly what we find.

Figure 4.9 juxtaposes the segment profiles for the product categories and shows not only the magnitude of the individual segments but also how they line up against one another. What we see is very compelling, and shows just how naive simple ethical consumer characterizations can be. What we see is that although the "social" segments are quite substantial – 22 percent in the case of athletic shoes and 54 percent in the case of batteries – they do not overlap in any predictive way. Indeed, 11 percent of the participants in study no. 2 fall into the "social" segment for both batteries and shoes – something we would have expected if the distribution was totally random; 11.8 percent = 54 percent × 22 percent. In essence, the horrible truth of this is that knowing that someone is in the "social" segment for one category has no predictive power in terms of indicating that s/he will be in the "social" segment for the other. Indeed, you would be better off predicting that, if individuals were in the "social" segment for batteries, they would be in the "brand" segment for athletic shoes.

108 *The Myth of the Ethical Consumer*

Segment size and country differentiation

The ethical consumer literature is replete with studies making comparisons between consumers in different countries (such as Sriram and Forman, 1993; Rawwas, 1996; Polonsky *et al.*, 2001; Al-Khatib, Starton, and Rawwas, 2005; Rawwas, Swaidan, and Oyman, 2005). The basic operative assumption is that individuals embedded in different cultures will exhibit different "ethical" customer profiles (see, for example, Srnka, 2004). As we have discussed in the prior chapters and earlier in this chapter, it is conceivable that much of what is being attributed to cross-country differences may be the result of the instruments used to assess the degree of "ethicality" in people's consumerism. For us, the question is whether more sophisticated analysis reveals anything different.

Table 4.11 provides information about the segment membership by country in two ways. The first three columns show the distribution by segment across countries (each segment column for each category adds up to 100 percent). The second three columns show the segments within each country (each country row adds up to 100 percent).

We see two phenomena going on. First, there are indeed country-level differences that appear to be material, but the segments are not, in and of themselves, country-specific. That is, all three segments have representatives from all six countries for both products, with the exception of the "social" segment for athletic shoes, which does not contain any respondents from South Korea. However, the figures also show fairly large differences in the proportions of respondents from specific countries in specific segments. For example, the "price" segments for both athletic shoes and AA batteries are clearly dominated by South Korean respondents, who comprise 38 percent of the segment for shoes and 45 percent of the segment for batteries. Similarly, Spanish respondents make up a much greater proportion of the "brand" segment for AA batteries (47 percent), while Turkish respondents dominate the "brand" segment for athletic shoes (41 percent).

Second, for their part, the "social" segments (for both shoes and batteries) show rather similar patterns of membership across the countries. Five countries – Germany, Spain, the United States, India, and South Korea – contribute very similar proportions of respondents to the two "social" segments. The first four countries contribute a relatively high and similar proportion of respondents to the two segments while

Table 4.11 *Distribution of country and segments*

| | Percentage of …. | | | | | |
| | Consumers in segment | | | Consumers in country | | |
	Brand	Price	Social	Brand	Price	Social
Athletic shoes						
Germany	15.7	8.8	27.7	30.1	16.9	53.1
Spain	11.4	13.3	27.6	21.8	25.4	52.8
United States	7.4	20.2	21.1	15.2	41.5	43.3
Turkey	41.2	7.2	3.1	80.0	14.0	6.0
India	20.4	12.6	20.4	38.2	23.6	38.2
South Korea	3.9	38.0	0.0	9.3	90.7	0.0
AA batteries						
Germany	9.2	5.5	24.9	23.2	13.9	62.9
Spain	47.1	4.3	17.8	68.1	6.2	25.7
United States	24.6	14.8	12.0	47.9	28.8	23.3
Turkey	17.4	8.8	22.7	35.6	18.0	46.4
India	0.3	21.7	20.7	0.7	50.8	48.5
South Korea	1.4	44.9	1.8	2.9	93.3	3.7

South Korea contributes a relatively low proportion of respondents. Turkey is the only country to show an inconsistent pattern of contribution, with a relatively high contribution for AA batteries (similar to Germany, Spain, the United States, and India) and relatively low for athletic shoes (similar to South Korea). These results suggest that preferences for social products may be much more global than previous research on C_NSR and consumer ethics has suggested. In other words, cultural differences may not impact the importance consumers place on social issues as much as has been suggested in previous work. This is something that will be seen again in Chapter 6, when we report on more research based on this six-country sample.

The importance of recall

The last issue we address in this chapter is the role of recall. We questioned consumers as to whether or not they could recall the attributes of the products that they had purchased in the product categories studied. Our concern here is to address the question "If

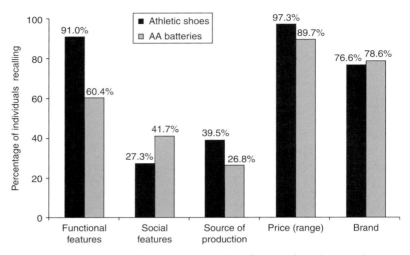

Figure 4.10 Percentage of consumers recalling features from last purchase

an individual indicated that s/he recalled a social or non-functional attribute – e.g. brand or country of origin – did that influence his/her choice when such a feature appeared in the choices available?". What this allows us to do is determine whether an individual who indicates that s/he can recall a social or non-functional attribute (e.g. child labor or brand) is more likely to choose an option that contains the "good" (e.g. no child labor) attribute or the same level (e.g. Nike) of that attribute. If the responses are believable, this suggests that prior action that is revealed through recall hints at something about the individual's deeper preferences. The details of the analysis are to be found in Auger *et al.* (2010).

Figure 4.10 provides information on simply whether people can recall the features of their last purchase in the product category. What stands out is that (1) brand and price can be recalled easily; (2) the functional features of athletic shoes are easy to recall; (3) the functional features of AA batteries are much less likely to be recalled, but are still recalled in a significant number of cases; and (4) the social features and source of production are always significantly less recallable than the functional features, brand, and price. The social features of AA batteries have a much greater recall rate than the social features of athletic shoes, which is not surprising given that the social features of the batteries are observable while those for the athletic shoes are not.

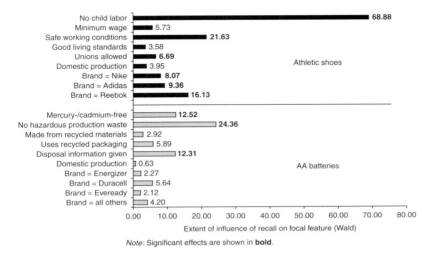

Figure 4.11 Influence of feature recall on focal product feature

Figure 4.11 provides the statistics for whether there is a relationship between feature recall and the influence of the focal feature on choice. The number on the X-axis is the Wald statistic, which measures the degree of statistical significance. The numbers in bold are the ones of relevance. For brevity, we include only the statistics for the non-functional features. First, there is a strong relationship between the recall of many of the social attributes and what a participant chose when faced with alternatives in the DCE. What these results reveal is that, of the non-functional attributes, the social attributes appear most salient, followed by brand in the case of the higher-involvement product, athletic shoes. There are also a few things that do not matter. Whether or not individuals indicated they knew the country of production of the products in either category was unrelated to whether they reacted to the country of origin manipulations in the experiment. In the case of AA batteries (when we reveal only the results for the major brands and aggregate all others for simplicity), remembering the last brand of battery did not influence whether the individual chose options with that brand in the experiment. However, a brand effect was evident in the case of athletic shoes; the brand of an individual's last purchase was related to a tendency to choose that brand in the experiment.

What this reveals is that, if a respondent has a proclivity for remembering whether or not his/her product is environmentally sound or labor-friendly, this is a strong indicator of purchase intention in the experiment. We should emphasize that this is not an artifact, as it would be very difficult for participants to link what they answered in the first part of the survey with what they were being asked to choose in the DCE (for which they had to make quite complex trade-offs). This potentially suggests that those who are cognizant of environmental and labor issues in products are indeed likely to respond to further propositions with respect to these issues.

Ethical consumerism in light of experimental reality

This chapter has presented a considerable array of studies, which give a remarkably enlightening picture of social consumption. In doing so, they go a long way to dispelling the myth of the ethical consumer. Individuals are revealed to be complex choosers, capable of nuanced decisions that bear little resemblance to the simplistic models of general moral decision making in the consumer context. However, we also see that characterizing individuals based on their willingness to incorporate social factors into their decisions is not impossible. It is just extremely difficult, because it is not possible with the standard mechanisms applied in the extant academic literature, or by market research practitioners.

We also see that the mythical character of the ethical consumer reveals itself when people are forced to make realistic choices involving substantial trade-offs. Our respondents are shown to be at one and the same time socially responsive and socially blind, focusing on price, brand, and the functional aspects of the products. They are fickle in that, when forced to give up functionality, they choose to dump their morals. If we give them the option to flee from a decision, some choose not to choose, while most others simply sacrifice their ethics for functionality. However, a small percentage of people still choose ethics over function. We also see that individuals either purposely overstate their social credentials or just want to look good in surveys, making it nearly impossible to believe what they say about their social proclivities. In other words, some people stretch the truth as it applies to their own good consumption intentions. More positively, we see that people in different countries do not behave all that differently – or not so differently that we require culturally distinct models – implying that a paradigm of $C_N SR$ could be effective globally.

Chapter 4 has given only part of the social consumption picture. With its focus on a more structured, quantitative approach to social product choice, the studies discussed here no doubt exaggerate some of the more subtle cultural and psychological factors influencing consumption. We will pick up this challenge in Chapter 5, in which we give social consumption (or the lack thereof) a more personal and cross-cultural flavor.

Given the complexity of what we have covered in this chapter, it is important to make sure that the lessons are clear. So what have we learned from this battery of studies?

First, some individuals in some contexts will take into consideration the social features of products. Although our estimates of the influence of the social features are no doubt high, they reveal that there clearly is some room in the market for products that incorporate more than functional features. At one level this is hardly surprising, since the vast majority of the value that consumers get from products and services, in general, is not purely functional. Our results merely imply that C_NSR is a potentiality of some significance in some markets if producers can create a value proposition that individuals are willing to accept, and one that does not force them to give up on the functionality and other things they have come to expect from the product.

It is also important to understand that the reasons consumers might accept the producer's social product proposition are not particularly relevant. We are not concerned about why they want to incorporate a social feature into their decisions, just that, within the context of their own self-image and value equation, they do. This is contrary to the role model aspect of the myth of the ethical consumer. For example, much of this rhetoric surrounding "ethical" consumerism is decidedly proactively political and pseudo-militaristic. The "ethical" consumer should not just be making a decision for him-/herself but making a difference to society by scaling the walls of global capitalism, like Frodo at Mount Doom in *The Lord of the Rings*. Typical ethical consumer rhetoric can be seen in knowmore.org:

One major issue with the concept of "ethical consumerism" is that it is based on the idea that we, potential buyers of goods, are defined as consumers. It is dangerous for a community of action-oriented people to limit their places in society to that of consumers only, instead of people with the free will to take more direct action. We are, after all, people, not consumers. If we see ourselves as consumers (or a collection of things we have purchased), then our corporate-dominated culture has already defeated us (and the poor people in sweat shops who will continue making shoes for the rest of Americans). Our responsibility does not end after we stop ourselves from buying the new Air Jordans. We need to stop Nike in order to end their abuse.

The consumers in our studies hardly fit this mold. They are just individuals making choices one product and one feature at a time, and doing so because they believe it is valuable or right to do so. However, they are consumers who are sufficiently open-minded to consider incorporating new features into their decisions. It is, very fundamentally, their decision, and their decision alone.

Second, what is clear from the results in this chapter is that simply appealing to the "ethicality" of the purchasing context is not going to be particularly effective. There are two reasons for this. First, individuals appear to be remarkably subtle in the extent to which they associate specific issues with specific contexts. The fact that we discovered that few individuals are "social" about both labor and environmental issues in every context implies that utilizing general ethical surveys to characterize an individual's proclivity to respond to social product positioning is going to be ineffective, because it is both theoretically and practically inappropriate. The value of social features is impossible to ascertain in the absence of the context in which the feature is embedded. Second, this last fact was confirmed by the degree to which general social surveys failed to provide information that was predictively useful. We saw this in the dismal degree to which the MORI poll predicted willingness to pay. Consumption is fundamentally a context-embedded phenomenon, and abstracting from the context is not only foolish commercially, it is dangerous intellectually. Utility is not an absolute construct, and the value an individual receives from the features of a product is not going to be independent of the purchasing and use context.

Third, a priori segmentation techniques prove to be particularly ineffective in the context of social consumption. A priori segmentation is done by relating observable characteristics of the individual – such as gender, where s/he lives, income, education, and so on – to specific behavioral outcomes. It typically ends with consumers being categorized in some pithy way – for example, "vocal activists," "principle pioneers," "onlookers," etc. (Tiltman, 2007). However, our results showed that nothing observable was related to the propensity to respond to the inclusion of social features in products. This does not necessarily imply that there are no observable characteristics that can be discovered with further research, but that the obvious ones are pretty ineffective in the contexts that we studied. Despite this, our results should imply that a degree of skepticism is called for when faced with such social survey data. As shown in Table 4.8, we can come up with quite nice little groupings of individuals that appear to have face validity and seem eminently logical. However, as our comparison of Utilitarians and Anti-utilitarians showed, despite the prettiness of the categories, they can be spectacularly meaningless.

Historically, research into "ethical" consumerism has focused on the role of values and beliefs and individual socio-demographic differences as the sources of the variance in "ethical" consumption – hence the heavy reliance on ethics scales and cross-cultural surveys. However, the implications of our last two points for this logic are dire. It is clear that the social preferences we discovered are not related to values and beliefs as generally characterized. It is very difficult to explain the outcomes seen throughout this chapter based on recourse to values and beliefs. Nothing that was done in the various studies influenced our subjects' values and beliefs, nor were we constraining behavior in any way that would imply significant moderating or mediating effects. Individuals simply chose to make different decisions when those decisions had a price, either directly or indirectly.

Fourth, we would argue that our results imply that the individual choice should take predominance in any examination of social consumption. This is both a logical issue and an empirical issue. Empirically, the fascination with psychometric methods that is common in the literature requires the level of analysis to be the group. This is simply a requirement that arises due to the inability to compare individual scale results (those issues of incentive compatibility, comparability, inference, and context we discussed in Chapter 3). We find that what is more interesting is the differences at the individual level – something that can be discerned much more effectively through experimental methods. Although we find that there are groups of individuals that can be characterized as segments, what is also true is that it is nearly impossible to tell who is in a particular group until they "behave" and reveal who they are. The fact that we find no covariates that matter implies that all the important differentiating variance is at the individual level. Our use of LCRA allowed us to discover this variance. Most other techniques would fail to see it, because they would be looking for observable patterns rather than those being revealed through the choices made in the experiments.

Fifth, and finally, our finding that information does not seem to influence choice hints at a more subtle decision model operating. This will be revealed in more detail in the next chapter, but two points are important. First, providing people with information about the social issues did not seem to influence their choice. This is contrary to many discussions about ethical consumer choice, in which there is a strong emphasis on the need for informed consumer choice. Indeed, it appears that most individuals understand the issues in play, be they those pertaining to labor rights or the environment. This will be seen in our qualitative research, described next. However, what is intriguing is our second finding on information: individuals who can recall the social features of their last purchase are more likely to utilize social features in their decision model. We therefore have two apparently conflicting results: on the one hand providing information does not matter, yet on the other hand those who can recall specific social product information make different decisions. Given that we already know that there is no observable difference between these groups of individuals, something more complex is clearly going on. It must be the case that the subjects who do not recall the social features are simply not investing in utilizing the specific information about the products, despite the fact that they are knowledgeable about the general issues and could source the information if they chose. They appear to be using their decisions to drive their choice of what information to recall rather than recalling information with which to make a decision.

Assessing the myth

As noted in Chapter 1, it is our thesis that the ethical consumer is mythical in three senses: (1) it is an idealization of heroic behavior that is unachievable in reality; (2) it is a role model for what society expects behavior should morally be; and (3) it is false when examined in the light of actual behavior. What we can say at this point is that few individuals behave in line with the strict moral or ethical consumption behavior that epitomizes the heroic idealized ethical consumer. Our findings show malleable individuals with complex decision models, who neither appear heroic in practice (although many did in the MORI poll) nor operate according to an unbending ethical code (otherwise Figure 4.9 would not look as it does). Of course, this should not be surprising.

5 | *Rationalization and justification of social (non-)consumption*

The hardest thing to explain is the glaringly evident which everybody had decided not to see.

Ayn Rand

Not "Seeing is believing," you ninny, but "Believing is seeing."

Tom Wolfe

Myths are public dreams, dreams are private myths.

Joseph Campbell

The previous chapter outlined in detail the findings of a number of experiments aimed at determining the extent to which social consumption serves as a motivator of choice and how we might attempt to characterize individuals who have proclivities toward social issues when it comes to consumption. We also revealed how general classifications of consumers as "ethical" have little validity when one examines behavior more closely. We can say that there are no doubt consumers who, in specific circumstances, take into account social issues when purchasing products/services, but that this is influenced by a complex combination of factors that belies simplistic theoretical and normative specifications. Additionally, the scale of the phenomenon is considerably smaller than the tidal wave of activism portrayed in popular polls.

However, the experimental methods we used are dominantly rational approaches that help us see behavior in more constrained circumstances, but do not reveal to us how people feel about their own behavior. In this sense, experimentation reveals the rational, analytic side of behavior while helping us get deeper into aspects of choice that may be unconscious or more personal, but it does not help us understand what the individuals themselves believe and think. Furthermore, the individual consumer approach applied in these experiments abstracts considerably from the role of the consumer in society. In other words, a narrow conceptualization of C_NSR is one based on purchasing alone; however, a more realistic and broader abstraction is one that accounts for the deeper meaning that individuals take from consumption, along with the broader implications that follow from their membership in a society. It is to this that we turn in this and the next chapter.

We are concerned with four issues in this chapter. First, we want to give a broader analysis of the issues highlighted in Chapter 4 by examining a greater number of social issues with consumers in a face-to-face situation. Our experiments were done in an impersonal context and, hence, one in which a dimension of realism was missing. Second, we want to apply an alternative, interpretative, method of investigation so as to loosen the dependence of our thesis on one specific methodological approach. This multi-method approach is unique, as research in consumer ethics tends to take either a quantitative approach or an interpretative approach, without combining the insights each can bring. Third, we want to begin broadening the perspective of what motivates behavior and where justification and excuse come into play. The myth of ethical consumerism holds that the consumer is the one empowered to make change; however, it may be that the consumer is simply waiting to be led, or is motivated more by logical consistency in his/her behavior being justifiable *ex post*. Fourth, we want to set the stage for expanding and embedding C_NSR within both CSR and the broader social agenda, the topic we will pick up in Chapter 6.

The contribution of interpretative methods to understanding C_NSR

As we have shown in the last chapter, asking consumers to make paper and pencil responses indicating how they feel about ethical dilemmas or trade-offs is not a very good predictor of their actual behavior in situations involving social consumption opportunities. Moreover, observing experimental and market behavior may, in specific circumstances, help us profile the potential green consumer, the potential activist consumer, or the potential vegetarian or vegan consumer, but it cannot reveal the reasoning that leads to these behaviors or the logic that often makes consumers behave in socially irresponsible ways despite endorsing socially responsible statements of belief. Qualitative methods such as case studies, phenomenological interviews, and focus groups can add considerable depth to understanding how consumers behave in ways they regard as responsible, how they account for behaviors that are inconsistent with their avowed beliefs, and what they know or think they know about the underlying issues (Belk, 2004; Harrison, Newholm, and Shaw, 2005). However, one must be careful not to be seduced by consumers giving what amounts to socially acceptable responses when they find themselves in a public forum, such as a focus group. Our approach mitigates this, particularly when taken in light of our experimental results.

Interpretative research is hermeneutic in character, meaning that it involves the interpretation of messages, texts, and human action in a context. As such, it is fundamentally about the building and enhancing of theory rather than the testing of theory. Hence, in our case, we are seeking to build a model of social consumption (or non-consumption) rationalization and justification within the contexts that we have set for those being studied. The work given in the prior chapter reveals the degree to which an attitude–behavior gap exists. Now we want to gain an understanding of how individuals justify that gap.

Interpretative research can capture the commonplace, everyday nature of human understanding, in which the individual is a participant. In this sense, we seek to understand consumers as they make sense of themselves and those around them. Following the interest in exploring the plurality of ethical consumer values with ethnographic and qualitative methodologies to address this complexity (Gurney and Humphreys, 2006; Tadajewski and Wagner-Tsukamoto, 2006), this chapter incorporates an interpretative approach based on consumer in-depth interviews in a cross-cultural context.

We set about doing this in two ways. First, we are trying to understand social consumption as it goes on unnoticed – a ubiquitous aspect of day-to-day behavior. Unconscious consumption is increasingly well understood by key researchers. As noted by Barnett, Cafaro, and Newholm (2005, p. 19):

This ... underscores the importance of taking account of the concerns that motivate ordinary consumption practices. Rather than thinking of "ethical consumption" being set off against "unethical" consumption, we might do better to recognize the forms of ethical concern always embedded in consumption practices.

Second, by applying an in-depth hermeneutic analysis, we are endeavoring to reveal what is being hidden from view and covered up by the consumer. This is particularly relevant in the case of social consumption, in which the morality of consumption (Borgmann, 2000) stands in opposition to the desire for consumption (Belk, Ger, and Askegaard, 2003).

An interpretative approach

Study no. 3 involved approximately hour-long depth interviews with twenty consumers in each of eight countries: Australia, China, Germany, India, Spain, Turkey, Sweden, and the United States. Details of the sample are given in Appendix 1. During these interviews, informants were presented with three scenarios, addressing qualitatively different consumer ethics situations. One scenario involved purchasing counterfeit products, one involved the purchase of a popular athletic shoe manufactured under conditions of worker exploitation, and the final scenario involved the purchase of a product that is potentially harmful to the environment or that uses animal by-products and animal testing. The scenarios are presented in Table 5.1.

The questions asked of the participants after they had read each scenario began in a projective manner and then narrowed down to more specific queries. The projective questions asked the respondents to tell the interviewer how they thought people from their country would respond to the issue involved in a scenario (see Appendix 4 for the semi-structured interview guide). The use of projective techniques is regarded as especially desirable when dealing with sensitive subject matters and topics that might lead to socially desirable but inaccurate answers in more direct questioning (Rook, 1988, 2001; Belk, Ger, and Askegaard, 2003).

Two versions of each scenario were created. Manipulations in the scenarios involved: the type of ethical breach – (1) environmental or animal-related in the case of bath soap, (2) worker-related (male or female) in the case of athletic shoes, and (3) trademark infringement on either a big-ticket or small-ticket item in the case of Louis Vuitton products. The combination of the second and third scenarios contrasted the country of origin of the corporations involved – developed or emerging market. One version of each scenario was shown to a participant, with the version systematically rotated across participants – that is, manipulations were partly within subjects and partly between subjects. This enabled us to see how these various types of ethical

Table 5.1 *Scenarios used for interviews*

Labor practices: Nike athletic shoe production

The product choice available to today's athlete – professional, amateur, or casual – is truly amazing. In addition, what was once a product for use only by the athletically inclined has become an everyday fashion item. The humble sneaker has come of age.

Today's sophisticated athletic shoes are made for many different people and purposes. Not only are they different in terms of comfort and cushioning, but they have many additional specialized characteristics. Shoes vary in their ability to ventilate your feet, whether they support your ankles, their weight, and the durability of the soles. Shoes are available in a variety of synthetic and natural materials, and in a variety of colors and styles. Finally, of course, shoes vary by brand, with the Nike brand name being the most well-known worldwide brand.

Most Nike athletic shoes are made in developing nations in south-east Asia, where a contracted manufacturing company can pay the female [male] workers substandard wages. The labor standards in these countries can also be quite lax. It is not uncommon to find that the shoes coming from countries in south-east Asia have been manufactured in factories with unsafe working conditions, by women [men] who are required to work long hours.

It was once the case that when you purchased a sneaker your choice was limited to a few standard options. Now only product design and marketing are done in the West, with production being carried out in south-east Asian factories that are quickly able to change to new designs and materials. As a result, the variety of athletic shoes available to today's consumer is a blistering array that is meant to satisfy almost any consumer's athletic or fashion requirements around the world.

Animal testing/environment: bath soap

Soap is one of the oldest and most basic commodities known to humankind. It exists in a variety of forms and is used by billions of people every day. Ordinary bath soap – that bar sitting in your bathroom – can be anything from the very simple formulation used, and perhaps made, by your grandmother to a quite complex mixture of ingredients.

Today's sophisticated soaps are made for many different people and purposes. Not only do they vary in terms of their fragrance and moisturizing capacity, but they have many additional medicinal characteristics. Some soaps are designed to keep the pores open and unclogged while others are specially formulated so as not to aggravate acne conditions. "All-natural" soaps avoid the use of non-natural ingredients and artificial coloring and "antibacterial" soaps aim to stop the spread of germs.

Table 5.1 (*cont.*)

Traditional soaps are made from animal by-products – e.g. from tallow, a rendering of beef fat. A concern for animal rights has had an effect on the lowly soap. Companies today market products guaranteed not to be tested on animals or to use any animal by-products. This way, the concerned consumer can be sure the soap manufacturer did not contribute to the harm of animals in any way. [**Concern for the environment has led to the development of soaps with biodegradable ingredients. This means the soap will dissolve safely into the local water supply after being used, and any chemicals that might be in the soap will not adversely affect local animal or human populations.**]

Counterfeit products: Louis Vuitton products

Luxury goods by famous designers are often available in counterfeit versions at much lower prices than genuine versions. One of the more common categories of goods for which this is the case is luggage [**wallets**]. For example, a genuine Louis Vuitton roll-on airline suitcase [**wallet**] would cost about US $1,100 [**US$300**]. However, fake bags [**wallets**] of the same size and appearance can cost as little as one-twentieth of this amount. The suitcase [**wallet**] has the same characteristic brown color with gold monogram "LV"s on it and the same gold clasps. It is the same size and has similar-appearing lining, handles, and wheels.

Some of these suitcases [**wallets**] are thought to be made in the same Chinese factories where the genuine suitcases are made under contract to Louis Vuitton. Other, less expensive suitcases [**wallets**] are clever unauthorized copies. Those making the fake luggage [**wallets**] are local Chinese individuals who either use the manufacturing facilities of companies under contract to Louis Vuitton (during off-hours, such as evenings and Sundays) or else set up separate manufacturing facilities in other plants. They sell the suitcases [**wallets**] through networks of small-scale dealers and distributors, who often set up temporary shops or work in bazaars and markets, and on the streets of large cities in Asia, Europe, Africa, and North and South America. Recently, some such bags [**wallets**] have also become available on the internet.

Even though companies such as Louis Vuitton have international copyrights on their designs and logotypes, it is difficult for them to stop this counterfeiting, because the makers move plants and are hard to locate. Although they occasionally succeed in shutting a dealer down, there are so many sellers and the scale of their individual operations is so small and mobile that this is a never-ending task.

Note: Second-version changes are shown in **bold**.

evaluations were interpreted both by the same respondent as well as by informants in various different cultures. All responses were audio- and video-recorded in digital video format in the native language and dialect of each locale, and translated into English later if needed.

To maximize cultural variance, we chose informants from developed and emerging markets in a variety of cultures from both the East and the West. These markets have substantial overlap with the locales used in the experimental studies described in Chapter 4, thereby allowing us to make substantive comparisons. Those selected in each country were high school graduates ranging in age from twenty to sixty, with an equal proportion of men and women. These ranges comprise the target market for the goods in the three scenarios. Respondents were from major urban areas in each country, with the sample reflecting the ethnicity and religions of the nation, as well as varying socio-economic levels.

After discussing the "grand tour" questions with the researcher, informants were presented with the three scenarios, one at a time. Which version of each scenario was given to the respondents was determined randomly. The order of the scenarios presented was rotated within each group of twenty. The analysis of the transcripts and videos was qualitative and hermeneutic (Arnold and Fischer, 1994; Thompson, Pollio, and Locander, 1994; Thompson, 1997). All the authors participated in the interpretative process, first individually and then in unison, in order to leverage our own cultural and individual differences (Belk, Ger, and Askegaard, 2003). A complete half-hour documentary capturing many of these interviews is available on the DVD included with this book.

Understanding varying social consumption rationales

We found, first, that there were considerable inconsistencies between beliefs and behaviors. Indeed, of the 120 interviewees, we did not find a single participant who revealed "ethical" consumption behaviors. All admitted purchasing counterfeit goods at some time and few indicated that the factors discussed mattered materially to them. What was surprising was the degree to which they considered themselves to believe in, and be knowledgeable about, the aspects of social or commercial justice that were embodied in the scenarios. In other words, although most of the subjects indicated that labor practices, the environment, and intellectual property theft were important to society, most did not consider them very relevant to them personally. In the end, they all indicated that, when it came to doing something, they did not act upon these beliefs.

The results indicate very starkly that, although individuals do not seem to be particularly concerned, except superficially, the justifications for the inconsistencies in their beliefs and behavior have a number of consistencies that are culturally based. Three justifications and rationales dominated: (1) economic rationalism, (2) governmental dependency, and (3) developmental realism.

The economic rationalists

In capitalist and individualist countries such as Australia and the United States, and to a great extent Spain, many of the rationales and justifications used were of an economic rationalist nature. In other words, consumers justified their behavior using rational arguments that focused on their own utility as consumers.

The economic rationalist justifications included citations of price as more important than any other consideration. These informants also asked rhetorically why, if the issue did not directly affect them, they should care about it at all. For example, in response to the scenario depicting non-biodegradable soap, one of our US informants said, "[I]t's not a big deal, it's hard to tell from packaging; not a big deal – cost is more important; it just doesn't matter to me." Another said, "I've never really noticed; it would take some kind of catastrophe to make me care." Similarly, another American said, "Fish would have to start dying for it to affect me – I have to be hit over the head." In justifying why he did not care whether his soap was biodegradable, another US subject brought in impression management concerns: "[P]eople can see your sneakers, but they can't see your soap."

In providing a justification for his lack of concern about testing soap on animals, an Australian participant espoused the utilitarian view that, if the benefits outweighed the costs, then his behavior was acceptable. He assessed the benefits of an ecologically sound soap in an overtly economic rationalist way: he would not pay more than 10 percent more for something that was biodegradable.

Of the three scenarios, our interviewees were least concerned about purchasing counterfeit goods – something most people consider "victimless." The most common account for this position was an inability to perceive any ethical problem with such behavior. We can, again, see economic rationality evidenced in the justifications offered by the Americans, Australians, and Spaniards. For example, one American said, "It's a waste of money, but no one's hurt; you get what you pay for; smart consumer." Another said, "[A] good deal; the consumer isn't being fooled." Another American called counterfeits "a bargain." One American participant did an implicit cost–benefit analysis and said, in discussing whether he would buy counterfeit products or not, "I'd only worry that the quality might not be good (or with pirated software that there might be a glitch)."

An Australian said, "If quality was an issue I would purchase the original, but if that was not the case the fake might be good enough." One Australian male related that the price of the original LV bag was too high based on the cost of the materials, and thus from an economic perspective it was rational to buy the fake. Similarly, as another argued, "[f]akes are not the same quality but price makes up for that," echoing the cost–benefit analysis mentality.

Finally, this type of rationale was also exhibited in the context of sweatshop labor (Nike sneakers) by Americans, Australians, and Spaniards. For example, an American said, "Most buyers are not aware of it [the labor conditions], and people 'over there' are willing to work under these conditions." Another said, "It's too bad, but all sneaker companies do this; Nike could do something but competitive pressures don't allow it." This economic rationality/cost–benefit analysis is again exhibited, but in a more macro way. For example, an Australian consumer, in discussing how factories operating under sweatshop conditions can be economically beneficial to the country in which it is located, said, "Part of this is a development issue. Years ago it was Japan, then Singapore and Malaysia. Now it is Vietnam and China. These countries need opportunities." One particularly rational Spanish woman noted that we cannot ask corporations to behave in ways that we ourselves do not: "Aren't we exploiting ourselves when we use cheap labor from migrants? If I have a cleaner to clean my place, I wouldn't get a Spanish cleaner, because I have to pay her €12 an hour; I get a Romanian one and I pay her €6 an hour. It's the same thing."

The rationale was not always monetary, but was sometimes based more on time utility. For example, an Australian said, "All things being equal, if this [the labor conditions] was the case, I would purchase another brand, but it is torture going out and buying joggers. So if I found a pair of Nikes that worked for me I would buy them." Because of the time and effort involved in buying new athletic shoes for her, she would buy Nike in spite of her professed concern about the labor issue if it met her purchasing criteria.

Similarly, one Australian participant said, "It is part of a process, and unfortunately such conditions appear to be necessary." Another articulated this line of thinking this way: "Most Australians are concerned about price, not the labor issues. Morals stop at the pocketbook. People might say something but, if they were to make them [athletic shoes] in Australia at twice the price, people would buy the foreign cheaper brand. These blokes [factory workers in south-east Asia] are lucky to have a job. If they weren't making them there these people would not have work. You would not want to upset the labor conditions in these countries [by paying them more]. The advantages to these people outweigh the costs." Finally, echoing an all-things-being-equal logic, another Australian noted that they "might consider a local brand not using bad labor practices, but it would have to be competitive in terms of all other factors."

Our American, Australian, and Spanish informants clearly view issues surrounding social and ethical consumerism through a lens of economic rationality. Knowing that this is the meaning being attached to the situations given in the scenarios offers a clear direction as to how to reach consumers in these countries, and how the message would need to be structured, to bridge the gap between their professing to care about the issues and their actual consumer behavior. For example, showing exploited factory workers or calling attention to the extent of their exploitation could heighten guilt, but it is something that these consumers could naturally ignore as they have powerful logic mechanisms to do so. Such tactics may, at the margin, raise the perceived benefit of avoiding products and companies involved in such exploitation, but they are not necessarily going to be a motivator to seek out products that possess these benefits.

The governmental dependents

In social democracies such as Germany and Sweden, and, again, to a lesser degree Spain, the justifications that consumers offer for their ethical beliefs and behavior tend to center on their lack of individual responsibility for the issues presented to them. They say, instead, that it is the role of the government to address the issues. They feel that legislation and laws are the way to fix things, and thus it is the role of politicians to debate and decide on ethical consumerist policies. If something is legally available to them, consumers in these countries feel it must be acceptable to buy it, since the government has sanctioned its sale. For example, a Swedish participant said, in relation to the issue of soap being biodegradable, "The government should protect the environment." Similarly, another Swede noted, "Now we're part of Europe, so it's Europe's responsibility."

Although still demonstrating a lack of individual responsibility, respondents did not always share the viewpoint that governments need to be the vehicle for addressing ethical issues. One Swede expected that "advertising should let us know about this." She still did not see it as her individual responsibility to be proactive but thought advertising should be *required* to inform consumers better so that they could choose. Similarly, another Swedish consumer noted that "[i]n Germany there is a duck on packages to mark 'green' products," suggesting that the Swedish government should enforce a comparable approach so as to make consumers aware of the issue.

In response to buying counterfeit goods, one Swede expressed a commonly held belief that "[i]f it's legal people should buy it, but if it is illegal they shouldn't." He equated the ethics of consumerism to the laws enacted by government – that is, if the government has decided that a particular product can be legally sold in the country, then the consumer does not have a responsibility to question that ruling. Similarly, another Swede felt that "[c]opyright infringement is a crime that should be stopped legally, not by consumer boycott" – that is, the government should be taking action, not consumers.

We also see a shifting of blame to the companies themselves, not just to the government. In discussing athletic shoes made in sweatshop conditions in south-east Asia, a Swedish participant said, "It's Nike's fault, not mine."

With German consumers, this lack of individual responsibility was revealed in what we call a traditionalist manner – that is, they felt that the expected pattern of government protection absolved them of responsibility; why should they waste time thinking about such issues or changing their consumption patterns? For example, one German said that the situations presented in the scenarios are "just the way things are." Another commented, "I cannot do anything about it, so why bother thinking about it?" Yet another followed this logic with a fairly typical remark: "Don't talk about things that don't concern you and you can do nothing about." Here we see that, because it is up to someone else instead of the individual consumer to address these issues, the question then becomes: why should anyone think, talk, or act about the issues at all? Although Germany and Sweden are considered to be green countries politically, there is a surprising lack of concern with the individual's responsibility to engage in C_NSR behavior.

The meanings that consumers in these countries attach to consumer ethical issues are filtered through a lens of holding other institutions responsible for addressing ethical, social, and consumer-related issues. Thus, even if they think that a particular practice is wrong, they do not see it as their responsibility to address the issue, or, amazingly, even to think about it. In trying to bridge that gap and encourage consumers in these countries to take a more agential role, a successful strategy might entail questioning whether the government, corporations, and institutions such as the advertising industry have motivations that may be antithetical to what is best for the consumer. If so, then there should be room and reason for the consumers themselves to have a voice on these issues.

The developmental realists

Consumers in emerging markets tended to have quite different justifications for their beliefs and behavior. Even if our urban, middle-class consumers from China, India, and Turkey perceived what was happening in the scenarios to be ethically wrong – and many of them did not – they saw breaching their own sense of morality as part of the price to be paid so that their country and its citizens could develop and grow economically. They tended to see the issues surrounding paying low wages to factory workers and providing bad working conditions, not being environmentally sensitive or animal-friendly, and manufacturing and purchasing counterfeit goods simply as examples of the way the world works. Because they are intimately familiar with these practices, and that is all they have known, they just accepted these practices. For example, in discussing the ethicality of buying soap that is non-biodegradable, Turkish participants were quite direct: "In Turkey people are too poor to worry about such ethical issues"; "Turkish people are not influenced by ethical concerns, price is more important"; and "[T]hese ethical issues are of no concern to people in the village; they only want a cheap, familiar soap that cleans."

Even though the scenario describing poor working conditions was set in south-east Asia, Turkish participants could relate to the situation. For example, as one explained, "Turkish people are much less sensitive considering the ethical values brought up in this scenario. These issues would get much more reaction in the developed Western countries. Questions like the oppression of workers and female workers who are required to work longer hours for substandard wages are less sensitive for Turkish people compared to Western countries." Another Turkish consumer said, "There are so many things like that in Turkey. There are so many places that sell good-quality products but they give low salaries to their workers," ending: "Living conditions, natural laws, and the rules of life are like this. We saw like that, lived like that."

Most of the Chinese consumers did not think there was an ethical issue at all in the labor condition scenario. They thought the pay was normal for the local area, and should not be compared to wages in other countries. Some of them also used their knowledge of how capitalism works to justify their lack of concern: "We should judge by the living level and its coverage salary in Jiangsu [a city in China that has a Nike factory]; you should compare with the ordinary family, not Europe or any other place." The same participant went on to say, "Normal? It's absolutely normal. And natural, since it's a market economy." Another Chinese consumer noted that "[t]o have exploitation of the workers is quite natural; this is the natural adoption of every business throughout the world." Another followed with a similar sentiment: "The capitalist class is quite oppressing. We learnt it when we were in primary school. We know what the capitalist class is from our politics lessons." With reference to other south-east Asian countries, this was echoed further: "They are the capitalist countries, and we are the socialist country. Our country has socialism, we don't have this problem." With reference to the specifics of Nike, another showed a clear understanding of free markets: "They are capitalists, so they will pursue high profits." Moreover, it seemed that this realism was not devoid of hard economic rationalism, as expressed by a young Chinese woman: "Most people know how Nike shoes are made. It's very normal. Some say it's a good thing. You will be laid off if you aren't oppressed by others. The boss gives money to you. The boss earns money, and then you have money. No one is hurt. Everyone has won."

The Indian participants echoed this acceptance of labor conditions in similar ways to the Turkish and Chinese. One said, "What can we do? It has nothing to do with us. Some people earn well. Some countries are poor. That is business. It's cheap for them [Nike]. If they try to do it in the US, they have to pay more. There is nothing wrong. If they [the workers] had no job, then how would it be? At least they have food to eat." One Indian justified her belief that the workers are not being underpaid on issues of currency conversion: "In America they pay people $5; that would be 250 rupees in India. You wouldn't pay that much for work. So the currency also plays a role. If workers here work for Nike, they would be paid 100 rupees. In America they would pay probably $4 or $5. And you can't pay the equivalent in India." Another Indian acquiesced to the reality that "basically, there are few opportunities to work. Therefore, they [the workers] are satisfied with whatever work they get. Something is better than nothing. Manufacturers take this as an opportunity to give them low wages. In this way, both manufacturers and labor benefit."

One Indian consumer related the labor situation to the reality of working life in southern Asia: "We don't have to be concerned with this issue so seriously. There is an employment problem in south-eastern countries. Even if somebody is not willing to work at a lesser pay, the other person is ready to take the job for the same amount of salary. People don't really realize about what they are paid and how much the product is sold for. So this issue doesn't really matter much. The worker is paid what he requires for his basic requirements. He doesn't bother much about the amount he deserves to be paid. Apart from food, clothing, and shelter they consider the other things to be luxurious. Moreover, a person creates his own competitor if he wants to quit the job because of less pay. The other person may work at even cheaper wages."

Some justifications surrounding why it is acceptable to buy counterfeit products centered on the ethicality of large corporations exploiting people by charging high prices, especially in Turkey. With reference to the ethicality of purchasing a fake Louis Vuitton handbag, one Turkish woman said, "Turkish people don't know much about Louis Vuitton, so why should they care if it's original or fake? And then, why should they worry about the ethical issues? I wonder how many people have ever heard about Louis Vuitton." Another said, "Because the registered owners of these brands are wealthy Americans or developed Western countries, people don't really care so much. They think these brands have come out by way of exploiting us. Rather, some people see counterfeits as a positive development against the exploitation. I heard about people talking positively about counterfeits. They hold negative attitudes towards America. There may be people even saying, 'Let these brands go belly-up – who cares?' That wouldn't affect me so much. I am not bothered as much about Louis Vuitton as about authorized dealers in Turkey. In the end, they are giant companies. How much loss would Louis Vuitton suffer? That is, Louis Vuitton would suffer only a small loss in the end. I think nothing would happen to Louis Vuitton."

Other justifications centered on the right of people in developed countries to say that buying a counterfeit is wrong, considering the economic conditions of the majority of the population. The Chinese consumers interviewed accepted counterfeit goods as a normal part of everyday life. One explained, "It's acceptable in China, but not abroad. We didn't know about copyright of music products. We thought it was normal to buy fake disks. We got the same result by paying less money. Consumers say it's unacceptable to pay 20 yuan for a real disc, but rather we pay 1–2 yuan for a fake. We earn RMB [renminbi – the Chinese currency], and American people earn dollars." He thought it was not fair to hold Chinese consumers to the same standards, considering their reduced ability to buy the real thing.

One Chinese woman explained how she felt about fake goods in the marketplace: "In fact, it's not good. But real disks are too expensive and worth several fake ones. If it is only one or two yuan dearer than the fake one, the real one may lose market share. Many people prefer to buy cheaper things instead of the expensive real one. I know it's not ethical. People would buy real disks if they're cheap." Another described this argument in these terms: "In China, most of the consumers are from the ordinary working class. They do not earn much and they have to spend money on life, so they will certainly mind the price as the first important thing. That's natural. The mass media say that we should be against pirated editions. But, from the economical background of most of the Chinese people, most of them will go to buy the fake things. Why do they support the fake? Just think of the price."

One Chinese participant related why Chinese people bought so many fakes compared to other countries to the high rate of savings in China – that is, in more developed countries, consumers can spend all their disposable income because they are confident they will replace it with their next paycheck; in China, people save because you never know what may happen next. This was advanced as the reason people prefer to spend less money on fakes rather than a substantial amount of money on real products.

The Indian consumers once again reiterated these justifications when discussing the ethicality of buying a fake Louis Vuitton bag. One said, for example, "How can you talk about ethics when the basic necessities are not met? You need a good bag; OK, a good bag is there. You can't afford a real one. And you are taking it. It's like you don't have a choice, to really sit and talk about ethics. You can talk about ethics when you have everything in front of you. When you don't have things and when you are running for things, trying to get things, get a bag, good bag, and all that, get a good lifestyle, you can't, you don't have the choice. You feel like getting the real thing but you can't, so you try to pacify yourself with this [the fake bag]."

In discussing the popularity of counterfeit goods in India it was noted that "[f]or people who make it [the fake bag], if they make something of a bad quality, the goods are not sold. That money is wasted. So they don't sell that kind of goods. They make goods that can be sold; the expenses are met and profit is made. If we get the same thing for half the price, why won't we use it?" Counterfeit goods are a part of everyday life for the majority of Indian consumers: "Well, I think in India, it's very normal and regular. Nobody cares that it is a branded [real] one or not because you know there are very few people, a handful of people, who can pay for that brand. Eighty percent of Indians are like this. They go for the counterfeit goods, and only 20 percent can afford the branded ones."

In India, China, and Turkey, consumers attach meanings to these ethical situations through the lens of their economic situation, political education, and intimate knowledge of the development and labor conditions in their countries. We can also see a current of resentment about how the media, NGOs, and other consumers from developed countries try to frame the issues, as it is so distanced from their reality. In trying to reach these consumers, this suggests that reframing the issues to point out how consumers' personal or countrywide economic conditions may be helped overall by changing their consumption behavior may be a successful strategy for reaching them – that is, they may begin to appreciate that higher wages and higher expenditures can benefit the economy.

Currents of logic and justification

We can see in study no. 3 a diversity of justifications for the consumer's lack of social and ethical consumption behavior. Although we have characterized the justifications by country, there are individuals who span these three logics in all the countries studied. However, in all cases, despite this diversity of logic, it does reveal a clear desire on the part of the consumer to pass the obligation for his/her own responsibilities on to other authorities. The most obvious authority is the government, although this was viewed warily. Few consumers were keen to restrict their choice (even in the case of the Germans and Swedes), and none appeared willing to sanction other consumers for making consumption choices that they themselves would not make. Although they wanted the government to lead, they also appeared to want to have sufficient latitude to resist what they considered unjustified political interference in what was, fundamentally, individual free choice.

The results also hint at how behavior is only weakly linked to beliefs and knowledge. In nearly all our interviews we found that knowledge was not lacking. Consumers had seen articles and documentaries on labor practices, or, in the cases of India, Turkey, and China, experienced it first-hand. They all indicated that they had purchased counterfeit goods (indeed, several of the female interviewees had their purchases with them), although most of the Swedes, Germans, and Americans had done so "victimlessly" while on holiday (including a police trainee). They all knew about the issues associated with the environment and animal testing. Hence, it was not knowledge that motivated these individuals. The information was there; they simply chose to put it out of their minds and not act upon it. When this dissonance was pointed out to them, there was a distinct uneasiness that was alleviated only by calling upon the most culturally amenable justification.

What these results also reveal is that consumers in developing countries such as India and Turkey – the developmental realists – are hostile to government social initiatives they feel are being imposed on them in a neocolonialist manner by bodies such as the WTO, the G8, the International Labour Organization (ILO), and others, which they see as advancing developed countries' agendas at their expense. As the prime minister of India, Manmohan Singh (Yergin and Stanislaw, 2001), has stated:

The American attempt at Seattle [the WTO ministerial meeting held there in 1999] to introduce these extraneous issues really created serious doubts in the minds of many developing countries that new protectionism was back in the West in the guise of labor standards, social standards, and environment. I sincerely believe that the West should resist using the WTO as an instrument to promote these causes.

This aspect of our work presents a different reading of the consumer-driven urge for social policy regarding social consumerism. Consumers such as governmental dependents, who assign culpability to institutions, are often unwilling to support policy initiatives, as the case of labeling shows. Therefore government legislation is, in many cases, likely to go unnoticed. For economic rationalists, who are already resigned to the realities of commercial activity and international trade, government legislation might appear to be little more than rhetoric at the expense of more pressing local issues. For developmental realists, who are already accustomed to the limitations of legislative action and unclear about the ethical principles involved, proactive policies might be interpreted as overtly anti-capitalist or a threat to economic growth.

Interpreting the myth

What was quite interesting from this aspect of our work was the degree to which none of the consumers interviewed readily identified with the mythical ethical consumer. When asked about their beliefs in an abstract manner, they would engage in "ethically correct" discourses. However, there was not a single case in which the consumer revealed himself or herself as actively engaging in behaviors normally associated with ethical consumerism. They understood these behaviors, and expressed sympathy, but, fundamentally, did not use them to motivate behavior. Almost all the consumers were aware of this gap, but produced varying justifications for it.

We can interpret this in a number of ways. First, we did not prime the consumer in a way that led to defensive masking of behavior. The interview protocol given in Appendix 4 reveals that we only slowly moved on to aspects of their behavior. Hence, we found little effective posturing and idealization of personal behavior, because we did not target the individual directly, thereby protecting his/her ego. Second, we did not seek to find individuals who had any particular proclivities toward the issues being investigated. Third, we were not attempting to understand what could be done to make consumers more socially responsible, but were simply concerned with how they interpreted existing behavior.

What we do see is that, yet again, there is little evidence that the "ethical" consumer stands as more than a mythological entity, very similar in many ways to the toiling workers in old communist posters. The analogy is apt in this case, because what we do see is that consumers are much more likely to want to be led on this dimension than to be active leaders. We can speculate as to why this would be the case, but three factors can be hypothesized as critical, two of which are rational and follow on from the experiments in Chapter 4, and one of which we can glean from our interviews here.

First, consumers are willing to engage in an active and costly search when functional aspects of the product/service are at issue. This has a direct relationship to their utility and presents them with clear returns that accrue to them. We can see the logic of this in Toyota's advertising campaign for the third-generation Prius. Ads for the car speak predominantly about its technological innovations and cool features. This is a direct appeal to car owners seeking car features. In addition, the perception of the car as a "chick vehicle" is being countered with the use of young, trendy males as drivers.

Second, consumers are unwilling to engage in costly social search and verification when the benefits from that search have only a marginal impact on the use value of the product/service in question. Again, using the Prius as the example, we see the information campaign as being quite simplistic when it comes to the environmental features of the automobile. Nearly all the environmental statements are functional and related to fuel usage. The consumer is willing to trust the source but certainly wants either verification that the source is valid (e.g. the government) or trustworthy (e.g. a well-established brand with skin in the game).

Third, consumers may, in circumstances in which their self-image and the image revealed by the social aspects of the product/service are linked, be willing to invest in social consumption activities. This is the quasi-rational co-production discussed in Chapter 3. As noted by Belk, Ger, and Askegaard (2003, p. 348) in discussing consumer desire:

The social nature of desire implies that preferences of consumers are far from being independent. [...] The mimetic aspect of desire creates difficulties for using individual attitude or intention measures to predict adoption of new products whose use will be visible. [...] The consumer, individually and jointly, has a role in constructing the object of desire, within a social context. What makes consumer desire attach to a particular object is not so much the object's particular characteristics as the consumer's own hopes for an altered state of being, involving an altered set of social relationships.

At this point we see in the Prius campaign a quite clear attempt to link the individual owner to a specific social niche by asking "Are you a Prius person?". By doing so, Toyota is subtly manipulating the image being presented, by allowing the consumer not to have to "sacrifice" anything (you get all those nifty features) but at the same time to engage in the co-production of an image the company wants to convey to the outside world.

These results are quite consistent with what we discovered through experimentation, with a few minor exceptions and revelations. An important revelation was the degree to which consumers understood the general facts underlying the issues investigated – working and environmental standards and counterfeiting – but chose either to ignore or downplay the relevance or applicability of that information to their specific circumstances. Furthermore, this was more than simply blind self-interest in the face of contrary evidence. Consumers were able to distance themselves and their consumption practices from the issues by distinguishing between idealized conceptions of what their behavior should be and what it was. As one of our Australian interviews showed:

Basically, you know as far as consumerism goes you would have to say I was pretty much an ethical vacuum. But in my defense I will say I'm conscious of it and I don't see it as a problem, I'm afraid. You know, for the Third World countries you can call it – a lot of people call it – exploitation, but we are all exploited one way or another every day of our lives and I think it's improving the standard of living, it's a step in the progress process.

This is consistent with the idealized, mythical ethical consumer as role model and the reality of the normal – conflicted and flawed – individual. As noted by Frankfurt (1971, p. 7):

Besides wanting and choosing to do this or that, men may also want to have (or not to have) certain desires and motives. They are capable of wanting to be different, in their preferences and purposes, from what they are.

We are able to understand a lot about C_NSR by understanding that consumption can be explained through the reasons and logic tied to that activity, not just via rational action. The experiments revealed how a rational perspective hinted at the potential for some social consumption by some people under some circumstances. The results here suggest that idealized notions of ethical consumption are understood at the mythical level – time and time again, our participants revealed to us that they understood the myth – but that they are just that: heroic ideals. And, as with all heroic ideals, they are something to which we aspire, and something we can explain away when we prove unworthy.

6 | *The ethical consumer, politics, and everyday life*

Man is a consuming and sportive animal as well as a political one.

John Dewey

Of course ... that's life. A series of trade-offs.

Meredith Johnson (Demi Moore) in *Disclosure*

The price of anything is the amount of life you exchange for it.

Henry David Thoreau

From the consumer context to the perspective of the citizen

A serious limitation of work in the field of ethical consumerism and social consumption is the contextualization of the research, be it survey, experimental, or ethnographic. Although one can largely remove aspects of bias by using increasingly ingenious approaches, it remains a reality of the work in this field that individuals will be primed simply by the context in which they are being studied. As noted again and again in earlier chapters, this means that the degree to which social consumption is estimated to occur will be related quite directly to the degree to which context is removed from the estimation process. Equally, the importance of political and social issues more generally will be influenced by the degree to which the questioning intimates their importance.

One concern that we have left until this chapter is the degree to which a cause, or cause category, focus inflates the importance that consumers place on the central issues under investigation. In other words, because nearly all studies of social consumption, including our own, concentrate on single issues, there is a concern that we are biasing the results by increasing the *salience* of whatever issue is being studied. For example, a considerable number of individuals might reveal a concern about genetically modified (GM) foods when questioned in a focus group on food safety. Slightly fewer might express concern when asked how "important" or "unimportant" GM foods are to them on a survey scale. An even smaller group would reveal a willingness to pay in an experiment in which GM food has to be traded off with other aspects of food quality and desirability. Finally, even fewer people would actively seek out and avoid genetically modified foods in the supermarket or restaurant when the cost of the search is quite significant. As a colleague once remarked in a seminar: "If you want to find the greatest number of ethical consumers, use a focus group. If you want to find the least, look at behavior." As Andrew Carnegie put it, "As I grow older, I pay less attention to what men say. I just watch what they do."

Much of what we are saying above parallels our discussion of bias in Chapters 3 and 4. However, the salience bias is germane to the generalizability and composition of the phenomena of C_NSR, and how we attempt to address it here further proves that the ethical consumer is a mythical notion. Following on from the above, the salience and resonance of the issue is reduced as it gets put into a context that demands more trade-offs. In focus groups and simple surveys and polls there are, effectively, no trade-offs (and potentially a lot of bias). Experimental approaches increase the trade-offs but do so in a controlled and artificial manner (and reduce bias when well constructed). Actual purchasing increases the trade-offs dramatically, but does so in a manner outside the control of the researcher (thereby potentially adding bias due to product availability, consideration set formation, and other factors whereby reality deviates from a natural experiment).

For the researcher, this creates two dilemmas of relevance to the topic of C_NSR. First, decisions made without trade-offs give biased information and inflate the importance of the concerns being investigated. Larger and more representative samples, and the typical statistical approaches used to beat sense out of data, do nothing to address this issue. Second, methods that reduce this bias – such as the experimental approaches we have applied – are typically fairly artificial, quite costly to implement, and hence use smaller samples, making it difficult to get the population-level estimates that are useful to policy makers. Indeed, one of the reasons simple opinion polling remains popular, despite its various failings, is the fact that it can be executed quickly and easily over a broad range of topics and populations.

In this chapter, we show how we can resolve these dilemmas by applying techniques that give us information involving trade-offs among a larger range of issues across a broader sample of people. In doing so, we also show that the complexity that we saw in individual decision making is in evidence at the macro level as well. Just as individuals refuse to follow the idealized patterns represented by "ethical consumerism" in purchasing, so, too, do they fail to conform to simple rules around general social, economic, and political preferences. Moreover, just as ethical consumerism is overestimated by naive polling, we show that the socio-political-based concerns for many ethical consumer and citizen-related issues are also probably dramatically overstated. In doing so, we show that, as the complexity of context rises, individuals reveal more about the structure of their "true" beliefs – beliefs that reflect something closer to the contexts in which they live their lives.

We present the results of two studies. The first is linked directly to study no. 2 from Chapter 4 and involves consumers in six countries – Germany, Spain, the United States, Turkey, India, and South Korea – and sixteen social issues that overlap with those examined in Chapters 4 and 5. The second study is a comprehensive omnibus examination of a population sample of Australians that examines not just social but political and economic issues as well. It examines sixteen categories of economic, social, and political issues, along with specific sub-issues within each category.

These final two studies are important to put the prior research in perspective and to move from the specific, in which individual decisions are made, to the general, in which policy issues are decided. As noted by Reich (2008, p. 178) in his book *Supercapitalism*, "There is a difference between the private wants of a consumer and the public ideals of a citizen." In this sense, there is no "ethical consumer" but a consumer who is a citizen and a citizen who is a consumer. Johnston (2008), Jubas (2007), and Soper (2004, 2007) are just three of many authors who point out that the notion of the citizen-consumer hybrid is a joining that is fraught with conflicts and contradictions. As Johnston (2008) observes, there is the unfortunate tendency to stereotype consumers as either "hapless dupes" – those suckers of mass consumption orchestrated by evil corporations – or "unencumbered sovereign agents in the global economy" – our mythical ethical consumer. Neither personification is realistic or useful.

The citizen-consumer suffers from ideological schizophrenia. The consumer personality focuses on self-interest and private choice. The citizen personality focuses on the common good and the need to ensure the survival and well-being of others. The consumer personality reveals itself at the grocery store and shopping mall, where everyday purchasing becomes the focus of attention. The citizen personality comes to life in political debates, polls, and reading the newspaper. The two personalities coexist. At times the two are in conflict. At times they are partners in cooperation. In what follows, we pull them together to get a picture of the degree to which otherwise disparate components of the individual's existence in the society – at the economic, social, and political levels – can be characterized and evaluated in a way that is useful in understanding the reality of C_NSR as a reflection of a broader range of individual preferences, and how the citizen personality can be seen as a component of the degree to which consumer action reflects social preferences.

A pound for human rights, a penny for genetically modified food: a glimpse at measuring social issue priorities

As discussed above, one major limitation to a product-by-product approach to understanding social consumption is that it focuses the consumer's consciousness on the social issues at hand and contextualizes the issues in a trade-off with functional attributes and price. Although this is more realistic at one level, it abstracts from the fact that individuals are faced with trade-offs amongst social causes when they reveal themselves as citizens as well as consumers. As we noted in our comparison between product segments, the idea that people care about everything is part of the mythical nature of ethical consumption. There is no doubt that individuals will express significant concern about a lot of things when there are no hard choices – as is the case when answering an opinion poll. However, in reality, we cannot care about everything equally and will not care at all about many things. What we seek here is a picture of what these trade-offs look like and, in doing so, to get into the individual's citizen personality.

   In the first of the studies we will discuss here, we are concerned with the individual's degree of concern about a set of sixteen social and ethical issues: (1) animal rights in product testing; (2) the use of animal by-products; (3) product biodegradability; (4) products made from recyclables; (5) the provision of product safety information; (6) human rights; (7) packaging recyclability; (8) product disposability;

(9) the payment of minimum wages; (10) whether unions are allowed; (11) whether minimum living conditions are met; (12) sexual orientation rights; (13) the guarantee of safe working conditions; (14) the use of child labor in production; (15) genetically modified material usage; and (16) gender, religious, and racial rights. We chose these issues on the basis of a review of the ethical consumerism literature and an examination of the broad issues of concern for business and consumers given in the popular press. They were also chosen purposely to include some of the social attributes used in discrete choice experiments discussed in Chapter 4, as we were interested in where the product-related issues investigated fit into the general range of social issues.

The approach used to determine importance was a best–worst (BW) experiment. Details of the mathematical and psychological characteristics of these experiments are given in Appendix 5, Marley and Louviere (2005), and Marley, Flynn, and Louviere (2008). A BW experiment presents the subject with a block of $N > 2$ items from which s/he must select the "best" and the "worst." The blocks are formed via an experimental design and represent a reduced form of discrete choice experimentation. As Finn and Louviere (1992) demonstrate, "BW models the cognitive process by which respondents repeatedly choose the two objects in varying sets of three or more objects that they feel exhibit the largest perceptual difference on an underlying continuum of interest." The approach has proven fruitful in a number of areas ranging from the assessment of values (Lee, Soutar, and Louviere, 2008) and healthcare economics (Flynn *et al.*, 2007) to the estimation of foreign direct investment choice by senior managers (Buckley, Devinney, and Louviere, 2007). It has also been shown to be effective in reflecting the preference patterns extracted from more complex discrete choice experiments (Buckley, Devinney, and Louviere, 2007).

The BW methodology gives the researcher a number of advantages when compared to standard opinion polls and importance surveys – advantages that are particularly germane to the study of social consumption in a cross-cultural context.

First, the issue of scale equivalence between individuals and cultures is reduced. For example, as noted before, the use of a Likert-type scale raises the immediate question of what the scales mean to the individuals, as it is well understood that individuals from different cultures use scales differently (see, for example, Baumgartner and Steenkamp, 2001,

Cohen and Neira, 2004, and Dolnicar and Grün, 2007). In the case of a BW experiment, this is not an issue, since "best" and "worst" are identical to everyone – that is, BW experimentation eliminates differences in the way that human subjects use rating scales, including cultural differences in rating styles, if they exist. Second, the importance measures derived consider all issues on a common scale, and the resulting scale has known measurement properties, either an interval or a ratio scale. In addition, interpreting the scale is relatively simple. Marley and Louviere (2005) show that the simple difference in BW scores (i.e. simply taking the number of times an item is considered "best" and subtracting the number of times it is considered "worst") is a close approximation of the true scale values that are estimated via multinomial logit regression. These properties allow for a quick and simple examination of the relative importance of an issue by simply scaling the number of times an issue is considered "best" against the number of times it is considered "worst."

Hence, unlike scales that ask people to rate importance, BW experimentation derives importance on the basis of the trade-offs made when different issues are presented in conflict. For example, standard surveys assume that one issue is more important than another simply because individuals rate it higher on the scale used (e.g. 3 = "not important at all" as compared to 4 = "somewhat important"). However, the individual filling in the survey is making an absolute judgment, which may or may not play out when trade-offs need to be made. Cognitively, for the absolute judgment to translate into a relative judgment, the individual would need to keep in his/her mind all his/her prior responses and know all his/her future responses and be able to calibrate them so that the ordering is correct – an absolutely impossible task even for the most committed survey respondent.[1] In the case of BW experimentation, the equivalent of this exercise is derived directly from the choices, thereby removing the cognitive burden from the participant.

The participants in the first BW study were the same 605 consumers from six countries involved in study no. 2. Each participant saw twenty blocks of four issues, presented after the discrete choice experiment. Table 6.1 provides the glossary of definitions of the sixteen issues while Figure 6.1 presents an example of the instructions and what the experiment looked like to the participants.

A BW score for each of the sixteen issues was obtained by subtracting the number of times an issue was selected as "Least important" (worst)

Table 6.1 *Sixteen issues considered in the six-country best–worst experiment*

Category of Issue	Definition
Animal by-products used	Indicates that the product is made using animal by-products such as animal fat or lard.
Animal rights	Describes the general treatment of animals for commercial purposes, such as the use of animals for product testing, the displacement or killing of animals for natural resource exploitation (e.g. logging), or the cruel use of animals for entertainment.
Child labor not used	Means that companies do not use workers under the minimum working age in the country(ies) in which they are operating.
Gender, religious, racial rights	Indicates that discrimination based on gender, religion, or race is not allowed.
Genetically modified material used	Indicates that the use of GM materials is allowed within a country and that companies use GM materials in their products.
Human rights	Describes the basic rights of all people as stated in the Universal Declaration of Human Rights, such as the right to food, clothing, housing, education, etc.
Minimum living conditions met	Means that companies supply their employees with basic and acceptable living accommodations when required.
Packaging recyclability	Indicates that part of or all packaging materials can be recycled for future use (e.g. product packages, food containers, shipping boxes, etc.).
Paying minimum wages	Signifies that companies adhere to the minimum wage standards of the country(ies) in which they are operating.
Product biodegradability	Indicates that the materials used to make a product can be broken down naturally and hence are safer for the environment.
Product disposability	Indicates that a product can be disposed of without causing undue damage to the environment.
Product safety information provided	Means that information about the safe use of a product and/or potential dangers from using a product is included with the product.

Table 6.1 (*cont.*)

Category of Issue	Definition
Products made from recyclables	Indicates that some or all of the materials used to make a product were obtained from recycled sources.
Safe working conditions	Signifies that companies follow a set of procedures to create a safe working environment for their workers.
Sexual rights	Indicates that discrimination against individuals in terms of their sexual orientation is not allowed.
Unions allowed	Indicates that unionization is legal within a country and that companies producing in that country do not attempt to prevent or curtail the unionization of their workers.

from the number of times that same issue was selected as "Most important" (best). The results of these calculations are individual-level scales (BW scores) for each of the sixteen issues that are easily comparable across the entire sample.[2] In this study, each of the sixteen issues appeared a total of five times in the experiment, so the individual-level scales for each issue can range from +5 to −5. For example, a value of +3 could be obtained if a respondent selected an issue as most important four times and selected the same issue once as least important. A score of −5 meant that every time the issue appeared it was rated least important.

Figure 6.2 presents the overall mean BW scores, calibrated so that a higher score is "better." The figure ignores, for the moment, the differences between countries. What we see is a clear differentiation between the issues. "Human rights" is a "category killer" social issue. Its score of 3.0 means that, when appearing against all other issues, it has a 60 percent chance of being chosen as most important. The four dominant issues are related to human and labor conditions ("no child labor" and "safe working and living conditions"). The least important issues are obvious with one exception: genetically modified food. Despite the activist agenda surrounding GM foods, there is relatively little resonance for the issue when it is compared to the others in the list – something we will discuss again shortly. What the score of −1.11

Instructions. In this section, we will present you with sixteen social and ethical issues. These will be organized in groups of four (a total of twenty groups or questions). For each group, select the **one issue** among the four that is **least important** to you and the **one issue** that is **most important** to you. Please make sure that you select only one least important and one most important for each group of four issues. We have included a description of the issues; please keep them in mind throughout the rest of this section.

—EXAMPLE—

In this example, sexual rights are least important and human rights are most important. Please notice that only **one issue** was selected in **each column** "(**Least important**" and "**Most important**").

	Least important		Most important
A	Only one ⟹ □ √ □ □	Animal rights Sexual rights Human rights Gender, religious, racial rights	□ □ √ ⟸ Only one □

Question no.	Which issue matters LEAST to you? (Tick ONLY ONE box for each question)	Sets of social and ethical issues for you to consider	Which issue matters MOST to you? (Tick ONLY ONE box for each question)
1	□ □ □ □	Animal rights Product biodegradability Products made from recyclables Product safety information provided	□ □ □ □
2	□ □ □ □	Human rights Product biodegradability Packaging recyclability Product disposability	□ □ □ □
3	□ □ □ □	Product biodegradability Paying minimum wages Unions allowed Minimum living conditions met	□ □ □ □
4	□ □ □ □	Sexual rights Product biodegradability Safe working conditions Animal by-products used	□ □ □ □
5	□ □ □ □	Gender, religious, racial rights Product biodegradability Child labor not used Genetically modified material used	□ □ □ □
6	□ □ □ □	Human rights Animal rights Gender, religious, racial rights Sexual rights	□ □ □ □
7	□ □ □ □	Animal rights Packaging recyclability Paying minimum wages Safe working conditions	□ □ □ □
8	□ □ □ □	Animal rights Product disposability Genetically modified material used Minimum living conditions met	□ □ □ □

Figure 6.1 Experiment instructions and example of the best–worst task

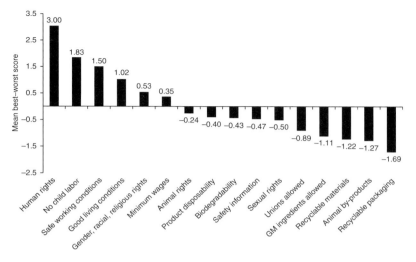

Figure 6.2 Mean best–worst scores across six countries

implies is that when "GM ingredients allowed" appears in a list it has a
22 percent chance of being chosen as least important by a randomly
selected individual. The other issues – from "gender, racial and religious
rights" to "sexual rights" – are all effectively of middling importance
and statistically indistinguishable.[3]

As we noted earlier, our sample is not representative of the population
in the countries studied. Hence, general conclusions about these findings
are limited to the domain that the sample represents, not the country as a
whole. However, the point that is brought out here is that the groups
being studied do make distinctions between the issues they are facing and
prioritize them clearly in terms of their importance. If every issue were
equally important then the profile seen in Figure 6.2 would be flat, but
this is not the case. Some issues plainly dominate others.

We should also emphasize the critical importance of the nature of
comparator groups when making assumptions about importance. In
other words, the fact that the issue of "human rights" dominates all the
other fifteen issues presented is conditional on the fifteen issues against
which it is being compared. We can be reasonably certain about the
prioritization of these sixteen issues, but that does not reveal to us
anything about other issues that we have excluded. Hence, the BW
method provides important information conditional on the domain of

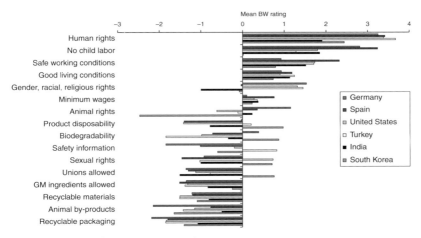

Figure 6.3 Mean best–worst scores by country

the issues being queried; the larger this domain, the more veracity there is in statements that can be made about the ordering of the preferences. We could not, for example, make inferences about the importance of climate change, even from information relating to the specific environmental issues included (such as biodegradability). However, if we knew that climate change was more important than child labor we would immediately know that it was more important than the issues that child labor dominates.

The results in Figure 6.2 gave a general picture of the trade-offs and prioritizations that the participants made, ignoring their country of origin. Figure 6.3 presents the BW scores differentiated by country. Basically, we see the same pattern as revealed earlier, with some additional twists. First, the top issues – "human rights" through "good living conditions" – are very much the same for all countries, in that they are generally all positive. Second, the low-rated issues – "recyclable packaging" to "GM ingredients allowed" – are the same across countries, in that they are generally all negative. Third, the differences between countries lie not in the major issues, but in what falls in the middle.

Table 6.2 allows for a closer examination of the structure of these more general social preferences by giving the mean BW scores for each country. For each country, the top four issues are indicated in bold, the bottom four in italics. The underlined numbers indicate a score of less than 2.0 in absolute value (meaning that they are marginally important

Table 6.2 *Mean best–worst scores by country*

Issue	Overall	Germany	Spain	United States	Turkey	India	South Korea
Human rights	**3.00**	**3.24**	**3.41**	**3.66**	**3.38**	**1.89**	2.44
No child labor	**1.83**	**2.82**	**3.24**	**1.28**	**1.80**	**1.85**	0.01
Safe working conditions	**1.50**	0.92	**2.31**	**1.71**	**1.74**	**1.51**	0.80
Good living conditions	**1.02**	0.93	**1.19**	1.24	0.90	**1.13**	0.73
Gender, racial, religious rights	0.53	**1.54**	−0.03	**1.45**	**1.32**	*−1.00*	−0.08
Minimum wages	0.35	0.10	0.76	0.35	0.26	0.37	0.23
Animal rights	−0.24	**1.16**	0.36	−0.11	−0.63	0.24	−2.47
Product disposability	−0.40	−0.03	*−1.41*	0.22	*−1.41*	−0.78	0.99
Biodegradability	−0.43	0.39	−0.71	*−1.83*	−0.98	−0.33	0.88
Safety information	−0.47	*−1.84*	−1.02	0.00	−0.18	0.82	−0.59
Sexual rights	−0.50	−0.93	*−1.46*	−1.03	0.73	−1.00	0.70
Unions allowed	−0.89	*−1.36*	−1.31	−0.78	−1.13	*−1.51*	0.76
GM ingredients allowed	*−1.11*	−1.35	*−1.51*	−1.38	*−1.32*	−0.82	−0.25
Recyclable materials	*−1.22*	−1.22	−1.22	*−1.50*	*−1.51*	−0.81	*−1.09*
Animal by-products	*−1.27*	*−2.15*	−0.76	*−1.43*	−1.15	−0.49	*−1.65*
Recyclable packaging	*−1.69*	*−2.19*	*−1.80*	*−1.85*	*−1.84*	*−1.07*	*−1.41*

or unimportant). If they were below 1.0 in absolute value they are considered as neither important nor unimportant.

What becomes obvious at once is the degree to which the South Korean participants stand out. Basically, their differential concerns center around two issues only: "human rights" (positively) and "animal rights" (negatively). Indeed, the rating of animal welfare is statistically identical in absolute value terms to the valuing of human rights. The other differences seen across the countries are matters of degree. Germans, Americans, and Turks tend to give slightly more preference to gender, racial, and religious rights, and the Germans value animal rights moderately more than middling. There are more differences at the bottom around the determination of what is least important than there are at the top about what is most important.

These results reveal two things. First, certain important issues resonate quite broadly across all groups. Although there are noticeable differences (in our case, seen in the South Koreans), the ordering of the most important issues is fairly consistent. Second, there is more variation around the degree to which an issue is least important. This is related to the fact that there are no "category killer" unimportant issues on which everyone can agree. People seem to agree much more on what is important than they do on what is unimportant.

It is valuable to note how a number of very emotive issues do not line up with preconceived notions of what "should be" important. Despite the considerable media interest and activity around issues such as GM food and animal welfare, there is considerably less resonance for these issues when they are put in opposition to other deserving or impactful social concerns. For example, GM food is considered fairly unimportant, despite the degree to which poll after poll shows considerable consumer angst over the topic, particularly in Europe. The Pew Global Attitudes Survey (2003) is just one example:

More than seven-in-ten in Germany (81%), Japan (76%) and Italy (74%) also take a negative view of scientifically altered produce. [...] Although opposition in the U.S. is less widespread, 55% of Americans also believe genetically modified foods are a bad thing.[4]

It is intriguing to note the consistency of our results with those of the two field studies on GM foods conducted by Mather, Knight, and Holdsworth (2005) and Mather *et al.* (2007) and discussed in Chapter 4.

The same can be seen in the case of animal welfare. According to our results, only the Germans give "animal rights" some consideration. This contrasts dramatically with a Eurobarometer survey that indicates that 73 percent of Turks, 64 percent of Spaniards, and 56 percent of Germans would "be willing to change [their] usual place of shopping in order to be able to buy more animal welfare friendly food products" (Eurobarometer, 2007). The same survey also finds that 72 percent of those surveyed believed that farmers should be compensated financially for the higher production cost, without, of course, indicating who should pay that higher price and how. This highlights the bias induced when surveys focus on causes, thereby signaling that the issue being studied is one of importance, otherwise it would not be studied at considerable cost by important organizations in the first place. Although our sample is not representative, it is certainly telling that, when 70 to 90 percent of people are indicating extraordinarily strong opinions about an issue in an unconstrained survey, we are finding that few, if any, people we studied seem to care when those issues are put into a situation in which simple trade-offs have to be made.

Our list of sixteen issues was not meant to be comprehensive but was intended to be broad in terms of the nature of the concerns. In this sense, it becomes much clearer where the issues we investigated in Chapters 4 and 5 in a purchasing context stand. Although more people appeared to be willing to consider environmental issues in their purchasing decisions (the environmental segment was larger in the case of AA batteries), as a general social cause many of the issues embedded in those products (e.g. product disposability, recyclable materials) do not have the magnitude of impact of the labor issues, such as child labor or safe working conditions, embedded in the purchasing of athletic shoes.

This last point can be seen in Tables 6.3 and 6.4, which present the mean BW scores for the specific product category segments estimated in Chapter 4. We see that, overall, the issues relating broadly to AA batteries are viewed as of less importance (hence the negative signs). However, we find that there is a tendency toward slightly less unimportance in the social segment. The aggregate score – which is just the sum of the individual scores of the five items for each individual – increases as we move from the "price" to the "brand" to the "social" segment. With labor-related issues we see the same trend but with more resonance on two issues: child labor and working conditions. Indeed, the "social" segment views unionization as unimportant, as it does the issue of minimum wages. However, the same tendency is seen: those in the "social" segment, as revealed through the purchase choice experiment, indicate overall preferences for labor-related issues in the BW experiment.

These results give us insights into where the divide between the citizen and the consumer comes into play. It is obvious that issues such as human rights and child labor are quite high in terms of their resonance with individuals as citizens, but that other issues arise in the immediacy and context of purchasing. This is a fact well understood and articulated by many writing in the field (such as Harrison, Newholm, and Shaw, 2005).

Table 6.3 *Mean best–worst scores by product category segment (AA batteries)*

	Price segment	Brand segment	Social segment
Product disposability	−0.79	−0.38	0.20
Recyclable packaging	−1.85	−1.61	−1.23
Safety information	−1.05	−0.50	−0.18
Recyclable materials	−1.41	−0.95	−1.05
Biodegradability	−0.67	−0.63	−0.22
Overall aggregate	−1.15	−0.81	−0.49

Table 6.4 *Mean best–worst scores by product category segment (athletic shoes)*

	Price segment	Brand segment	Social segment
Minimum wages	0.48	0.32	−0.03
Unions allowed	−0.41	−1.75	−1.33
Good living conditions	1.27	1.16	0.80
Safe working conditions	1.16	1.45	1.81
No child labor	1.27	2.09	3.00
Overall aggregate	0.75	0.75	0.85

However, there is a degree of consistency, in that two alternative methods reveal that the fundamental parameters influencing the prioritization of social ideals are aligned. This, we believe, is where the approaches discussed here and standard surveys and polls deviate. Surveys and polls do not deal with the reality of trade-offs. Although our list of social issues was very limited and the sample restrictive, we see much less evidence of an attitude–behavior gap precisely because we formulate a methodology that mimics the trade-offs inherent in realistic decisions, be they decisions made when the individual is using his/her consumer personality or when the individual is acting in the role of citizen.

This does not, of course, mean that there are no inherent flaws in the BW approach to preference analysis. Although we are able to get a picture of the relative importance of specific social causes, we do not know the absolute level of those preferences. For example, it is possible that people *do* care about everything. The approach to BW experimentation used here will, by definition, not reveal this to us, although, as we noted, advances in the technique make this more likely now. In the approach used here, if individuals care about every issue *equally*, the preference profile will be flat. Nonetheless, we cannot get a picture of the absolute level of preference without a broader analysis that widens the set of trade-offs – something we do in the next section. However, we again reveal why the context is so important. Without trade-offs, understanding value is impossible, since value is embedded in the context in which decisions are being made. As the quote by Sowell in Chapter 4 says, "There are only trade-offs."[5]

Seeing the citizen: estimating general societal preferences

The first study is very limited and was meant to link our information about social consumption with more general characterizations of the individual's preference in his/her role as citizen. However, as we noted, our sample is not representative of any of the countries investigated, and the domain of the issues is seriously limited. To get a better picture of societal preferences requires that we not only look at a range of social issues but also include economic and political issues. This is more realistic in a number of ways, and also allows us to come closer to the mixture of social, economic, and political concerns that dominate policy making, both locally and internationally.

To do this, we apply the BW logic from the first study to a comprehensive omnibus survey of sixteen categories of social, economic, and political issues using a representative sample from Australia to capture preferences more in line with the total populace. The goal here is to push the logic of trade-offs further, closer to the reality faced by the citizen-consumer. The survey is an omnibus in that it captures not only information about preferences using the BW methodology but also information about the participant's voting and political activities, religious beliefs and practices, and donating and volunteering activities. In addition, the sixteen general categories include a total of 121 subcategory issues that are themselves prioritized using BW methods. In the end, we have a picture of *general preferences* (e.g. the extent to which environmental sustainability is important relative to global security), *specific preferences* within each category (e.g. the extent to which climate change or loss of biodiversity is more important within the category of environmental sustainability), and how these relate to actual related behaviors (e.g. religious practices and voting).

Table 6.5 provides a listing and simple definitions of the sixteen general categories of social, economic, and political issues. Appendix 6 provides more detail on the sub-issues investigated within each category. Our discussion here focuses mostly on the category-level preferences, with a few examples from some of the more interesting categories. The categories themselves were chosen following an examination of routine opinion polls (e.g. Eurobarometer), discussions with political and social writers and academics, and a scan of the research on social, economic, and political causes and issues. The categories also span four important dimensions: (1) the *local* to the *global* (e.g. local crime and public safety versus global security); (2) the us to the others (e.g. individual economic well-being versus societal economic well-being); (3) *general* to *specific* rights (e.g. civil and personal liberties versus minority rights); and (4) the *social* to the *political* to the *commercial* (e.g. rights to basic services versus commercial rights). The individual sub-issues in each category were assigned on the basis of a pilot examination by academic and practitioner experts.[6]

Individuals were sampled via an online panel that is used routinely for political polls. The study was conducted in February 2007. The sample was chosen to be representative of the Australian voting-age population (eighteen and over) on four criteria: (1) age, (2) gender, (3) income, and (4) location (by state and city/rural/suburban). In total, 1,508 individuals provided usable responses. The survey had five parts.

(1) A BW experiment that involved trade-offs amongst the sixteen categories of issues. This is the focus of our discussion here.
(2) Eight BW experiments that involved trade-offs amongst the sub-issues in eight of the sixteen categories, the eight being chosen on the basis of an experimental design.
(3) A values questionnaire (Lee, Soutar, and Louviere, 2007) and Machiavellianism scale (Christie and Geis, 1970).
(4) A group of demographic and social and political questions that captured religiosity and political opinion, as well as tracking individuals' religious activity and their voting.
(5) A questionnaire that captured individuals' donating and volunteering activity across fifteen general categories, from working with schools and sporting organizations to being involved with homeless shelters, healthcare organizations, environmental groups, and other categories of NGOs.

Table 6.5 *Categories of social issues*

Issue category	Definition
Civil and personal liberties	Includes issues associated with individual rights and freedom, such as the right to life, the right of free speech/opinion/expression, and freedom from harm and from cruel, inhumane, or degrading punishments.
Equality of opportunities	Consists of freedom from discrimination based on a variety of criteria, such as age, gender, sexual orientation, and religion.
Commercial rights	Focuses on issues associated with commerce and ownership and includes physical property rights and intellectual property rights.
Worker/employment rights	Includes those rights and freedoms of workers exclusive of those covered by normal commercial rights, such as freedom to engage in a trade, profession, or occupation, the right to form/join a labor union, and the right to strike.
Rights to basic services	Addresses access to basic services and includes the rights to benefits of last resort (e.g. welfare, dole, etc.), access to healthcare, and the right to a basic education.
Animal welfare	Consists of issues dealing with the treatment of animals and preservation of animal species. It includes both the rights of an individual animal and the protection of a species.
Environmental sustainability	Focuses on issues associated with the protection of the natural environment. It includes issues relating to the recycling of materials, industrial and personal pollution, and climate change.
Minority rights	Deals with the rights and protection of minority groups within a society and includes the right to cultural expression in public, the right to engage in cultural practices, and the right to speak a foreign language.
Local crime and public safety	Relates to issues associated with local societal crime and safety, and contains protection from violent crime, child pornography, and sexual exploitation, and protection from bribery and corruption.
Food and health	Deals with major health issues that affect the society and includes obesity, abortion rights, and the use of GM foods.

Table 6.5 (*cont.*)

Issue category	Definition
Individual economic well-being	Focuses on economic issues that affect the individual and his/her family. These contain issues such as inflation, the cost of daily living, housing affordability, and taxation.
Societal economic well-being	Involves economic issues at the country (societal) level that may affect the individual and his/her family, but do so less directly. Such issues include economic growth, unemployment, poverty, and government debt.
Societal social well-being	Deals with social issues at the country (societal) level that may affect the individual and his/her family. These issues include the quality of schooling, public transport, immigration, and income inequality.
Global economic well-being	Focuses on economic issues at the global level that can affect the individual and society. It contains issues such as global growth, free trade policy, and Third World debt.
Global social well-being	Considers issues of social well-being at the global level, abstracting from the economic issues given earlier. It includes concerns about global poverty, income inequality, and war.
Global security	Includes issues associated with security at the global level and involves issues such as genocide, terrorism, religious extremism, and unilateral military actions.

The BW experiments looked identical in form to the one given in Figure 6.1, with the exception that instructions now read as follows:

In the conduct of our everyday lives a host of social and economic issues are important. Some are important in a more immediate sense; others are important in a more general societal sense but affect us all. In this section, we will present you with ... issues. These will be organized in groups of ... For each group, select the **one issue** among the ... that is **least important to you in the conduct of your life as a member of the society** and the **one issue** that is **most important to you in the conduct of your life as a member of the society**. Please make sure that you select only one least important and only one most important for each group of issues. We have included a description of the

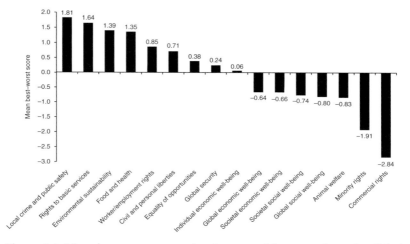

Figure 6.4 Mean best–worst scores for sixteen social, economic, and political issues

issues; please keep them in mind throughout the rest of this section and refer back to them as needed.

The main difference is in the statement "to you in the conduct of your life as a member of society," which changes the cognitive perspective of the individual from a self-interested orientation (e.g. as a consumer) to a citizen-based orientation.

For the trade-offs amongst the sixteen categories, the participants received a BW experiment identical to that used in the first BW study: twenty blocks with four issues in each block. For the other sixteen BW experiments on the category sub-issues, different designs were applied to generate the maximum efficiency for that set.

The results of the overall category choices are shown in Figure 6.4, which simply replicates the form of Figure 6.2 with the new categories. We immediately see a number of very clear patterns. First, issues that are near to the individual, in the sense that they are locally salient, are quite dominant – local crime and public safety, rights to basic services, food and health, and labor rights. Second, environmental sustainability comes out as quite important, even in competition with many individual issues. Third, commercial rights and those of minorities are very much at the bottom in terms of consideration, even lower than concerns about animal welfare!

We can drill down further into the categories and get a picture of the preferences in the sub-issues that make up the categories. It is impossible in one chapter to go over all the sub-issues, so we will focus on four categories: environmental sustainability, food and health, rights to basic services, and worker/employment rights. The preferences in these categories are shown in Figure 6.5.

In the case of environmental sustainability, we see a generally flat profile, indicating that no single issue dominates. Industrial pollution and deforestation are important, as are the issues of climate change and alternative energy. With food and health, water and sanitation dominates. Once again, GM foods, although a very emotive political issue according to the polls, is dead last amongst the twelve issues. In the case of basic services, it is access to healthcare and food that dominates, with welfare benefits considered less material. Finally, we see in worker and employment rights what was revealed in our discrete choice experiments: safe working conditions and child labor stand out, while the right to join a union is quite low. Minimum wages and retirement benefits are important, but not as much as the first two. Appendix 6 presents information on all the other category sub-issues.

Although these results are interesting, it is more relevant to look at a number of ways in which the findings can be linked to behavior. In this case, we can examine two types of behaviors that are important: voting and donating/volunteering.

In the case of voting preferences, we asked the participants to which party they gave their first vote in the last Australian federal election[7] and which party is closest to their own political and social philosophy (as well as whether or not they were a member of a party and which one). Figure 6.6 provides the category BW scores as to which party they voted for in the last Australian federal election.[8] Australia has three major party groups: the Liberals/Nationals (conservative and in power at the time of the survey; the Nationals are a rural partner party); Labor (a social democratic party and about to be elected into office); and the Greens (a left-wing environmental party with enough support to be a spoiler party).

The Liberals and Labor are mainstream parties, and are the only ones with any chance of forming a government. Hence, one would expect that they would have overlapping support groups, since to get into office they must convince middle-ground swing voters. This is quite clearly seen to be the case. On almost all issues, Liberal and Labor

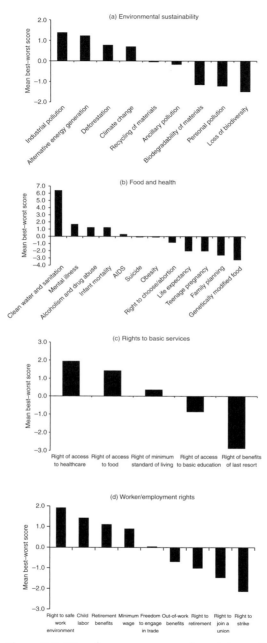

Figure 6.5 Mean best–worst scores for sub-issues in four categories

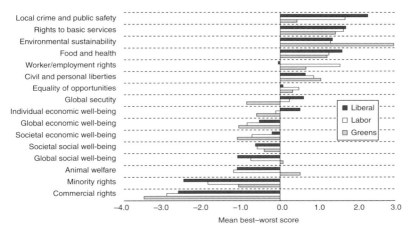

Figure 6.6 Social, economic, and political preferences by party vote

voters are in agreement in terms of the order of the issues. What is high for Liberal voters is generally high for Labor voters, with a few key exceptions that reflect their core supporters. Labor voters, unsurprisingly, rank "worker/employment rights" an equal first with "local crime and public safety" and "rights to basic services." Liberal voters focus more on "individual economic well-being" and "global security." However, the Green voters are an entirely different story. Again, unsurprisingly, they support "environmental sustainability", but they do so in a manner that nearly overwhelms the next two issues combined, "rights to basic services" and "food and health." Even more surprising is the fact that Green voters rate "animal welfare" slightly higher than "local crime and public safety" and rate "commercial rights" so low that the issue would be rated as least important in 75 percent of the cases.

We can take this sort of analysis further by examining volunteering and donation behavior and its relationship to the preferences revealed by the BW experiment. We will do this by focusing on two groups: human rights organizations and animal welfare organizations. Tables 6.6 and 6.7 show the BW scores for individuals based on whether or not the individual had donated and/or volunteered for an organization associated with human rights (e.g. Amnesty International or Human Rights Watch) or animal welfare (e.g. PETA, the Royal Society for the Prevention of Cruelty to Animals [RSPCA], the Humane Society). Fourteen percent of respondents donated to a

Table 6.6 *Best–worst scores based on human rights activities*

	Neither donate nor volunteer	Donate	Volunteer	Both donate and volunteer
Civil and personal liberties	0.65	1.02	0.73	2.10
Rights to basic services	1.63	1.68	1.09	2.10
Equality of opportunities	0.34	0.59	0.05	1.57
Environmental sustainability	1.35	1.62	1.14	1.00
Global social well-being	−0.91	−0.24	−0.05	1.00
Worker/employment rights	0.90	0.54	0.82	0.86
Local crime and public safety	1.97	0.93	0.82	0.43
Global economic well-being	−0.66	−0.63	−0.09	0.29
Individual economic well-being	0.14	−0.40	0.09	0.00
Societal economic well-being	−0.67	−0.60	−0.46	−0.29
Food and health	1.44	0.85	1.36	−0.57
Societal social well-being	−0.85	−0.15	−0.18	−0.72
Global security	0.32	−0.21	0.50	−0.72
Minority rights	−2.04	−1.22	−1.64	−1.14
Animal welfare	−0.82	−0.79	−1.32	−2.57
Commercial rights	−2.81	−3.00	−2.86	−3.14

human rights organization, 4 percent volunteered, and 2.5 percent did both. Thirty-two percent of participants donated to an animal welfare organization, 3.5 percent volunteered, and 2.1 percent did both.

The alignment between the importance of the issue category and the behavior is very tight in both cases. Volunteering or donating tells much less about preferences than both donating and volunteering, which represents the application of both financial and human capital and clearly identifies the individual as lying at the extreme of the population preference

Table 6.7 *Best–worst scores based on animal welfare activities*

	Neither donate nor volunteer	Donate	Volunteer	Both donate and volunteer
Animal welfare	−1.60	0.55	0.56	3.20
Environmental sustainability	1.28	1.55	1.03	3.05
Rights to basic services	1.72	1.54	0.84	1.10
Worker/ employment rights	0.91	0.73	0.84	1.00
Local crime and public safety	1.77	1.94	1.50	0.80
Food and health	1.45	1.17	1.28	0.80
Civil and personal liberties	0.80	0.54	0.60	0.65
Equality of opportunities	0.41	0.31	0.84	−0.05
Individual economic well-being	0.19	−0.16	−0.25	−0.30
Global economic well-being	−0.59	−0.77	−0.34	−0.95
Global social well-being	−0.75	−0.87	−0.89	−1.10
Global security	0.27	0.23	0.41	−1.15
Societal economic well-being	−0.55	−0.84	−0.94	−1.25
Societal social well-being	−0.62	−0.98	−0.66	−1.25
Minority rights	−1.91	−2.00	−1.09	−1.35
Commercial rights	−2.79	−2.95	−2.63	−3.20

distribution with respect to a specific issue. Those committing themselves to a human rights organization in this manner reveal quite clearly that they value fundamental rights (civil and basic services) and equality of opportunities. Those committing themselves to an animal welfare organization signal their support for animal welfare, and also seem to signal something about concern for the environment (not unexpected, given what we saw with respect to the preferences of supporters of the Green party). However, what is quite interesting is that those with a strong support for human rights have very little support for animal welfare (it is second to last in Table 6.6). Those strongly supporting animal welfare have a moderately low measure of the importance of those things that the human rights supporters value. This is seen in Table 6.7, where the BW scores of the animal welfare donators and volunteers are on par with, or below, the scores for those that neither donate nor volunteer.

This last point recalls the finding from Chapter 4 that the fact that a consumer was in the AA batteries "social" segment did not help to predict whether s/he would be in the athletic shoes "social" segment. In other words, concern revealed about the environment implied nothing about concern for labor rights when that concern was expressed through product choice, and vice versa. In this case, the same phenomenon arises. Concern for animal welfare does not imply concern for human rights, nor does concern for human rights imply that one will be concerned about animals. Indeed, if anything, the results indicate that general social proclivities are much more complex and do not follow simple stylized rules. These results should remind the reader of the work of Laury and Taylor (2008) discussed in Chapter 4.

The consumer as citizen: linking social and consumer preference

We could delve deeply into the data from this study; however, our point has been to show the degree to which there is a link between stated preferences and revealed preferences, and how this links back to the notion of C_NSR and the concept of the citizen-consumer.

Much of the literature on the citizen-consumer highlights the conflict between the individual's activities as a consumer and his/her role and attitudes as a citizen. What we have suggested here is that this is potentially misleading and arises because of a misunderstanding based on uncontextualized data. When considered in the circumstances in which trade-offs must be made, we see that the nature of the trade-offs that individuals make as citizens and decision makers is much more in line with the trade-offs that they make as consumers than has been supposed. The problem is not that people are "radicals in opinion polls but conservatives at the checkout line," but that the opinion polls are fraught with errors and biases that make it difficult to get an accurate picture of what an individual's opinions really are. There is a statement used in computer science that is quite apt in this situation: "Garbage in, garbage out," or GIGO. Uncontextualized opinions and attitudes are basically GIGO. It may be highly statistically accurate to ±x percent (as is normally the case with opinion polls) but it is little more than accurate garbage when it comes to investigating issues that are socially laden, and that depend on contexts to be actualized.

Our quick analysis of donations and volunteerism suggests that this may also be related to the way in which individuals reveal their social preferences through financial and human capital. What we have is a picture of a multifaceted consumer-citizen who chooses to reveal social preferences in many different ways, in many different places, and at many different times. In addition, the preferences are not themselves fixed or settled, nor, as the recursive model implies, even subject to a strict linear pattern. Indeed, the individual may not even know what his/her preferences are for a specific issue in a specific context at a specific point in time. Similarly, social preferences divulged in the context of voting as a consumer do not align with preferences on the same topics made known in the context of voting as a citizen. This arises because, even though the labels may be the same, the actual concepts are different. Acting as an environmentalist in purchasing, when there are considerable trade-offs in terms of product functionality, personal image, and price, is simply not the same thing as acting as an environmentalist when donating to Greenpeace or when voting for a candidate who supports carbon emission trading schemes as a means of reducing climate change. What we have shown in this chapter, we hope, is that the closer one can make the construct that the individual is evaluating similar in contexts that tap the same cognitive processes (e.g. in making trade-offs), the more consistency one sees in terms of what people disclose about themselves.

How does this relate to the myth of the ethical consumer? It does so in two ways. First, a parallel to the myth of the ethical consumer is the myth of the moral citizen (Clarke *et al.*, 2007, p. 5), who

strides forward, the bold embodiment of the republican tradition. S/he self-confidently articulates political views, engages productively in public discourse and makes demands of the state as of right.

Just as the ethical consumer is mythical in being a fictionalized idealization and unattainable role model that is dramatically inconsistent with reality, so, too, is the moral citizen. The hollowness of the moral citizen is seen in the humorous anecdote proffered by Sagoff (1988, p. 52):

Last year I bribed a judge to fix a couple of traffic tickets, and was glad to do so because I saved my license. Yet, at election time, I helped to vote the corrupt judge out of office. I speed on the highway, yet I want the police to enforce laws against speeding. I used to buy mixers in returnable bottles – but who can bother to return them? I buy only disposables now, but to soothe my conscience, I urge my state senator to outlaw one-way containers. [. . .] I send my dues to the Sierra Club to protect areas in Alaska I shall never visit. . . And of course, I applaud the Endangered Species Act, although I have no earthly use for the Colorado Squawfish or the Indiana bat. . . I have an "ecology now" sticker on a car that drips oil everywhere it's parked.

We have mythicized the ethical consumer by failing to recognize that we are basing him/her on a more general, and equally erroneous, conception of what the role of the individual is in society.

Second, it is the conjunction of these two myths that creates real and perceived conflict between what individuals advertise that they want and what they do when the economic times are hard. The assumption is, of course, that it is the stated opinions that are correct and it is the consumer personality that is being influenced by evil corporate and self-interested hedonist forces that do not allow the true "ethical" nature of the consumer to come forward. It is believed that it is only right and proper that the consumer personality subsume itself to the citizen personality. This is unfortunate, as it implies a fundamental attempt to "enhance the value of public affairs by positing the moral weakness of consuming" (Schudson, 2006, p. 202). Soper's (2007, pp. 210–11) position, unlike many writing in this genre, is more balanced: according to her,

[T]he "citizen" concern with freedom, environmental preservation and sustainability is altogether more intimately bound up with the consumer practices and conceptualizations of the "good life" related to the maintenance of living standards. He or she [the ethical consumer] would be someone whose own pleasures were felt to have been compromised through the quest for ever enhanced "living standards" defined in terms of disposable income. . . For such an individual, certain forms of consumption would have become a site of problematic pleasure or means of satisfaction. Here, then, there is no longer so clear a distinction to be drawn between what the individual values and what he or she self-interestedly pursues as a "maintainer of living standards", and the consumption choices such a person makes are likely to reflect this more integral conception.

The picture of the citizen-consumer we have drawn is one of schizophrenia on the one hand and a modicum of consistency on the other; but it is one that is closer to reality than gross idealizations that will only disappoint us when we look at the data. It points out that consumption is a socio-political phenomenon, whether we want it to be or not. The consumer is, again, a co-producer of his or her own image, and that image sometimes allows more of the consumer personality out and at others gives prominence to the citizen personality. In addition, this discussion highlights that, while one might want to expect a concurrence of political and social attitudes and behaviors with economic and consumer preferences and behaviors, one can only hope at a degree of overlap. As noted by Sassatelli (2006, p. 225):

[C]onsidering consumption as politics, as a new but powerful means of political participation, we may both underestimate the role that the "political" has to play in translating ordinary practices into politically consequential ones and lose sight of the politics of consumption, ranging from social distinction to the realization of intimate aesthetic experiences.

The mythical ethical consumer and the moral consumer are like the Eve Black and Eve White in the film *The Three Faces of Eve*. Commenting on the two extreme alternative personalities, Dr. Luther remarks:

The truth is, neither Eve Black nor Mrs. White is a satisfactory solution. Neither of them is really qualified to fill the role of wife, mother, or even responsible human being. A victory for either would be disastrous. No solution whatever.

7 | *Tastes, truths, and strategies*

It is not to be forgotten that what we call rational grounds for our beliefs are often extremely irrational attempts to justify our instincts.

Thomas Huxley

Old beliefs die hard even when demonstrably false.

E. O. Wilson

I am much more radical in my beliefs than my products represent me to be.

Isabella Rossellini

De gustibus non est disputandum

In Robert Heinlein's 1961 classic *a Stranger in a Strange Land*, the tale of a human orphan raised on Mars and then returned to Earth, two characters – the young Ben Caxton and the older Jubal Harshaw – discuss the complexities of morality and tastes (Heinlein, 1999, pp. 550–2):

Caxton: I had to leave.
          . . .
Harshaw: Let's see first if you've got it analyzed correctly. Just what aspects of the situation did you find disquieting?
Caxton: Why. . .the whole thing!
Harshaw: So, in fact wasn't it just *one* thing? And that an essentially harmless act. . . To put it bluntly son, – what are you belly-aching about?
Caxton: Well for cripe's sake, – Jubal would you put up with it, in *your* living room?
Harshaw: Decidedly not, – unless perhaps. . .no one noticed. . . If such be the case, – no skin off'n my nose. But the point is that it was not my living room. . . So what business is it of mine? Or *yours*? You

	go into a man's house, you accept his household rules – that's a universal law of civilized behavior.
Caxton:	You mean to say you don't find it shocking?
Harshaw:	Ah, you've raised an entirely different issue... A very large minority – possibly a majority – do not share my taste in this matter. [. . .] But shocking? My dear sir, I can be shocked only by that which offends me ethically. Ethical questions are subject to logic – but this is a matter of taste and the old saw is in point. . .*de gustibus non est disputandum.*
Caxton:	You think [it] is merely "a matter of taste"?
Harshaw:	Precisely. In which respect I concede my own taste, rooted in early training, reinforced by some three generations of habit, and now, I believe, calcified beyond possibility of change, is no more sacred than the very different taste of Nero.
Caxton:	Well, I'll be damned.

This little play between the two characters comes close to encapsulating the conceptual logic of much of our discussion. Caxton witnesses something that offends him and turns away from it. Harshaw, more seasoned, walks him through the act of revulsion he feels. For the young Caxton, everything is an emotional reaction underscored by what is right and wrong. For the seasoned Harshaw, there are two separate issues: one is a fundamental conflict of ethics, and can be solved logically; and the other is an issue of tastes, which can be accepted only as something that is. *De gustibus non est disputandum* – there is no accounting for tastes. As noted by George Stigler and Gary Becker (1977, p. 76), two Nobel-Prize-winning economists, in an article entitled with the dictum, there are two ways to think about tastes:

Tastes are the unchallengeable axioms of a man's behavior: he may properly (usefully) be criticized for inefficiency in satisfying his desires, but the desires themselves are data. Deplorable tastes may be countered by coercive and punitive action, but these deplorable tastes, at least when held by an adult, are not capable of being changed by persuasion.

Our title [*De gustibus non est disputandum*] seems to us to be capable of another and preferable interpretation: that tastes neither change capriciously nor differ importantly between people. On this interpretation one does not argue over tastes for the same reason that one does not argue over the Rocky Mountains – both are there, will be there next year, too, and are the same to all men.

Our conceptual argument is based on the supposition that individual consumption behavior, in its complexity and beauty, is best understood without recourse to preconceived notions of right and wrong, ethical and unethical, moral or immoral. Indeed, to do so – to propose that some tastes are "better" than others, or that individuals who hold to those desires are somehow superior for being more socially conscious – argues for a degree of moral absolutism that is contrary to modern democratic and libertarian traditions. Furthermore, it argues for a standardization of behavior and norms that demeans the role that the individual plays in defining his/her society by his/her actions, independent of what others in that society may believe. To maintain that there is such a thing as "ethical" consumption is to relegate all other consumption into the unethical, less than ethical or non-ethical categories, and to brand the individuals who choose to engage in such heinous consumption as somehow different from their enlightened "ethical" co-consumers. Although our argument appears in line with Barnett, Cafaro, and Newholm (2005, p. 21), who hold that "to cast everyday consumption as unequivocally unethical threatens to alienate ordinary people rather than recruit them," it differs in that we contend that all people are "ordinary" and that any idea of recruitment implies that "conversion" is both socially desirable and morally right.

We also assert that many of the premises underlying the utility of ethical consumerism are logically inconsistent. For example, much of the popular positioning of ethical consumerism is geared around the rhetoric of "empowerment." The Ethical Consumer Research Association, the publisher of *Ethical Consumer* magazine in the United Kingdom and a host of rating tools, views its purpose as "empower[ing] the consumer to become a driving force for change through ethical consumerism." In the United States, Greening America views one of its missions as "to empower people to take personal and collective action."

The irony is that those uttering the rhetoric of ethical consumerism are assuming that consumers are not already empowered to use their wallets in the manner that they see fit, and to use that power with an open mind. In other words, those advocating the strict interpretation of ethical consumerism are assuming that individuals are empowered only when they act in line with the rhetoric, and that their lives up to that point have been little more than examples of blind and sheep-like consumption orchestrated by self-interested firms. This creates an obvious logical conflict. If consumer choice is the key to ingraining a social conscious into purchasing, how is that possible in a world in which consumers are actively being duped or manipulated by corporate interests? Is ethical consumerism just the replacement of one consumer controller by another? Are consumers, once ethically guided, cognitively different – superior and freed from their human biases? This dilemma leads inevitably to a picture of the consumer as potentially powerful, but neutered by a lack of information. Therefore, the refrain switches to the claim that being an ethical consumer is about "being informed" – e.g. "We aim to put power back in your hands by providing the information you are looking for in order to make conscious and informed choices that will affect positive change" (www.ethicalconsumer.ca) – or that latent ethical consumers are demanding more information with which to make their informed decisions – e.g. a survey by Consumers International reported that 60 percent of consumers wanted product-related climate change information at the point of purchase (Lazzarini, 2007).

However, as our research in Chapter 5 revealed, most people are informed to a reasonable level – they certainly are not ignorant of the issues and can discuss them quite intelligently – but nearly all choose to behave "unethically." Indeed, they are just as capable of discussing the social issues involved as they are the functional features of the products being evaluated. The research covered in Chapter 4 showed that (1) the majority of individuals will still not consider the social features even when fully informed, and (2) providing additional information does not influence choice differentially. This evidence is brought to the surface in a personal example that is particularly enlightening. One of the authors was on a panel with a leader of a well-known global NGO and asked this person: "Suppose that you communicated to a consumer everything you knew about [the subject] but in the end the consumer chose to behave in a way that was counter to what you felt was correct? How would you feel?" The response was telling, to say the least: "They could not possibly have understood what I was communicating and behaved in that manner. It would not have made any sense to have done so. The facts are the facts."

It is important to understand what we are saying here and what we are not saying. We are not saying that individuals are cognitively infallible and endowed with perfect foresight. Nor are we saying that they are nothing more than petty, selfish, and narrow-minded utilitarians. Equally, we do not underestimate the degree to which individuals are purposeful and act to achieve an end that is meaningful *to them*. To quote the Austrian economist Ludwig von Mises (1996 [1949], p. 26):

But what is essential in such a [product] and distinguishes it from other [products] cannot be described without entering into the meaning which the acting parties attribute to the situation. No dialectical artifice can spirit away the fact that man is driven by the aim to attain certain ends. It is this purposeful behavior – viz., action – that is the subject matter of our science. We cannot approach our subject if we disregard the meaning which acting man attaches to the situation, i.e., the given state of affairs, and to his own behavior with regard to this situation.

What we are saying is that people engage in consumption to satisfy their own needs, but are free to define those needs broadly so as to incorporate the welfare of others, even those unseen and at a great distance. This may include their incorporating environmental, labor, and other social components into their decision calculus; equally, it may be that they choose not to incorporate this information. However, it is not an issue of being informed or manipulated. It is simply an issue of the nature of what diverse individuals find desirable and acceptable. There is no accounting for tastes (even bad ones). Ethical consumerists argue for the ethicality of one set of tastes over another, but to do so is to assume an absolutist nature of tastes. Again, Jubal Harshaw explains (Heinlein, 1999 [1961], p. 553):

You are not a prude Ben. A prude is a person who thinks his own rules of propriety are natural laws. You are almost entirely free of this prevalent evil.

Nor is social consumption an issue of the alignment of consumer choice with values. As noted in Chapter 3, it is very difficult to find a line of sight from basic values to behavior. It is relatively easy to find a link between what individuals say in a survey about what they believe their values are (on whatever scale the researcher considers "valid") and what they believe they will do in such-and-such a situation. For some people, this may actually be a reasonable representation of what they hold dear and what they do every day. However, for most people, in most practical situations, this information is meaningless and naive. It is meaningless because it fails to account for the context, and it is naive in terms of its conceptualization of a causal relationship. For example, our finding in Chapter 4 – that an individual's consideration of labor issues in the purchase of athletic shoes was unrelated to his/her consideration of environmental issues in the purchasing of AA batteries – shows that values were not a determinant. Otherwise, these groups would have been related quite strongly, since the underlying values cannot have changed from one part of the experiment to another. This is confirmed further by our comparison of the MORI poll, the ethical disposition survey, and the individual's willingness to pay for social features. These were unrelated precisely because the general nature of the poll and scales provides little information that captures the structure or components of the decision model in operation. In the first examination, the "values" of the individuals did not change, only the product context. In the second situation, the values differed, but they proved useless in distinguishing between individuals who were willing to make sacrifices to get the good social attributes and those who were not.

What, then, is the lesson? Briefly, that individual "tastes" for social issues are not very different from their "tastes" for other aspects of their existence, even for the very mundane features of the products that they purchase. Practitioners and researchers in this field want to believe that social tastes are something different, operating at a higher level of consciousness because they are somehow more important to the investigator or activist; but this is a delusion. They are more important only when individuals, comparing them to all the other things that have value to them, determine that they are more important. As we have shown repeatedly, for some people this is the case, but for most others it is not. For those strict adherents to the religion of ethical consumerism, this will sound like heresy. How can it possibly be that the color of a sneaker is more important than the conditions under which the sneaker is made? However, our point has not been to debate the moral merits of arguments such as this, but simply to point out that ordinary people in ordinary circumstances, for whatever reason, are saying "It just is." Some people like Coke, some like Pepsi, some like Dr. Pepper, and some drink no soda at all, viewing it as an unhealthy alternative to water, fruit juice, or beer. Some people are concerned about animal rights, others about workers, still others about the environment; and some are not particularly concerned about any social issue.

This does not, of course, imply that individual tastes cannot be altered with time and persuasion, as well as education and regulation, nor that consumer choice is arbitrarily limited by the inability and unwillingness of firms to test the market with more products with clear social positioning. In holding that tastes can change, we differ very basically from Stigler and Becker (1977). Nevertheless, it is this that is yet another one of those ironic aspects of research in this field. If one believes that values are critical to social product decisions – as those researchers using values and belief scales as core independent variables in their research do – then the only effective way to change behavior is to change people's values. However, if we believe that values are "core" to who an individual is, changing him or her is one of the most difficult things to do in life; hence the conundrum. Those promoting the role of values as important to decision making are stuck with the fact that changing behavior is well-nigh impossible without individuals experiencing the equivalent of a religious conversion of sorts. Harshaw's expression "rooted in early training, reinforced by…generations of habit, and now…calcified beyond possibility of change" sums up the problem. However, if you believe that values are unimportant (or only marginally so) in determining tastes – i.e. if you are a values atheist – then creating an environment for social consumerism becomes much easier. The first thing that matters is changing behavior as a precursor to influencing tastes. As our discussion in Chapter 3 showed theoretically, and our analysis in Chapter 5 showed empirically, the complexity of how individuals rationalize the consistency between what they do and why they do it will go a long way to addressing the rest of the cognitive chain that makes their decisions look logical to them.

The inconvenient empirical truths

Although we have spent a considerable amount of time discussing conceptual issues, past literature, and the practical aspects of social consumption, the validity of our thesis comes down to the empirical evidence we can put onto the table that confirms the mythical nature of ethical consumerism and presents a more realistic picture of social consumption. We admit that our own work is not definitive in any way, shape, or form. It points to gaps in understanding and limitations of methodology, which we encourage others to investigate, but more and better work needs to be done. That said, we believe that our findings do create a series of inconvenient empirical truths that deserve an airing. They do not, in themselves, imply that notions of social product demand are fallacious, but instead they provide a cautionary tale of how easy it is to misestimate and misinterpret results, particularly when the subject of the investigation is a socially laden topic, and those doing the investigating at times have a vested interest in the outcome (Devinney, 2009).

Intentions without trade-offs are suspect. The vast majority of research on social consumption uses simple intention scales that do not account for the extent to which actual behavior involves trade-offs of valuation. Cotte's (2009) extensive survey of the literature shows that only 23 percent of the studies examined used experimental methods and these were mostly either very old (before 1980) or very recent (after 2000). The vast majority of research relies on self-reports (47 percent) and interviews (9 percent). Intention surveys not only suffer from the problems of incentive compatibility, comparability, inference, and social acceptance bias that we discussed in Chapter 3, but also fail to provide operational and realistic data on which to make decisions. As noted by John Drummond, CEO of Corporate Culture, a CSR consultancy, "Most consumer research is highly dubious, because there is a gap between what people say and what they do" (Murray, 2005), making corporate product development decisions based on information such as this well-nigh impossible. This is further evidenced by the almost crazily confusing information that continues to be generated by popular polls from "respected" market research firms. For example, athletic shoe manufacturers are pilloried non-stop in the press for the use of "sweatshop" labor, and this appears to be in line with Fraser Consultancy's list of the least ethical firms, as viewed by UK consumers: McDonald's, Nike, Shell, Adidas, Barclays Bank, Coca-Cola, BP, Camelot, American Express, and Nestlé (in that order) (Walsh, 2006). However, if you want completely different information, you can just look at another poll by another research organization. According to a study carried out at approximately the same time by GfK NOP, the brands perceived as the most ethical in the United States, France, Germany, and Spain included Nike, Adidas (no. 1 in Germany), Puma, Nestlé (no. 1 in Spain), and Coca Cola (no. 1 in the United States), although none were on the top of the UK list (Grande, 2007). It is inconceivable that these differences represent anything that is truly meaningful intellectually, or useful to the managers of these companies or the consumers of their products.

Values and beliefs are overrated, particularly when context comes into play. The vast majority of research into social consumerism puts considerable faith in the veracity of values and beliefs, particularly as measured by ready-made scales. Our findings reveal that the fluidity of social consumption is inconsistent with a model that gives pre-eminence to values and beliefs as antecedents to behavior. It would be unfair not to note that many studies argue this as well, but they invariably rely on the crutch of mediating and moderating variables to explain why values and beliefs lack validity. Our argument is simpler: the scales on which values and beliefs are being measured are fundamentally flawed, both at the individual level and the group level. At the individual level they attempt to represent values as immutable and absolute, when they are measurable only in comparison to other values. At the group level they lose validity through a lack of incentive compatibility, comparability, and inference, but also because they assume that values do not interact with context.

The role of the group is overstated and the role of the individual understated. Much of the research on social consumption is based on the ability to make statements about groups with different intentions or values based on survey responses. These responses overstate the degree to which group similarity matters, and the degree to which observable factors – such as gender, age, education, and so on – serve as a differentiator of choice in more realistic settings. In none of our studies did we find that any observable factor mattered as a segmentation differentiator. When we did find that such demographics mattered, they did so as a distinguisher between survey responses that were themselves unrelated to choice and willingness to pay. In other words, the grouping of responses on scale A was related to the grouping of responses on scale B, but neither scale A nor scale B revealed anything meaningful about people's choices or willingness to pay. This suggests that what is really being found is not meaningful differences in behavior, but meaningless differences in response styles to surveys.

The analog to this point is that the role of the individual is being understated. Our finding – that no demographics matter as a differentiator of choice – can be counterposed against the findings in Chapter 6 – that other "related" behaviors are differentiators for social consumption. This hints at two important facts. First, much of the heterogeneity in choice is to be found in the individual, and not in arbitrary groupings based on survey results. Second, what homogeneity exists is revealed by groups of related behaviors, as, for example, our findings in Chapter 6 – that individuals who indicate relative preferences for certain social issues reveal this in related behaviors, such as donating, volunteering, and voting, and that the intensity of their preferences is related to the intensity of the other behavioral manifestations.

What this discussion hints at is that a priori segmentation is inferior to behavioral segmentation, particularly in the social contexts we have examined. As discussed in Chapter 4, a priori segmentation occurs when the observable characteristics of respondents (consumers) are used to characterize a group in which those in the group possess similar traits but those traits differ from those in other segments. Behavioral segmentation looks for individuals with similar behavioral patterns, or, in our case, similar choice models. There is no stipulation that the similarities have to be related in any way to observable characteristics; all that matters is that the decision models used are the same, and this is derived directly from choices. Hence, our finding that related social behaviors seem to correlate well would suggest to those interested in finding the social consumer that the key is not untrustworthy surveys on beliefs and intentions, but a closer examination of behavior that is likely to be tapping the same basic decision calculus.

Related to this last point, cultural agglomeration is less useful than believed. As Chapters 4, 5, and 6 have revealed, the degree of cultural differentiation is much lower in our studies than is normally seen in the literature. The most obvious reason for the quantitative findings in Chapters 4 and 6 is that the methods we use mitigate methodological biases that are related to culture. Although this does not imply that cultural or country aggregation has no value, it implies that more predictive accuracy is achieved by focusing on the individual first. In Chapter 5 we found that culture is related mostly to justification, explanation, and persuasion, not to behavior – the implication being that culture plays less of a core role in choice behavior, and more of a role in how the individuals perceive their behavior and justify it to others.

Social consumption does not defy the law of demand. Stated simply, the demand for social issues responds to prices. The existence of a WTP reveals not just what individuals are willing to pay to acquire a good social feature, but also the reservation price beyond which no smart firm should go. We noted in Chapter 4 that our WTP results represent maximal estimates that should be considered what an average consumer would pay under perfectly ideal circumstances, including complete information and the optimal mix of functional features. This is a much more limited and cautious statement than what is normally seen in the press and periodically arises in many academic articles, where it is erroneously assumed that consumers *will* pay the estimated price premia independent of any other intervening circumstances. As noted by Levitt and List (2007, p. 154), when discussing laboratory experiments, "the basic strategy underlying laboratory experiments in the physical sciences and economics is similar, but the fact that humans are the object of study in the latter raises special questions about the ability to extrapolate experimental findings beyond the lab, questions that do not arise in the physical sciences." Experimental results provide a window on demand but must be used sensibly. Thus, although one might quibble with the absolute level of our estimates, and the magnitude of the social feature and product demand that we find, there is evidence that a demand for social features is there and that it behaves in a manner similar to the demand for other components of product demand.

Function trumps ethics. Perhaps the most expected result is that people will not sacrifice function for ethics. This shows up in our work in three ways. First, in the most clear-cut example, we show that, when faced with a choice of good ethics for bad function or good function for bad ethics, individuals overwhelmingly choose good function and bad ethics. Second, when examining the social segment for both AA batteries and athletic shoes, we see that individuals in these segments also value the functional features to a significant degree. In essence, there is no "only ethics" "social" segment, but a segment that reveals slightly less price sensitivity, which shows up in a higher WTP for social features. Third, in our ethnographic study discussed in Chapter 5, nearly all the consumers interviewed showed a reluctance to give up product functionality. They revealed a remarkable reluctance to consider social product features as anything but secondary to their primary reasons for purchasing the products in question.

The convenient empirical truths

Although we have set a high bar in terms of proof that consumers will respond to social product features and will take an interest in the nature of the production processes of the products that they purchase, there is one clear and convenient truth: *some consumers in some situations are clearly willing to give consideration to more than purely functional aspects of the products that they purchase.* Hence, despite the critical commentary of the last section, it is obvious that there is a latent social product feature demand that can be tapped under the right circumstances. In other words, some consumers will ascribe value to social features, and that value can be tapped through the configuration and pricing of the product or service. However, what is important is to understand what we mean when we say that a tendency toward C_NSR exists in some people in some circumstances.

First, it is clear that ***whoever is in this group is in it contextually.*** In other words, looking for individuals who are category-independent, circumstance-independent social consumers is highly problematic. What makes a consumer willing to consider accommodating the social features of a product into his/her decision model is a complex combination of the social features in question – the social features must resonate with that consumer – and the context in which the purchasing is occurring – the circumstances must make it easy for the latent demand to be revealed in actual purchasing. It is less important to want to characterize these people than it is simply to allow them to reveal themselves by creating circumstances in which this is possible.

Second, the ***passive application of information loses to active persuasion.*** However, by "active persuasion" we do not mean overt proselytizing associated with the goodness or morality of a cause. For example, in all the work discussed here we found that passive information provision did little to influence choice. However, there is a difference between active and passive persuasion. In a small trial consulting field study carried out by one of the authors and a few students, individuals were given the opportunity to request a socially "enhanced" version of a product at no additional cost, and without any active persuasion. Fewer than 1 percent of people did so. However, it took very little prompting at the ordering counter for the number accepting the socially acceptable product to jump dramatically (to over 30 percent). What was most interesting was that, when questioned about why they chose the socially enhanced product (the individuals were identifiable by the packaging in which the product was consumed), all of them were very articulate (and even passionate) about the need to support the social cause. Of course, what was unknown to them was that, had they not been "gently persuaded" at the ordering counter, more than 99 percent of them would not have chosen to consume the socially enhanced product, even at a zero price premium! We call this the McDonald's strategy; we employed the social equivalent of asking whether you wanted to "upsize your meal" or have "fries with your Coke."

Third, ***what matters most to understanding social consumption is other social choice.*** People opt for consistency between related behaviors – a fact seen clearly in the evidence presented in Chapter 6. Hence, from a practical perspective, what it is important to discover is not the link between what people say they value and what they do, but the link between the different manifestations of what they value by what they do across a broad range of contexts. We call this the Amazon strategy. If you go onto Amazon.com the model that applies is behavior-based, and the ideal (and optimal) segment has one customer in it – you (see, for example, Bonhard *et al.*, 2006). Amazon uses what you search for and what you bought in the past as a signal for what else you will search for and potentially buy (Macleod, 2006). This allows Amazon to create dynamic web pages that, in theory, can differ for every customer coming onto their site. Of course, this can be wrong from time to time, particularly when you branch out and search for new things. However, for long-term customers, the logic is simple and works well and can even anticipate variety seeking. Initially, you are segmented according to what others like you have done. However, as more information becomes available about your specific purchasing and search behavior, the less the system relies on potentially inaccurate data based on extrapolations from what others do and the more it relies on more accurate extrapolations based on data about what you do. Our logic is similar.

Fourth, although consumers may not be willing to pay a higher price for a product with better social features, ***they may be prepared to reward the company in other ways***. The question is whether or not this is sufficient to compensate for the additional costs faced by the firm. Although we do not report on this here, in another consulting project using the DCE approach we refined our work and showed how this might arise. A property developer found that selling "green" homes at a premium was, basically, impossible. Consumers were unwilling to pay more for the supposedly energy- and water-efficient homes the developer was required to build under the stringent building regulations placed on new developments (for example, the co-generation of power was required – which was done with solar cells and gas conversion – as was water recycling on site, and so on). We found that purchasers used two logics in their decision models. The first was simple: they compared the land, layout, and space to the next best home using "old" technology (some of which were only one block outside the development). Second, they looked at the technologically sophisticated homes in much the same way that consumers of technology products look at computers, TVs, and other gadgets. In seven to ten years' time, the average turnover time for a home, the technology-laden, energy-efficient homes would possess obsolete technology that would have to be replaced/upgraded in order for it to be sold (or the house would sell at a discount). In other words, in addition to looking at the new homes as saving them money on energy and water usage, purchasers were also incorporating technological obsolescence into their decision rules. In their simple calculus, the energy savings would be offset by the need to upgrade the technology when the time came to sell the property. The solution the developer used, which was based on extensive experimentation with home buyers, was (1) to remove the ownership of the technology from the home owner and attach it to the body corporate (the owner of the common property) and then rebate the consumer for natural resource savings, and (2) to focus on inventory turnover rather than price. (1) involved taking the technological obsolescence out of the purchaser's decision equation by giving owners options on the energy efficiency of the community; (2) recognized that, once the "green" issues had been removed, potential buyers could use the same decision criteria they were using with all other properties, hence reducing their cognitive load when comparing homes. The result was that the efficient homes sold under the new scheme turned over one third more quickly, reducing inventory costs and more than compensating for the additional cost of meeting the resource usage regulations.

Strategies for enhancing $C_N SR$

The convenient and inconvenient truths revealed in this book open up the possibility for developing effective $C_N SR$ strategies. The overall logic is simple: utilize the convenient truths while avoiding the pitfalls of those that are inconvenient.

The most obvious lesson can be summarized in two core empirical propositions. The first is to apply rigorous behavior-based approaches when examining social consumption. Such approaches involve forcing consumers to make difficult and inconvenient choices from which preferences can be gleaned, as seen in our applications of DCE, and by working them through deep and contesting analyses that reveal inconsistencies between what they say and what they do, as seen in our ethnographic work. The second is not to rely on a single method or a single study to guide your strategy. Part of the problem with this field is the fact that, until recently, nearly all the research in the field has been survey-based, leading to all its results being conditional on a single dominant methodology (Cotte, 2009). Uniquely for work in this field, we have brought to bear very different methodologies that provide a convergent perspective.

With that as a basis, we argue for a series of progressive ideas to be applied. Note that we are not saying anything about the morality or ethicality of choices, and are not presupposing that it is good or bad that individuals choose to behave one way or another in a purchasing context. Ultimately, we are arguing that it is up to the socio-economic and socio-political marketplace to decide what is justifiable and sustainable. Our purpose is simply to highlight how to compete in that marketplace in the most effective, efficient, and fair manner.

First, *focus on the behavioral outcome, not the reason for the behavior.* The key in the first instance is to create opportunities in which individuals can reveal latent social preferences without coercion. This may involve persuasion, advertising, social network interactions, and so on, and may also be linked to individual, family, network, and collective social decisions. Related to this is the need not to focus on singular opportunities (such as might exist with cause-related marketing campaigns), but to keep in mind the fact that different individuals will manifest their behavior in different contexts. Hence, having multiple means by which this can occur not only maximizes the likelihood that an individual will reveal his/her social desires, but also allows the company to test which combination of the many opportunities presented is the best to use.

Second, *focus on the ties and interactions with functionality.* As noted many times throughout the book, consumption is contextual, and abstracting social consumption from the functional aspects of a product/service or its category assumes that C_NSR is simply an "add-on" to traditional consumption. Individuals willing to respond to social positioning are responding to both social *and* functional positioning. Therefore, the product or service proposition must be presented to the customer holistically. As we found in our behavioral segmentation, those in the "social" segments possess a functional product preference profile. In the green homes example just given, the developers were able to sell the homes effectively because they understood how they fitted into the purchaser's decision calculus.

Third, *engage in small-scale experimental steps that allow the consumer both to learn and to co-produce.* One of the great difficulties in developing a strategy for enhancing C_NSR is that it is a nascent technology. Consumers do not necessarily know the product/service norms (e.g.

what is "good" labor practice, or what does it mean for an animal not to suffer when killed?), nor do they have any reason to put their trust automatically in the verifiers, if there are any at all. Typically, the verifiers are the corporation, the corporation's auditors, or third-party organizations that are unlikely to be unbiased because they are selling consulting services or directly promoting specific social causes they consider to be important above all else. Hence, consumers have to build up a knowledge base of what they consider to be acceptable product/service standards, and which organizations are best able to provide them with that information. Note that this goes far beyond the never-ending discussion of certification and labeling, and, indeed, should not even be thought about in those terms. What we are arguing here is that, if C_NSR is going to be a co-evolutionary reality involving many players, then the ultimate best outcome is one in which the consumer is an independent, knowledgeable participant, not a reader of labels or a reactor to certification.

Linked to this is the co-production aspect of consumption, whereby consumers are co-producing consumption meanings in tandem with brands. Socially recognized self-expression is a strong motivation for consumption (Arvidsson, 2008). We noted in Chapter 3 how consumers create their own identity through co-production, using a combination of things that they consume. In developing C_NSR, organizations need to understand how they fit into the co-production equation. We have used the third-generation Prius advertising campaign slogan, "Are you a Prius person?," many times, and it is a good example of the logic of co-production for an individual image. Toyota shows a distinct understanding of not just how to sell a vehicle, but how consumers use vehicles for socially recognized self-expression.

Fourth, *utilize persuasion and reinforcement to link behavior back to motivations*. Ultimately, estimates based on our experimental methods are good predictors of trial and short-term repeat buying, but in the end it is interaction with the product or service that will drive long-term usage. Hence, it is important that behavior is reinforced. The reinforcement serves two purposes. First, it tightens the cognitive and emotional link between the behavior and what the individual perceives as the rationales and motivators behind it (even though these may really be effects). Such linkage goes a long way toward making C_NSR a more routine and habitual act. For example, acts such as wearing seat belts or recycling are individually motivated actions that became engrained slowly.

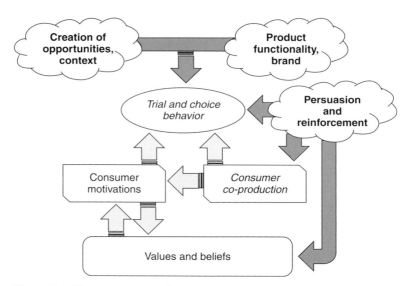

Figure 7.1 The components of a C$_N$SR strategy

Similarly, societies in which a majority of adults smoked, even in hospitals and schools, have become, in the space of two decades, places where smokers huddle together in doorways like banished heretics. Second, it solidifies the behavior so that, when it comes into competition with other, conflicting, cognitive and market demands, it is the behavior that wins out (or at least holds out). Indeed, it is precisely this issue that makes social consumption so difficult to create in the first place: it is running up against decades of individual consumption and purchasing habits, not to mention tastes "calcified beyond possibility of change."

Figure 7.1 gives a graphical representation of aspects of the logic of the four points of this strategy. The items in the clouds and in bold represent the factors over which the firm has primary control – creating context, product/service offerings, opportunities to purchase, and reinforcement and persuasion. The items in italics are those factors that represent consumer choice – to purchase or not, how the product/service is used in conjunction with the other products and services. The items in plain text are the consumer rationalizations – the motivators and values and beliefs the consumer associates as coming into play. The heavily colored arrows are the initial primary factors influencing choice (e.g. trial and initial repeat purchases of the product/service). The lightly colored arrows represent second-order, and later, factors that the consumer incorporates into his/her decision calculus.

Figure 7.1 does not, of course, represent a complete behavioral model; rather, it is meant to explicate a set of logical premises. First, it serves to highlight a key difference between value-driven "ethical" consumerism and behavior-driven C_NSR. Ethical consumerism assumes that the motivations arise with fundamental values and beliefs, and that external factors serve to limit the ability of those values being realized in consumption. C_NSR assumes that behavior is a response to circumstances, aspects of which can be orchestrated and controlled, along with long-term interactions between the individual, the suppliers of products and services, and the general environment (e.g. other consumers and potential reinforcers and persuaders). Its ethicality or morality arises only secondarily as part of the consumer's rationalization process. Second, it shows the progression of a C_NSR strategy from the initial seeding of behavioral opportunities through the subsequent consumer justifications and motivations and recall of the values and beliefs that align best with the decisions being made. Third, it hints at why researchers can overestimate the importance of values, beliefs, motivations, and culture. For example, the study discussed in Chapter 5 showed how culture worked at the level of justification but that behavior appeared to be quite consistent – something also found in Chapters 3 and 6 in different ways. Here we can now see why. Because persuasion and reinforcement, along with the creation of purchasing opportunities and co-production, are very culturally embedded – for example, they are based on language, social interaction, and physical environment – researchers taking a cross-sectional slice of reality at a single mature point in time will perceive more variance in the factors at the bottom of the figure. However, these are the aspects of consumption that are being localized by the producers in order to enhance their market, and self-localized by the consumers in the process of justification and rationalization. Hence, the role of the secondary factors is overemphasized.

Jettisoning the myth

The work in this book is in no way conclusive but points to a direction of research and thinking that represents a deliberate, multi-method, multidisciplinary approach to the phenomena of social consumption. To date, work in this field has been compartmentalized into different disciplines using discipline-based methods and has rarely cited the work outside the researcher's primary field. What we have done, we hope, is opened up a realm of possibilities for academics and social and corporate practitioners alike by showing the validity of a multidisciplinary, multi-method perspective on social consumption – and, by the very nature of our commitment, "created more and more questions" that demand answers (Allport, 1983). Some reading this book will consider what we have done to be equivalent to the opening of an intellectual Pandora's box, and will no doubt be quite critical of the logic and findings we present. This is good, and part of the give and take of scientific debate. However, we believe that the linking of ethicality and morality with consumption, as has been done in the case of the "ethical" consumer, has muddied the waters of intellectual discourse, and taken what should be a logical and practical decision by consumers and firms and suffused it with quasi-religious and political rhetoric.

We should emphasize that, although most of our results reveal a remarkable reluctance on the part of the majority of consumers to make consumption choices that include a social dimension, we do not rule out the correctness or efficacy of their doing so today or in the future. Nor do we argue that, when acting as groups, activist organizations and their supporters do not have a role to play in what Keane (2009, p. xxvii) calls "monitory democracy" – a "post-Westminster form of democracy in which power-monitoring and power-controlling devices have begun to extend sideways and downward." All we have done is provide a more rigorous and scientifically skeptical lens with which to peer into the life and mind of the individual consumer as it is today. If, over time, more consumers choose to incorporate a social dimension into their consumption choices, there is nothing at all wrong with this.

Nor would we disagree with those who argue for more open debate about the role of social consumption and the importance of consumers, firms, government, and NGOs in promulgating social experimentation (such as Kysar, 2004, Barnett, Cafaro, and Newholm, 2005, Reich, 2008, and Keane, 2009). Our point throughout the book has been one of objectively examining the facts in the most critical and contestable manner possible, rather than using facts to support a predetermined viewpoint. We are, according to Thomas Huxley, engaged in "the great tragedy of science...the slaying of a beautiful theory by an ugly fact." However, science is a social process, and it is impossible to remove the investigator, and his/her biases, from the investigation. We have given our perspective and put our facts, ugly as they may seem, on the table.

It is our argument that the notion of the "ethical" consumer needs to be jettisoned. In Chapter 1 we based the mythical status of the "ethical" consumer on four premises. The first is the simplest; it is mythical in the sense that it fails to conform to the reality of everyday consumption; in other words, it is false. Second, it is mythical in the sense that it represents a "heroic" character. Third, it is mythical in being a role model for what some in society believe to be morally correct behavior. Finally, it is mythical in the sense that it represents idealizations that open to contestation the existing flawed behavior of members of society. Hence, the ethical consumer is an ideal, embodied in a hero who holds to a moral standard sufficiently high that it creates the guilt surrounding our obviously flawed, self-interested behavior.

Clearly, myths serve a social purpose. There is no doubt that having heroes and idealizations of behavior are motivators to us fatally flawed, ordinary human beings. Zimbardo (2007) has coined the phrase "the banality of heroism" to denote this arguing that we are all "heroes in waiting." Similarly, there may be a benefit in pointing out to people that they are fundamentally flawed and behave in ways that need correcting. As noted by Zimbardo, heroism involves "resisting the impact of situational influences," or, in our terminology, having internal motivations sufficiently strong that they overwhelm the external context in which behavior is occurring. However, the analogy can be carried too far. It needs to be remembered that what we are discussing is not heroism reflected in the few, but the common, everyday economic activity of the masses (Holt and Thompson, 2004).

Although one can justify wanting to hold onto the myth as a propaganda tool for social change, it is when social expedience turns into an uncritical belief that the myth is real that serious problems arise. We can look at this in two ways.

First, although myths may serve a social purpose, they do not serve a scientific purpose. For example, one of the authors was involved in a doctoral consortium in which an interesting exchange occurred. One of the professors leading the program asked the aspiring academics, "How many of you are studying in this field [social responsibility] because you want to use your results to engender social change?" Nearly a half of them raised their hands. The professors leading the program were uniformly shocked, with one asking, "How, then, can you be objective? What if the results of your research simply do not support your beliefs in this area?" At this point, science is abandoned and the enterprise becomes a plaything of "politics and religion," as aptly characterized by Sagan (1987):

In science it often happens that scientists say, "You know that's a really good argument; my position is mistaken," and then they actually change their minds and you never hear that old view from them again. They really do it. It doesn't happen as often as it should, because scientists are human and change is sometimes painful. But it happens every day. I cannot recall the last time something like that happened in politics or religion.

Second, as noted by Triandis (2009), "humans tend to confirm their point of view by selecting only the evidence that supports it" and engage in "motivated irrationality," whereby information that can be used to improve outcomes is ignored (Abelson and Levi, 1985). These tendencies, along with many other psychological biases, lead individuals to engage in *cognitive simplification* and *self-deception*. Cognitive simplification can be seen in two illustrative examples. The first is in the theoretical and empirical logic behind much of the research in ethical consumerism, with its emphasis on the primacy of values and beliefs and a directed approach to behavior. The second is in the structural dichotomy seen between "ethical" consumption and the ordinary non- or un-ethical consumer (Lévi-Strauss, 1983). Self-deception arises when we "see the world according to our needs, wishes and hopes rather than according to the way it is" (Triandis, 2009, p. 32). Our argument is that much of the evidence relating to the ethical consumer has been colored by the wishes and hopes of those involved in the study of social consumption – wishes and hopes that are based on a cognitively simplified model of human behavior.

It is because of these two factors that we argue for jettisoning the myth of the ethical consumer and focusing instead on social consumption or $C_N SR$. The value of concentrating on $C_N SR$ is threefold. First, it represents a more realistic conceptualization of the consumer's potential use of consumption opportunities for social value creation. It says nothing about ethics, morality, right or wrong, or good or bad. Its focus is squarely on the individual's willingness to ascribe value to a feature that happens to be social rather than functional, and how individuals make complex value trade-offs. Second, it aligns the consumer much more clearly with general notions of CSR. As shown in Chapter 2, value creation from CSR is impossible without $C_N SR$. It is also important to align CSR and $C_N SR$ to counter the anti-corporate rhetoric pervasive throughout the realm of "ethical" consumerism. Third, it allows for a broader interpretation of the individual in the society at large. C_NSR is about revealing the individual more holistically through an examination of the context of purchasing and consumption. As we hope Chapter 6 showed, we can expand the idea of C_NSR to discuss the social responsibility of the citizen (perhaps C_ZSR!). Social consumption then becomes part of the role of the individual in a monitory form of democracy, one in which there are no illusions. For Keane (2009, pp. 854–5; emphasis in original), such

democracy is born when people are disposed to speak and act as if they are subjects of this world, in all its flesh and blood complexity, rather than as objects dangling on some other-worldly or super-worldly dynamic. [...] It therefore implies that the mundane realities are "up for grabs", that is, are capable of ordering and reordering by humans beings whose eyes are fixed for at least some of the time on *this* world and not *that* world extending through, above and beyond human intervention. [...] Democracy recognizes that although people are not angels or gods or goddesses, they are at least good enough to prevent some humans from thinking they *are* angels or gods or goddesses.

We can therefore speak about the individual as having a variety of social responsibilities – as consumer, citizen, worker, investor, and so on – each of which gives us a different angle on the complex embodiment of the individual in the different roles and contexts. As the quote from Isabella Rossellini at the beginning of this chapter shows, looking at consumption is only one window on the individual. But it is a window worth looking through.

Appendix 1
Description of country choices
and participant sampling

This appendix describes the samples used and gives some basic information about the individuals participating in the three major studies described in the book.

Study no. 1

As noted, study no. 1 involved three samples in two countries as well as a follow-up experiment (which we will discuss here as study no. 1+).

Country choice

The initial country choices represent samples of convenience, but ones that offered a wide range of variability on key variables. By focusing on Hong Kong (HK) and Australia (A), the intent was to have variability that accounted for differences on several key dimensions. Countries were chosen on the basis of two criteria. The countries chosen were meant to achieve the following.

- Generate variance in orientation on traditional cultural distance scales:
  - individualism: A > HK;
  - power distance: HK > A;
  - uncertainty avoidance: HK > A; and
  - masculinity: A > HK.
- Generate variance in social environment and practices. Hong Kong was perceived to be more commercial, with greater emphasis on consumption and brands, particularly within the student sample.

Group sample

Three groups were examined. Undergraduate students in Hong Kong, MBA students in Australia, and supporters of Amnesty International in

Australia. The three samples were chosen mainly to determine the range of effects that it was possible to find. The undergraduates in Hong Kong were expected to be the least sensitive to social positioning and the most price- and brand-sensitive. The AI supporters sample was chosen as a group that had revealed preferences for supporting a social cause (although not one that is immediately and intimately related to the products and issues being examined). The Australian MBA sample was considered to be a middling sample that included potential middle- to high-income consumers. In addition, these individuals were expected to (and did indeed) differ significantly on extant survey scales related to ethics and social interaction.

Participant sample

The participant sample were all contacted via mail, either through a direct mailing via the post, in the case of the Amnesty International sample, or via internal mail, in the case of the Hong Kong undergraduate and Australian MBA samples. In the two student cases, the universe was sampled, in that all the third-year undergraduates and all the MBA students available received a survey. In the case of the AI sample, 500 supporters were chosen at random on the basis of a geographic representation across Australia. Respondents in the student samples were entered into a lottery that awarded them one of five monetary awards: A\$250, A\$125, A\$75, A\$25, A\$5 (or their Hong Kong dollar equivalent). The AI supporters had A\$5 per completed survey given to Amnesty International in their name.

Response rate

In total, 1,253 people were studied: 396 undergraduate students in Hong Kong, 357 MBA students in Australia, and 500 AI supporters (also in Australia). One hundred and eleven instruments were completed and returned from the Hong Kong students (28 percent), 162 from the Australian MBAs (45 percent), and 172 (34 percent) from the AI supporters.

Study no. 1+

The sample in this sub-study included only MBA students in Australia (although at a different university). Students who participated in the sub-study received two free movie tickets worth approximately A$15. The sample totaled 122 subjects from a total population of 450 (27 percent). The response rate was slightly lower in this study, on account of the fact that only one reminder was sent. The simplicity of this experiment meant that the sample received was sufficient to estimate the effects under investigation.

Study no. 2

As noted, study no. 2 covered six countries, with all the participants being involved in an experiment focusing on athletic shoes (as in study no. 1) and one-half of the participants being involved in an experiment focusing on AA batteries. The other half examined laundry detergent products, and the information from that experiment is not included here for proprietary reasons.

Country choice

Countries were chosen on the basis of four criteria. The countries chosen were meant to achieve the following.

- Generate variance in terms of the level of development and income:
  - more developed = United States (U)/Germany (G);
  - intermediate development = Spain (S)/South Korea (K); and
  - less developed = India (I)/Turkey (T).
- Generate variance in orientation on traditional cultural distance scales:
  - individualism: $U > G > S > I > T > K$;
  - power distance: $I > T > K > S > U > G$;
  - uncertainty avoidance: $S > K = T > G > U > I$; and
  - masculinity: $G > U > I > T > S > K$.
- Generate variance in religious practices and historic traditions. Three countries (Spain, the United States, and Germany) were dominantly Christian and Western (one Catholic, one Protestant, and one a mixture). One country was Muslim and Middle Eastern (Turkey). One country was south Asian and Hindu with a Muslim minority (India). One country was Asian with a mixture of Buddhist and Taoist traditions (South Korea).
- Generate variance in education/literacy. The countries ranged from high to low literacy. This was used as a surrogate for the availability

of educational opportunities. However, it was expected that the less developed the country, the more likely the sample would be to include more educated individuals.

- Generate variation in political development/freedom. This was aimed at picking up the salience of economic traditions. The Index of Economic Freedom from the Heritage Foundation was used in the first instance (the scores are from 2004). This revealed three group-ings (free and mostly free = United States [78.7]; intermediate freedom = Germany [69.5], Spain [68.9], South Korea [67.8]; low freedom = Turkey [52.8], India [51.5]). Note that this is an "eco-nomic" and not a "political" measure.

In addition, the products under investigation needed to be widely available in the country. Finally, we had to have the availability of a professional local market research team who could execute the experi-ments successfully. Our original intention was to include China, Australia, Canada, Denmark, South Africa, the United Kingdom, and Egypt in the sample. We reduced the sample for (1) financial reasons (e.g. data collection costs in Denmark and Egypt were very high); (2) political reasons (e.g. it was difficult to get approval for a study on labor rights in China); (3) logical comparison reasons (e.g. the United States was considered similar to Australia and the United Kingdom); and (4) logistical reasons (e.g. we were unable to secure a base from which to operate in South Africa).

Participant sample

The participant sample was generated by using the most appropriate means for collecting such data within each country. For this, we took the advice of the market research firms utilized (Heaken QuickTest, AC Nielsen, and Research International). Mall intercepts were used in the United States, Germany, Spain, and India. In Turkey, individuals were interviewed in their homes after being contacted via telephone. In South Korea, they were interviewed either in their homes or office. Our con-tract with the research firms was to receive 100 usable responses in each country. The sampling frame was set simply (as mall intercepts do not allow for precise targeting). A quota sheet was used that targeted individuals based on four initial criteria, in this order: (1) they should have purchased within the product categories in the last six months;

(2) they should fit in an age distribution; (3) there should be a balance of gender; and (4) we aimed for a mix of incomes consistent with the middle range (US$15,000–25,000) with the exception of the United States and Germany (where that range was US$25,000–40,000). In reality, the choice of the sampling locations was chosen to drive the targeting.

In the United States, samples of twenty-five participants were secured at four shopping mall locations, one each in Chicago, Los Angeles, Houston and Washington, DC. In Germany, participants were secured along a well-traveled shopping street in Hamburg (Grindelalle). In India, participants were secured at shopping locations in Mumbai. In Spain, they were secured in the area around the Grand Via and the El Corte Inglés department store. In South Korea, participants were contacted in advance and the experiments were conducted at their office or home.

The participants were instructed as to the intent of the project and told to read and evaluate each question carefully. They were told that the entire survey would take between half an hour and forty-five minutes to complete. They were paid the equivalent of US$30 for their participation (and were told that this was conditional on their being truthful and answering every question carefully).

As individuals were approached, it is impossible to know what would constitute an effective "participation" rate. However, in no case did an individual who agreed to participate choose not to complete the experiment. As experiments were returned to us they were checked for consistency. Inconsistency arises when the decisions made are intransitive or the individual just randomly answers questions. This occurred in between 1 and 7 percent of the cases, and the research company secured additional participants. Ultimately, rechecks indicated that one additional US participant's results were not useful while several of the Spanish participants we initially rejected had useful data.

Overall, the Turkish sample was the most accurately targeted, as it was the only one in which we could preselect individuals. In the case of Germany, our participants were slightly poorer than targeted. In most cases we had a slightly female-skewed level of participation, a result driven mainly by the first targeting criterion. Only in South Korea was there a major issue. The research firm struggled to find male participants who purchased the two products being investigated. Ultimately, we abandoned this criterion in the case of the South Korean sample.

Study no. 3

Study no. 3 involved 160 participants from eight countries.

Country choice

As in study no. 2, the countries were chosen on the basis of four criteria, allowing for overlap between the samples. The countries chosen were meant to achieve the following.

- Generate variance in terms of the level of development and income:
  - more developed = Australia/Germany/Sweden (Sw)/United States;
  - intermediate development = Spain (Sp); and
  - less developed = India/Turkey/China (C).
- Generate variance in orientation on traditional cultural distance scales:
  - individualism: $U = A > Sw > G > Sp > I > T > C$;
  - power distance: $C > I > T > Sp > U > A > G > Sw$;
  - uncertainty avoidance: $Sp > T > G > A > U > I > C > Sw$; and
  - masculinity: $G = C > U = A > I > T > Sp > Sw$.
- Generate variance in religious practices and historic traditions. Five countries (Spain, Australia, the United States, Sweden, and Germany) were dominantly Christian and Western (one Catholic, two Protestant, and one a mixture). One country was Muslim and Middle Eastern (Turkey). One country was south Asian and Hindu with a Muslim minority (India). One country was Asian with a mixture of Buddhist and Confucian traditions (China).
- Generate variance in education/literacy. The countries ranged from high to low literacy. This was used as a surrogate for the availability of educational opportunities. However, it was expected that the less developed the country, the more likely the sample would be to include more educated individuals, as with study no. 2.
- Generate variation in political development/freedom. This was aimed at picking up the salience of economic traditions. As before, the Index of Economic Freedom from the Heritage Foundation was used in the first instance (2004 scores). This revealed three groupings (free and mostly free = United States [78.7], Australia (77.9); intermediate freedom = Sweden [70.1], Germany [69.5], Spain [68.9]; low freedom = Turkey [52.8], China [52.5], India [51.5]). This is an "economic" and not a "political" measure.

- Generate variation in the degree of economic development. The United States, Australia, Germany, Sweden, and Spain represented developed economies. Turkey, India, and China represented emerging market economies.
- Generate variation in political orientation. The aim here was to account for the degree to which state intervention and control were important. The Freedom House Index of Political Freedom (which has a political liberties and civil liberties component) was used. This leads to three general categories (the political liberty/civil liberty ranks [1–7] for 2004 are used): free: Australia (1/1), Germany (1/1), Spain (1/1), Sweden (1/1), USA (1/1); intermediate: India (2/3), Turkey (3/3); not free: China (7/6).

In addition, the products under investigation needed to be recognizable to the participants and available in the country. Finally, we had to have the availability of a professional local market research team who could execute the interviews in the local languages (AC Nielsen, Ipsos, and Market Vitamins).

Participant sample

Those selected in each country were high school graduates ranging in age from twenty to sixty, with an equal proportion of men and women. A professional market research firm contacted all the participants, and the interviews were conducted either in their home or at a pre-arranged research location. At least one of the authors conducted an extensive, day-long training session with the local qualitative researcher who would conduct the interviews in each non-English-speaking country. This was to ensure that identical procedures were followed in all locations, with the same instructions given to all participants. In Australia and the United States, the interviews were conducted by one of the authors. The cities included in the sampling were Sydney (Australia), Beijing and Shanghai (China), Hamburg (Germany), Mumbai and Hyderabad (India), Madrid (Spain), Gøteborg (Sweden), Istanbul and Ankara (Turkey), and Salt Lake City (United States). Participants were paid for travel and given compensation that ranged from US$10 to US$50 for their time.

Appendix 2
Ethical disposition survey: the MORI poll and ethics scales

The ethical disposition survey consisted of three parts. The EDS was administered to participants separately, with some receiving the EDS before the experiments and others receiving it after the experiments. A control group did not receive the EDS.

The EDS appeared to participants in two sections. Section 1 included forty statements, to which the reader responded on a five-point Likert scale. Section 2 included the three questions found in the MORI poll.

MORI poll

This consisted of three blocks of questions aimed at measuring the extent to which various factors influenced purchase intention.

(1) If you were buying a product (for example, a pair of shoes, clothes, or fruit) that had been produced in a developing country, which, if any, of the following would you take into consideration when you were buying it? (Please choose as many or as few as you like.)

(a) Appearance/fashion/style or trend, (b) availability, (c) brand name, (d) quality, (e) that the people who had produced it were paid enough money to live on, (f) that it caused as little damage as possible to the environment and that its production processes were environmentally friendly, (g) that the people who produced it worked in an environment that did not affect their health, (h) that the product had not been tested on animals (or had not used new ingredients tested on animals), (i) the human rights record of the country of origin, (j) your need (for buying it), (k) none of the above, (l) don't know.

(2) Do you think companies should have a minimum agreed standard of labor conditions (for example, on health, safety, pay, and working hours) for their workers in developing countries? (Tick the appropriate box.)
(a) Yes, (b) no, (c) don't know.

(3) If you were buying a product that had been made in a developing country, which, if any, of the following things about the people who made the product would affect your decision to buy it? Would you still buy it, would you still consider buying it but may not, would it make no difference to you either way, or would you definitely not buy it? Circle the appropriate number (1 = would still buy it, 2 = would still consider buying it, 3 = would make no difference, 4 = would definitely not buy, 5 = don't know) if the people who produced it:
   (a) were forced to work overtime;
   (b) did not earn enough wages to live off;
   (c) had no job security;
   (d) could be sacked if they became pregnant, and were subjected to forced pregnancy testing;
   (e) found their health to be in danger;
   (f) had no holidays or days off;
   (g) were not allowed to join a union;
   (h) had no right to sick pay;
   (i) were subject to discrimination or harassment;
   (j) were under the legal minimum age to work.

Machavellianism scale

The scale used was MACH IV, developed by Christie and Geis (1970). It consists of twenty statements, to which the subject responded on a five-point scale from 1 = strongly disagree to 5 = strongly agree.

(1) Never tell anyone the real reason you did something unless it is useful to do so.
(2) The best way to handle people is to tell them what they want to hear.
(3) One should take action only when sure it is morally right.
(4) Most people are basically good and kind.
(5) It is safest to assume that all people have a vicious streak and it will come out when given the chance.
(6) Honesty is the best policy in all cases.
(7) There is no excuse for lying to someone else.
(8) Generally speaking, people won't work hard unless they're forced to do so.

(9) All in all, it is better to be humble and honest than to be important and dishonest.
(10) When you ask someone to do something for you, it is best to give the real reasons for wanting it rather than giving reasons which carry more weight.
(11) People who get ahead in the world lead clean, moral lives.
(12) Anyone who completely trusts others is asking for big trouble.
(13) The biggest difference between criminals and others is that the criminals are stupid enough to get caught.
(14) Most people are brave.
(15) It is wise to flatter important people.
(16) It is possible to be good in all respects.
(17) Barnum was wrong when he said that there's a sucker born every minute.
(18) It is hard to get ahead without cutting corners.
(19) People suffering from incurable diseases should have the choice of being put painlessly to death.
(20) Most people forget more easily the death of their father than the loss of their property.

Ethics position questionnaire

The ethics position questionnaire of Forsyth (1980) was used to gauge moral relativism/absolutism and ethical idealism. It, too, involves twenty statements, to which the subject responded on a five-point scale from 1 = strongly disagree to 5 = strongly agree.

(1) A person should make certain that their actions never intentionally harm another even to a small degree.
(2) Risks to another should never be tolerated, irrespective of how small the risks might be.
(3) The existence of potential harm to others is always wrong, irrespective of the benefits to be gained.
(4) One should never psychologically or physically harm another person.
(5) One should not perform an action that might in any way threaten the dignity and welfare of another individual.
(6) If an action could harm an innocent other, then it should not be done.

Table A2.1 *Correlation matrix of MORI poll responses (all respondents)*

	Which, if any, of the following would you take into consideration when you were buying it?										Which, if any, of the following things about the people who made the product would affect your decision to buy it?									
	1. Appearance/style	2. Availability	3. Brand	4. Quality	5. People paid enough to live on	6. Little damage to environment	7. Work environment healthy	8. No animal testing	9. Human rights record of country	10. Need for the product	11. Forced to work overtime	12. Did not earn enough wages to live off	13. Had no job security	14. Could be sacked if they became pregnant	15. Found their health to be in danger	16. Had no holidays or days off	17. Were not allowed to join a union	18. Had no right to sick pay	19. Were subject to discrimination or harassment	20. Were under the legal minimum age to work
1	1.00																			
2	0.33	1.00																		
3	0.20	0.28	1.00																	
4	0.33	0.26	0.15	1.00																

5	−0.08	−0.06	**−0.36**	−0.18	1.00														
6	−0.05	0.01	**−0.25**	−0.14	*0.65*	1.00													
7	−0.05	0.02	**−0.23**	−0.06	*0.72*	*0.67*	1.00												
8	−0.02	0.04	**−0.27**	−0.06	*0.46*	*0.52*	*0.49*	1.00											
9	−0.04	0.01	−0.14	−0.03	*0.45*	*0.39*	*0.49*	*0.37*	1.00										
10	0.18	0.19	0.07	0.15	−0.11	−0.14	−0.11	−0.02	−0.14	1.00									
11	−0.11	0.02	**−0.27**	−0.12	0.37	0.28	0.32	0.29	0.36	−0.01	1.00								
12	−0.06	0.07	**−0.22**	−0.12	*0.50*	0.33	0.30	0.36	0.28	−0.07	*0.46*	1.00							
13	−0.04	0.02	**−0.20**	−0.07	*0.42*	0.22	0.26	0.24	0.33	0.09	*0.54*	*0.53*	1.00						
14	−0.06	−0.01	−0.16	−0.12	*0.42*	0.16	0.35	0.23	0.29	−0.10	0.30	*0.49*	0.39	1.00					
15	−0.04	0.04	**−0.25**	−0.09	0.40	0.33	0.34	0.32	0.30	−0.12	0.35	*0.54*	0.30	*0.63*	1.00				
16	−0.09	0.05	**−0.28**	−0.15	*0.48*	0.34	0.43	0.35	0.27	−0.07	*0.48*	*0.67*	*0.53*	*0.57*	*0.56*	1.00			
17	−0.07	−0.02	**−0.34**	−0.21	*0.50*	0.33	0.46	0.38	0.34	0.02	*0.47*	*0.55*	*0.62*	*0.47*	*0.44*	*0.67*	1.00		
18	−0.13	0.04	**−0.21**	−0.14	*0.51*	0.33	0.44	0.38	0.35	−0.01	*0.51*	*0.61*	*0.57*	*0.52*	*0.57*	*0.68*	*0.70*	1.00	
19	−0.02	0.07	**−0.21**	−0.04	0.41	0.29	0.37	0.29	0.31	−0.01	0.37	*0.51*	*0.45*	*0.60*	*0.62*	*0.64*	*0.51*	*0.66*	1.00
20	−0.04	−0.01	−0.17	−0.11	0.39	0.28	0.28	0.25	0.31	−0.10	0.38	*0.55*	*0.42*	*0.59*	*0.64*	*0.49*	*0.45*	*0.50*	*0.60*	1.00

Notes: **Bold** implies p < 0.05. ***Bold italics*** implies p < 0.01.

(7) Deciding whether or not to perform an act by balancing the positive consequences of the act against the negative consequences of the act is immoral.

(8) The dignity and welfare of people should be the most important concern in any society.

(9) It is never necessary to sacrifice the welfare of others.

(10) Moral actions are those which closely match ideals of the most "perfect" action.

(11) There are no ethical principles that are so important that they should be a part of any code of ethics.

(12) What is ethical varies from one situation and society to another.

(13) Moral standards should be seen as being individualistic; what one person considers being moral may be judged to be immoral by another person.

(14) Different types of moralities cannot be compared as to "rightness."

(15) What is ethical for everyone can never be resolved since what is moral or immoral is up to the individual.

(16) Moral standards are simply personal rules which indicate how a person should behave, and are not to be applied in making judgments of others.

(17) Ethical considerations in interpersonal relations are so complex that individuals should be allowed to formulate their own individual codes.

(18) Rigidly codifying an ethical position that prevents certain types of actions stands in the way of better human relations and adjustment.

(19) No rule concerning lying can be formulated; whether a lie is permissible or not permissible totally depends upon the situation.

(20) Whether a lie is judged to be moral or immoral depends upon the circumstances surrounding the action.

Table A2.1 provides the detailed correlation matrix of the MORI poll responses summarized in Chapter 4.

Appendix 3
Latent class finite mixture modeling

Mixture models are useful in estimating the likelihood that a specific individual fits into a class of individuals for which a particular model applies (see Wedel and Kamakura, 2000, for a general explanation). More specifically, mixture models assume that we are interested in decomposing a population of individuals (indexed by k), for which we have a set of n observations $y_n = (y_{nk})$, that we believe is a mixture of S segments in proportions $\pi_1, \ldots, \pi_S$ (note: all indicators in **bold** are vectors). A priori we have no idea from which segment each particular individual comes but we do know that the likelihood of the individual coming from each of the segments is constrained to be one – i.e. $\sum_{s=1}^{S} \pi_s = 1$. Given that the observations y_{nk} come from segment s, the conditional distribution function of y_n can be represented as $f_s(y_n \mid \boldsymbol{\theta}_s)$, where $\boldsymbol{\theta}_s$ is the vector of unknown parameters associated with the specific density function chosen – e.g. normal, Poisson, multinomial, Dirichlet, exponential gamma, or inverse Gaussian. Mixture models are estimated using maximum likelihood, where the vector $\boldsymbol{\phi} = (\boldsymbol{\pi}, \boldsymbol{\theta})$ is estimated based on the likelihood of $\boldsymbol{\phi}$ being $L(\boldsymbol{\phi}; y) = \prod_{n=1}^{N} f(y_n|\boldsymbol{\phi})$, where $f(y_n|\boldsymbol{\phi}) = \sum_{s=1}^{S} \pi_s f(y_n|\boldsymbol{\phi}_s)$ represents the unconditional probability of y_n given $\boldsymbol{\phi}$. Once an estimate of $\boldsymbol{\phi}$ is obtained, it is a simple matter of using Bayes' theorem to calculate the posterior probability that any individual n with y_n comes from any segment s, $p_{ns} = \pi_s f(y_n|\boldsymbol{\theta}_s) / \sum_{s=1}^{S} \pi_s f(y_n|\boldsymbol{\theta}_s)$.

Mixture regression models, the procedure used here, are estimated identically to mixture models except that we are interested in predicting the means of the observations in each segment by using a set of explanatory variables (Wedel and DeSarbo, 1995). We can therefore identify, for each segment s, a linear predictor, η_{nsk}, that is the product of a set of

P explanatory variables, $X_p = (X_{nkp})$, and parameters, $\beta_s = (\beta_{sp})$, such that $\eta_{nsk} = \sum\limits_{p=1}^{P} X_{nkp}\beta_{sp}$. η_{nsk} is related to the mean of the distribution, μ_{sk}, through a link function $g(\bullet)$ that varies with the distribution chosen.[1] In the mixture regression case, the parameters being estimated are once more $\phi_s = (\pi_s, \theta_s)$, with $\theta_s = (\beta_s, \lambda_s)$, where λ_s is a measure of dispersion in the distribution of segment s (in the case of the normal distribution, λ_s would be the variance of the observations in the segment).

Like any clustering technique, the appropriateness of mixture models is determined first by theory and second by the ability to find meaningful and significant differences in the population at hand. There is no single criterion for the choice of the number of segments. One such set of criteria, known as information criteria, is based on assessing the degree of improvement in explanatory power adjusted for the number of degrees of freedom taken up by the estimation of additional parameters (essentially, adjusting for over-parameterization): $C = -2*Ln(L) + Pd$, where L is the likelihood, P is a penalty equal to the number of parameters estimated and d is a constant. The most common information criteria are the Akaike (1974) information criterion (AIC), which arises when $d = 2$, and the consistent Akaike information criterion (CAIC), where $d = Ln(N+1)$ and N is the number of individuals.[2] CAIC is more conservative and is skewed to models with fewer segments, as it imposes an additional sample-size penalty. In addition to dealing with over-parameterization as the number of segments increases, one needs to be sure that the segments are sufficiently distinctive. To do this, one needs to compare the estimated posterior probabilities of segment membership. Celeux and Soromenho (1996) propose a normed entropy criterion, $NEC(S) = E_S/[lnL(S) - lnL(1)]$, where E_S is an entropy measure[3] accounting for the separation in the estimated posterior probabilities and $[lnL(S) - lnL(1)]$ adjusts for over-parameterization relative to a single segment model. E_S is measured as $1 - \sum\limits_{n=1}^{N}\sum\limits_{s=1}^{S} -p_{ns}ln(p_{ns})/N$, where p_{ns} is the posterior probability of individual n being in segment s.[4]

The problem ultimately comes down to the fact that no single criterion appears able to determine the "correct" number of segments and one therefore must rely on these criteria, as well as the structure of the models arising and how they relate to the theory being tested.

Appendix 4
Semi-structured interview guide used in all countries

Questions for the Nike scenario

- What do you think [insert country name] people think about Nike sport shoes?
- Are they likely to buy Nike sport shoes?
- Which factors will be most important when they are evaluating which brand of sport shoes to choose?
- Who is typically with someone when they are deciding which brand of sport shoes to purchase?
- Who pays attention to which brand of sport shoes someone is wearing?
- What do your family and friends think about Nike sport shoes?
- Tell me about what the Nike brand symbolizes compared to other brands.
- What would they think about you if you were wearing Nike sport shoes?
- If you were wearing some other brand?
- Tell me about a recent experience you have had purchasing sport shoes. Where did you purchase them? Who was with you? How did you make the decision? Which were the most important attributes?
- Are the ethical concerns brought up in the scenario of much concern to [country name] people?
- Do you think [country name] people are aware of the conditions the shoes are made under?
- Do you think about these labor issues when you are making your purchasing decision? Do others?
- Who, if anyone, is hurt by Nike paying substandard wages to male or female factory workers who are working in factories without high labor standards?
- Who, if anyone, benefits from Nike paying substandard wages to male or female factory workers who are working in factories without high labor standards?

- Have you read any articles or seen any shows on TV talking about the types of ethical concerns brought up in this scenario? What did you think when you read or saw them?

Questions for the soap scenario

- How do most [country name] people decide on which type of soap to use?
- Which factors are the most important when [country name] people are deciding on which type of soap to use?
- Do people ask each other what kind of soap they purchase?
- Tell me about a recent soap purchase you made. Where did you buy the soap? Which attributes were important to you? How did you make the decision?
- Tell me about your soap usage. Where do you use soap? How often?
- Are the ethical concerns brought up in the scenario of much concern to [country name] people?
- Do [country name] people discuss these concerns with each other?
- Who, if anyone, is hurt by soap being tested on animals? By soap not being biodegradable?
- Who, if anyone, benefits from soap being tested on animals? By soap not being biodegradable?
- Have you read or seen any programs or information about the type of ethical concerns brought up in this scenario? What did you think about the programs or articles?

Questions for the counterfeit goods scenario

- What do you think [country name] people would think about counterfeit goods like fake Louis Vuitton luggage or wallets?
- What factors do you think would be most important to them in deciding whether or not to buy such fake bags or wallets when they encounter them?
- If they have such a bag or wallet, are they likely to tell other people that it is a fake?
- Could other people tell it is a fake?
- How would they know it is a fake?
- How would you feel if someone gave you such a bag or wallet as a gift?

- Would you consider purchasing a counterfeited piece of luggage or a wallet? How would you make the decision whether to purchase it or not?
- Do you know anyone who has counterfeit luggage or wallets?
- Are the ethical concerns brought up in this scenario of much concern to [**country name**] people?
- Do people discuss these concerns with each other?
- Who, if anyone, is hurt by counterfeit Louis Vuitton luggage or wallets?
- Who, if anyone, benefits from these counterfeits?
- Have you read articles or seen TV shows about counterfeit goods such as this? What did you think of those articles or programs?

Appendix 5
The logic of best–worst scaling

Best–worst scaling (hereafter, BWS) is a fairly general scaling method that extends Thurstone's (1927) model based on random utility theory for paired comparison judgments to judgments of the largest/smallest, best/worst, most/least, etc. items, objects, or cues in a set of three or more multiple items. Specifically, BWS assumes that there is some underlying subjective dimension, such as "degree of importance," "degree of concern," "degree of interest," etc., and the researcher wishes to measure the location or position of some set of objects, items, etc. on that underlying dimension. We refer to the process of assigning numerical values that reflect the positions of the items on the underlying scale as "scaling." The BWS approach is based on the view that such measurement arises from theory, and that theory and associated measurement are inseparable. Thus, the scale values derived from BWS are those that best satisfy a theory about the way in which individuals make best–worst judgments.

To begin, we assume that there is a master set of K items to be scaled, $[I_1, I_2, \ldots, I_K]$. The items are to be placed in C subsets, $[i_1, i_2, \ldots, i_C]$, and some sample of individuals of interest is asked to identify, respectively, the best and worst items in each of the subsets (or in each of some subset of the subsets). If there are K total items to be scaled, then the total number of subsets that could be presented to the individuals is 2^K, minus all subsets that are null (1), singles (K), or pairs (K(K−1)/2), which grows exponentially with K. Thus, one needs some systematic way to pick the subsets that make sense, and, as noted by Finn and Louviere (1992), constructing the sets from a 2^K orthogonal main effects design, or some higher-resolution design in the 2^K family of designs, is a good approach, and one that coincides nicely with previous design theory for the case of only "best" choices (Louviere and Woodworth, 1983). There are other ways to construct appropriate sets, such as balanced incomplete block designs (BIBDs), and we illustrate the use of such designs in this appendix.

Thus, BWS assumes that there is some underlying dimension of interest, and one wants to assign scale values to the K items on that single underlying dimension. It assumes that the choice of a pair of items from any subset is an indicator of that pair of items in that subset that are the farthest apart on the underlying dimension. In other words, in any subset, say the c–th subset, if there are P items, there are P(P–1)/2 pairs of items that could be chosen best and worst, and an additional P(P–1)/2 pairs of items that could be chosen worst and best. Thus, for any given subset presented to an individual like the c–th subset, the individual implicitly chooses from 2 × P(P–1)/2 pairs. Let us denote the quantity 2 × P(P–1)/2 as M, and, for ease of exposition (and because it reflects the case in this appendix), we assume that P is constant in every subset (e.g. balanced incomplete block designs lead to subsets of fixed size, M). Now we can formulate this choice process as a random utility model as follows:

$$D_{ij} = \delta_{ij} + \varepsilon_{ij} \qquad (A5.1)$$

where D_{ij} is the latent or unobservable true difference in items i and j on the underlying dimension;

δ_{ij} is an observable component of the latent difference that can be observed and measured; and

ε_{ij} is an error component associated with each ij pair.

Because of the presence of the ε_{ij} component, the choice process of any individual is stochastic when viewed by the researcher, because it is impossible to know what the individual is thinking. Thus, we can formulate the model as a probability model to capture the probability that the individual chooses the ij pair in each subset:

$$P(ij|C) = P[(\delta_{ij} + \varepsilon_{ij}) > \text{all other M-1 } (\delta_{ik} + \varepsilon_{ik}) \text{ pairs}] \qquad (A5.2)$$

where all terms are as previously defined. This problem can be solved by making assumptions about the distribution and properties of ε_{ij}. A simple assumption that leads to a tractable model form that has seen many applications in the social and business sciences is that ε_{ij} is distributed independently and identically as an extreme-value type 1 random variate (equivalently, as a Gumbel, Weibull, or double exponential). It is well known that these assumptions lead to the multinomial logit (MNL) model (see, for example, Louviere, Hensher, and Swait, 2000), which is the form of analysis used in this appendix. In other words, the choice probabilities can be expressed as

$$P(ij|C) = \exp(\delta_{ij})/\Sigma_{ik}\ \exp(\delta_{ik}), \text{for all M } \delta_{ik} \text{ in } i_c. \qquad (A5.3)$$

We can express δ_{ij} as a difference in two scale values, say s_i and s_j, or $s_i - s_j$. Hence, we can rewrite the model as

$$P(ij|C) = \exp(s_i - s_j)/\Sigma_{ik}\ \exp(s_i - s_k), \text{for all M } \{s_i, s_k\} \text{pairs in } i_c$$
$$(A5.4)$$

Thus, the scale values of interest are s_i and s_j, which reflect the location of each item on the underlying scale.

If the subsets are constructed in such a way that the joint probability of choosing items i and j across all subsets can be estimated independently of the marginal probabilities (e.g. by using a 2^K orthogonal main effects design plus its foldover, or a BIBD plus its complement), then the model implied by equation (A5.4) can be estimated directly from the observed counts associated with each best–worst, worst–best pair summed over all subsets in the experiment. If the experiment does not allow one to calculate the total choices of all implied best–worst, worst–best pairs across the subsets (e.g. if one uses only the orthogonal main effects design or only the BIBD, as discussed by Finn and Louviere, 1992), one can approximate the desired scale values by taking differences in the marginal best and worst counts for each item. In other words, the simple score $\delta(b_i w_i)$ = total best i – total worst i approximates the unknown difference $s_i - s_j$ for each individual or subset of individuals who exhibit the same underlying ordering of the items (apart from judgmental errors).

We state this without proof, but note that one can easily see that this must be true by constructing an experiment that permits the joint choice probabilities for all the implied pairs to be estimated independently of the marginal probabilities, assuming an ordering of the items in that experiment, and simulating choices of the items with the highest and lowest rank in the order in each subset. It is easy to show that the total choices over all subsets for the implied pairs will be consistent with MNL, and, once one obtains the MNL estimates, one can easily see that the $\text{best}_i - \text{worst}_i$ differences are perfectly proportional to the MNL estimates.

Appendix 6
Australia omnibus social, economic, and political preference study

Individuals were sampled via an online panel provided by Research Now, a local Australian market research firm. The study was conducted in February 2007 and was completed within two weeks from the start to the end of sampling. The sample was chosen to be representative of the Australian voting-age population (eighteen plus) on four criteria: (1) age, (2) gender, (3) income, and (4) location (by state and city/rural/suburban). In total, 1,508 individuals provided usable responses out of a total sample of 1,751. Survey respondents were compensated for their participation.

The survey had five parts.

(1) A best–worst experiment that involved trade-offs between the sixteen categories of issues.
(2) Eight BW experiments that involved trade-offs between the sub-issues in eight of sixteen categories, the eight having been chosen on the basis of an experimental design.
(3) An ethics scale (Forsyth's moral relativism/ethical idealism scale).
(4) A group of demographic and social and political questions that captured religiosity and political opinion as well as tracking individuals' religious activity and their voting activity.
(5) A questionnaire that captured individuals' donating and volunteering activity across fifteen general categories, from working with schools to being involved with homeless shelters, healthcare organizations, environmental groups, and other categories of NGOs.

Table A6.1 provides information on the socio-demographics of the sample.

Table A6.2 gives the sub-categories underlying each category, along with the mean BW scores for each of the sub-issues. In each case the sub-issues were compared only against the other issues in the category. The maximum and minimum score is given in parentheses in the "Issue category" column, as well as the block size and number of blocks.

Table A6.1 *Socio-demographics of the Australia omnibus study*

Male (percentage of sample)	44.0
Age (percentage of sample)	
≤30	18.4
31–45	25.6
46–55	19.8
56–65	29.2
>65	7.0
Employment (percentage of sample)	
Full-time	37.5
Part-time	20.2
Home worker, unemployed, or retired	37.7
Student	4.6
Education (percentage of sample)	
No formal education	0.7
Primary school	1.3
High school	35.8
Technical school or some university	31.7
University degree	13.1
Postgraduate degree	3.5
Income (percentage of sample)	
<A\$20,000	19.1
A\$20,000 ≤ I ≤ A\$40,000	24.7
A\$40,000 ≤ I ≤ A\$60,000	18.8
A\$60,000 ≤ I <A\$80,000	16.3
≥A\$80,000	18.2
Lifestyle (percentage of sample)	
Single	21.3
Married	48.4
Divorced or widowed	13.1
Cohabiting	9.4
Percentage with no children	30.6
Median number of children, given children	2.0
Home ownership	
Own outright	37.6
Mortgage	29.0
Rent	33.4
Belief in afterlife (percentage of sample)	
Absolutely certain	34.7
Fairly sure	17.5

Table A6.1 (*cont.*)

Do not believe	16.9
Attendance at religious ceremonies in last year (percentage of sample)	
Regular	13.4
Periodic	30.3
Never	45.2
Political party closest to your beliefs (percentage of sample)	
Liberal/National	23.8
Labor	28.6
Greens	7.2

Table A6.2 *Sub-issues by category with mean best–worst score*

Issue category	Sub-issue (in order of the mean BW score)	Mean BW score
Civil and personal liberties (±11; 22 blocks of 6)	Legal rights	2.76
	Freedom from harm	2.68
	Right to life	1.64
	Right of association	1.60
	Right of free speech	0.92
	Right of identity	0.88
	Marital rights	0.09
	Right of liberty	−0.14
	Right to a nationality	−1.78
	Right to religious freedom	−2.62
	Right to vote	−2.94
	Freedom of movement	−3.08
Equality of opportunities (±7; 14 blocks of 4)	Age (both young and old)	1.26
	Disabilities	0.99
	Gender	−0.01
	Marital status	−0.17
	Racial/ethnic background	−0.27
	Sexual orientation	−0.89
	Religion	−0.92

Table A6.2 (*cont.*)

Issue category	Sub-issue (in order of the mean BW score)	Mean BW score
Commercial rights (±6; 10 blocks of 3)	Physical property rights	3.09
	Freedom to start/own a business	0.93
	Intellectual property rights	0.44
	Freedom to trade	−0.69
	Right of commercial domain	−3.77
Worker/employment rights (±4; 12 blocks of 3)	Right to safe work environment	1.89
	Child labor	1.39
	Retirement benefits	1.08
	Minimum wage	0.88
	Freedom to engage in trade	0.02
	Out-of-work benefits	−0.69
	Right to retirement	−1.00
	Right to join a labor union	−1.45
	Right to strike	−2.13
Rights to basic services (±6; 10 blocks of 3)	Right of access to healthcare	1.94
	Right of access to food	1.43
	Right to minimum standard of living	0.36
	Right of access to basic education	−0.86
	Right to benefits of last resort	−2.86
Animal welfare (±6; 10 blocks of 3)	Freedom from animal cruelty	2.40
	Protection of endangered species	1.87
	Protection against overhunting/-fishing	−0.87
	Humane farming	−1.35
	Freedom from animal testing	−2.05
Environmental sustainability (±4; 12 blocks of 3)	Industrial pollution	1.36
	Alternative energy generation	1.20

Table A6.2 (*cont.*)

Issue category	Sub-issue (in order of the mean BW score)	Mean BW score
	Deforestation	0.76
	Climate change	0.69
	Recycling of materials	−0.01
	Ancillary pollution	−0.15
	Biodegradability of materials	−1.14
	Personal pollution	−1.20
	Loss of biodiversity	−1.52
Minority rights (±6; 10 blocks of 3)	Right to cultural preservation	2.71
	Right to engage in cultural practices	1.33
	Right to cultural expression	−0.49
	Right to speak a foreign language	−1.71
	Right of secession	−1.84
Local crime and public safety (±7; 14 blocks of 4)	Child pornography	3.45
	Protection from violent crime	2.56
	Protection from terrorism at home	0.05
	Human slavery	−0.06
	Right to private protection	−0.36
	Safety of personal property	−0.85
	Freedom from harassment	−2.27
	Protection from corruption	−2.52
Food and health (±11; 22 blocks of 6)	Clean water and sanitation	6.35
	Mental illness	1.60
	Alcoholism and drug abuse	1.18
	Infant mortality	1.18
	AIDS	0.28
	Suicide	0.01
	Obesity	−0.05
	Right to choose/abortion	−0.78
	Life expectancy	−2.00
	Teenage pregnancy	−2.01
	Family planning	−2.53

Table A6.2 (*cont.*)

Issue category	Sub-issue (in order of the mean BW score)	Mean BW score
	Genetically modified food	−3.23
Individual economic well-being (±6; 10 blocks of 3)	Cost of daily living	4.06
	Housing affordability	−0.18
	Freedom from excessive taxation	−0.20
	Interest rates	−1.59
	Inflation	−2.10
Societal economic well-being (±3; 7 blocks of 3)	Poverty	1.35
	Unemployment	0.49
	Energy prices	0.38
	Economic growth	0.32
	Stability of currency	−0.19
	Balance of payments	−1.15
	Government budget deficit	−1.20
Societal social well-being (±4; 10 blocks of 3)	Quality schooling	1.81
	Youth inactivity	0.82
	Social isolation	0.80
	Income inequality	−0.37
	Public transport	−1.41
	Immigration	−1.65
Global economic well-being (±4; 10 blocks of 3)	Depletion of energy/resources	3.22
	Stability of financial system	0.97
	Population growth	−0.26
	Global economic growth	−0.74
	Third World debt	−1.45
	Free trade policy	−1.74
Global social well-being (±6; 10 blocks of 3)	Peace	2.84
	Diseases	1.46
	Third World poverty	0.13
	Income inequality	−2.13

Table A6.2 (*cont.*)

Issue category	Sub-issue (in order of the mean BW score)	Mean BW score
	Population growth	−2.30
Global security (±4; 10 blocks of 3)	Global terrorism	1.78
	Nuclear weapons proliferation	1.39
	Genocide	0.49
	Religious extremism	0.12
	Unilateral military action	−1.86
	Global criminal syndicates	−1.92

Notes

1 The appeal and reality of ethical consumerism

1. See www.csrwire.com/press/press_release/18938-GMI-Poll-Finds-Doing-Good-Is-Good-For-Business.
2. See www.ipsos-mori.com/researchpublications/researcharchive.aspx.
3. Prester John was a mythical figure who arose in the twelfth century. He was a supposed ruler of a Christian nation situated to the east of the Saracens. It was expected that he would ride to the rescue of the beleaguered crusaders. The quote is from the letter of Prester John sent to Emanuel of Constantinople in 1165. See www.graveworm.com/occult/texts/pjohn.html.

2 Social consumerism in the context of corporate responsibility

1. "Look for the union label" was the famous slogan used by the International Ladies Garment Workers Union in a series of commercials in the 1970s and 1980s.
2. We can complicate this further by separating the processes from the resources. This would be more correct technically and would account for the fact that the same resources might be involved in more than one process. However, nothing is gained from adding that complexity here, and we have opted for keeping the simplest specification between the functional attributes of the product/service and the resources that do not possess direct functional aspects.
3. It is possible that some resources may also be functional attributes, as would be the case in the provision of services when labor may be observed directly in the form of customer service. For simplicity, we will keep the specification of production resources and product/service attributes separate.
4. Note that we have not imposed any equilibrium conditions on this specification, as this does not impact on the logic of the argument we are making at this point.

3 Are we what we choose? Or is what we choose what we are?

1. See www.sustainablebusiness.com/index.cfm/go/news.display/id/14351.
2. See www.nationalgeographic.com/greendex.

216

3. See www.ipsos-mori.com/researchpublications/researcharchive.aspx.
4. See www.irishhealth.com/article.html?id=7880.
5. See http://lists.envirolink.org/pipermail/ar-news/Week-of-Mon-20040621/026152.html.
6. See www.gallup.com/poll/118546/Republicans-Veer-Right-Several-Moral-Issues.aspx.
7. See www.ethicalconsumer.org.

4 *Ethical consumers or social consumers? Measurement and reality*

1. See http://news.bbc.co.uk/2/hi/asia-pacific/6378161.stm.
2. For the PETA campaign, see savethesheep.com. For press coverage, see, for example, "US fashion store boycotts Australian wool," *Sydney Morning Herald*, October 15, 2004 (www.smh.com.au/articles/2004/10/15/1097784008200.html?from=storylhs), and "Australian wool in animal rights row," BBC Radio 4's *Crossing Continents*, July 21, 2005 (http://news.bbc.co.uk/2/hi/programmes/crossing_continents/4699931.stm).
3. "Australian wool wins historic agreement with PETA on mulesing," Goliath, June 30, 2007 (http://goliath.ecnext.com/coms2/gi_0199–6692167/Australian-Wool-Wins-Historic-Agreement.html).
4. Those wanting to examine the details of the studies summarized here or wanting to see related and more recent work can find information at http://mythoftheethicalconsumer.com.
5. This and related materials can be found at http://mythoftheethicalconsumer.com.

6 *The ethical consumer, politics, and everyday life*

1. One solution to this would be to continue to cycle through the questions until the survey participant was happy that every n[th] question was answered with the full information of the answers to all the other n-1 questions.
2. Direct estimation of the scales is done via multinomial logit regression. Auger, Devinney, and Louviere (2007a) provide an analysis of the information discussed here using multinomial logit estimation. They also provide a more comprehensive analysis of this data.
3. It is important to note that issues that appear in the middle – for example, those that might score 0.0 – are there for one of two reasons: either they were never chosen as most important or least important or they were chosen as most important and least important the same number of times. We can determine which of these is the case by examining the variance of the individual scores. However, for brevity we are excluding this aspect from our discussion.

4. See http://people-press.org/commentary/?analysisid=66.
5. Recent work is moving toward a point at which more absolute utility positions can be assessed. However, these developments post-date the work discussed here. See, for example, Orme (2009).
6. It is logical to believe that many sub-issues would span categories. However, this complicates the BW design and creates complexities in terms of analysis. For simplicity, we assumed that each sub-issue belonged to only one category.
7. Australia uses a voting preference system. Rather than voting for a single candidate, the voter expresses his/her preferences by ranking candidates or accepting the voting preference indicated by his/her party of choice. Such a system avoids the Arrow voting paradox problem.
8. Australia has a compulsory voting requirement for all elections. You are fined if you do not vote and all voting-age adults are required to be registered. Hence, using the actual vote does not create the voter participation problem that would arise elsewhere.

Appendix 3 Latent class finite mixture modeling

1. For example, in the case of the normal distribution the link function would be, simply, $\eta_{\mathrm{nsk}} = \mu_{\mathrm{sk}}$.
2. All these criteria have limitations, and there are numerous others that have been proposed. The general rule is that those based on a variant of the likelihood ratio test, such as AIC or CAIC, are to be used in conjunction with more sophisticated approaches (Deb and Trivedi, 1997).
3. The entropy measure is bounded between zero and one, with lower values indicating smaller separation between the segment identities as measured by the posterior probabilities.
4. NEC(S) is shown to perform in a similar manner to Bozdogan's (1994) information theoretic measure – a measure that is more robust than CAIC or AIC since it is based on the properties of the information matrix – for mixtures of normal distributions. Hence, although NEC(S) is not a general measure, it is applicable here since we are using mixtures of normal distributions.

References

Aaker, J. L. 1997. "Dimensions of brand personality," *Journal of Marketing Research* **34**: 347–56.

1999. "The malleable self: the role of self-expression in persuasion," *Journal of Marketing Research* **36**: 45–57.

Abelson, R. P., and A. Levi 1985. "Decision making and decision theory," in G. Lindzey and E. Aronson, (eds.). *Handbook of Social Psychology: Theory and Method*, 3rd edn., vol. I, 231–309. New York: Random House.

Adriaenssens, S., and J. Hendrickx 2008, "The income of informal economic activities: estimating the yield of begging in Brussels." Unpublished manuscript, European University College, Brussels.

Agnone, J. 2007. "Amplifying public opinion: the policy impact of the US environmental movement," *Social Forces* **85**: 1593–620.

Akaike, H. 1974. "A new look at statistical model identification," *IEEE Transactions on Automatic Control* **19**: 67–75.

Al-Khatib, J. A., A. D. Stanton, and M. Y. A. Rawwas 2005. "Ethical segmentation of consumers in developing countries: a comparative analysis," *International Marketing Review* **22**: 225–46.

Al-Khatib, J. A., S. J. Vittel, and M. Y. A. Rawwas 1997. "Consumer ethics: a cross-cultural investigation," *European Journal of Marketing* **31**: 750–67.

Allport, G. W. 1983. *Becoming: Basic Considerations for a Psychology of Personality*. New Haven, CT: Yale University Press.

Anderson, R. C., and E. N. Hansen 2004. "Determining consumer preferences for ecolabeled forest products: an experimental approach," *Journal of Forestry* **102**: 28–32.

Argenti, P. A. 2004. "Collaborating with activists: how Starbucks works with NGOs," *California Management Review* **47**: 91–115.

Arnold, S. J., and E. Fischer 1994. "Hermeneutics and consumer research," *Journal of Consumer Research* **21**: 55–70.

Arvidsson, A. 2008. "The ethical economy of customer coproduction," *Journal of Macromarketing* **28**: 326–38.

Atkinson, A. B., and J. E. Stiglitz 1980. *Lectures on Public Economics*. New York: McGraw Hill.

Auger, P., P. F. Burke, T. M. Devinney, and J. J. Louviere 2003. "What will consumers pay for social product features?," *Journal of Business Ethics* **42**: 281–304.

Auger, P., and T. M. Devinney 2007. "Do what consumers say matter? The misalignment of preferences with unconstrained ethical intentions," *Journal of Business Ethics* **76**: 361–83.

Auger, P., T. M. Devinney, and J. J. Louviere 2007a. "Using best worst scaling methodology to investigate consumer ethical beliefs across countries," *Journal of Business Ethics* **70**: 299–326.

2007b. "Measuring the importance of ethical consumerism: a multi-country empirical investigation," in J. Hooker, J. F. Hulpke, and P. Madsen (eds.). *Controversies in International Corporate Responsibility*, 207–21. Charlottesville, VA: Philosophy Documentation Center.

2009. "Global strategies for social product consumption: identifying the socially conscious consumer." Unpublished working paper; available at: http://mythoftheethical consumer.com.

Auger, P., T. M. Devinney, J. J. Louviere, and P. F. Burke 2008. "Do social product features have value to consumers?," *International Journal of Research in Marketing* **25**: 183–91.

2010. "The importance of social product attributes in consumer purchasing decisions: a multi-country comparative study," *International Business Review* (in press).

Austin, J. E., and J. Quinn 2007. *Ben & Jerry's: Preserving Mission and Brand within Unilever*. Boston: Harvard Business Publishing.

Bachelard, G. 1984 [1934]. *The New Scientific Spirit*, trans. A. Goldhammer. Boston: Beacon Press.

Baker, L. R. 1989. *Saving Belief: A Critique of Physicalism*. Princeton, NJ: Princeton University Press.

Barnett, C., P. Cafaro, and T. Newholm 2005. "Philosophy and ethical consumption," in R. Harrison, T. Newholm, and D. Shaw (eds.). *The Ethical Consumer*, 11–24. London: Sage.

Barthes, R. 1972. *Mythologies*. New York: Hill and Wang.

Bascom, W. 1965. "The forms of folklore: prose narratives," *Journal of American Folklore* **78**: 3–20.

Baumgartner, H., and J.-B. E. M. Steenkamp 2001. "Response styles in marketing research: a cross-national investigation," *Journal of Marketing Research* **38**: 143–56.

Belk, R. W. 2004. "The human consequences of consumer culture," in K. M. Ekström and H. Brembeck (eds.). *Elusive Consumption: Tracking New Research Perspectives*, 67–85. London: Berg.

Belk, R. W., G. Ger, and S. Askegaard 2003. "The fire of desire: a multi-sited inquiry into consumer passion," *Journal of Consumer Research* **30**: 326–51.

Belk, R. W., P. Østergaard, and R. Groves 1998. "Sexual consumption in the time of AIDS: a study of prostitute patronage in Thailand," *Journal of Public Policy and Marketing* **17**: 197–214.

Bem, D. J. 1972. "Self-perception theory," in L. Berkowitz (ed.). *Advances in Experimental Social Psychology*, vol. VI, 1–62. New York: Academic Press.

Berreby, D. 2005. *Us and Them: Understanding Your Tribal Mind*. London: Hutchinson.

Bettman, J. R., E. J. Johnson, and J. W. Payne 1991. "Consumer decision making," in T. S. Robertson and H. H. Kassarjian (eds.). *Handbook of Consumer Behavior*, 50–81. Englewood Cliffs, NJ: Prentice Hall.

Bierce, A. 1911. *The Devil's Dictionary*. New York: Doubleday, Page and Co.; available at www.gutenberg.org/etext/972.

Bishop, G. F., R. W. Oldendick, A. J. Tuchfarber, and S. E. Bennett 1980. "Pseudo-opinions on public affairs," *Public Opinion Quarterly* **44**: 198–209.

Bonhard, P., C. Harries, J. McCarthy, and A. M. Sasse 2006. "Accounting for taste: using profile similarity to improve recommender systems," in *Proceedings of the SIGCHI Conference on Human Factors in Computing Systems*, 1057–66. New York: Association for Computing Machinery.

Borgmann, A. 2000. "The moral complexion of consumption," *Journal of Consumer Research* **26**: 418–22.

Boulstridge, E., and M. Carrigan 2000. "Do consumers really care about corporate responsibility? Highlighting the attitude–behavior gap," *Journal of Communication Management* **4**: 355–68.

Bozdogan, H. 1994. "Mixture model cluster analysis using model selection criteria and a new informational measure of complexity," in H. Bozdogan (ed.). *Multivariate Statistical Modeling*, 69–113. Dordrecht: Kluwer.

Buckley, P. J., T. M. Devinney, and J. J. Louviere 2007. "Do managers behave the way theory suggests? A choice-theoretic examination of foreign direct investment location decision-making," *Journal of International Business Studies* **38**: 1069–94.

Callebaut, J., H. Hendrickx, and M. Janssens 2003. *The Naked Consumer Today*, 2nd edn. Antwerp: Garant.

Capron, M., and F. Quairel-Lanoizelée 2004. *Mythes et Réalités de l'Entreprise Responsable*. Paris: La Découverte.

Carrigan, M., and A. Attalla 2001. "The myth of the ethical consumer: do ethics matter in purchase behavior?," *Journal of Consumer Marketing* **18**: 560–77.

Celeux, G., and G. Soromenho 1996. "An entropy-based criterion for assessing the number of clusters in a mixture model," *Journal of Classification* **13**: 195–212.

Chandon, P., J. W. Hutchinson, E. T. Bradlow, and S. H. Young 2008. "Does in-store marketing work? Effect of the number and position of shelf facings on attention and evaluation at the point of purchase." Unpublished working paper, Center for Global Research and Education, INSEAD–Wharton School Alliance, Fontainebleau.

Chavis, L., and P. Leslie 2009. "Consumer boycotts: the impact of the Iraq war on French wine sales in the US," *Quantitative Marketing and Economics* **7**: 37–67.

Christie, R., and F. L. Geis 1970. *Studies in Machiavellianism.* New York: Academic Press.

Clarke, J., J. Newman, N. Smith, E. Vidler, and L. Westmarland 2007. *Creating Citizen-consumers: Changing Publics and Changing Public Services.* London: Sage.

Cohen, S. H., and L. Neira 2004. "Measuring preference for product benefits across countries: overcoming scale usage bias with maximum difference scaling," in *Excellence in International Research 2004*, 1–22. Punta del Este, Uruguay: ESOMAR Publications.

Corporate Crime Reporter 1999. "Monsanto officials join leading consumer, environmental groups," *Corporate Crime Reporter*, May 10.

Cotte, J. 2009. "Socially conscious consumers: a knowledge project for the RNBS." Unpublished working paper, Richeral lvey School of Business, University of Western Ontario, London.

Crew, L. 2004. "Unraveling fashion's commodity chains," in A. Hughes and S. Reimer (eds.). *Geographies of Commodity Chains*, 195–214. London: Routledge.

Darley, J. M., and C. D. Batson 1973. "From Jerusalem to Jericho: a study of situational and dispositional variables in helping behavior," *Journal of Personality and Social Psychology* **27**: 100–8.

Datamonitor 2005. *Natural and Ethical Consumers 2004.* London: Datamonitor.

Davis, M. A., M. G. Anderson, and M. B. Curtis 2001. "Measuring ethical ideology in business ethics: a critical analysis of the ethics position questionnaire," *Journal of Business Ethics* **32**: 35–53.

Dawkins, R. 1995. *River Out of Eden.* New York: Basic Books.

Deb, P., and P. K. Trivedi 1997. "The demand for medical care by the elderly: a finite mixture approach," *Journal of Applied Econometrics* **12**: 313–36.

Devinney, T. M. 2009. "Is the socially responsible corporation a myth?," *Academy of Management Perspectives* **23**: 44–56.

Devinney, T. M., P. Auger, G. M. Eckhardt, and T. Birtchnell 2006. "The other CSR: consumer social responsibility," *Stanford Social Innovation Review* **4**: 30–7.

Dickinson, R. A., and M. L. Carsky 2005. "The consumer as economic voter," in R. Harrison, T. Newholm, and D. Shaw (eds.). *The Ethical Consumer*, 25–36. London: Sage.

Dolnicar, S., and B. Grün 2007. "Cross-cultural differences in survey response patterns," *International Marketing Review* **24**: 127–43.

Donelson, R. F., E. H. O'Boyle, and M. A. McDaniel 2008. "East meets West: a meta-analytic investigation of cultural variations in idealism and relativism," *Journal of Business Ethics* **83**: 813–33.

Drakeford, M. 1997. *Social Movements and Their Supporters*. London: Macmillan.

Economist, The 2006. "Chinese cinema. No direction. Everyone is in love with Chinese cinema. Except the Chinese," *The Economist*, April 27; available at www.economist.com/businessfinance/displayStory.cfm?story_id=E1_GRGDNVJ.

Erikson, R. S., and C. Wlezien 2008. "Are political markets really superior to polls as election predictors?," *Public Opinion Quarterly* **72**: 190–215.

Etgar, M. 2008. "A descriptive model of the consumer co-production process," *Journal of the Academy of Marketing Science* **36**: 97–108.

Ettenson, R., and J. Klein 2005. "The fallout from French nuclear testing in the South Pacific: a longitudinal study of consumer boycotts," *International Marketing Review* **22**: 199–224.

Eurobarometer 2007. *Attitudes of EU Citizens towards Animal Welfare*. Brussels: European Commission.

Fehr, E., and C. Camerer 2004. "Measuring social norms and preferences using experimental games: a guide for social scientists," in J. Henrich, R. Boyd, S. Bowles, C. Camerer, E. Fehr, and M. Gintis (eds.). *Foundations of Human Sociality: Economic Experiments and Ethnographic Evidence from Fifteen Small-scale Societies*, 55–95. Oxford: Oxford University Press.

Fehr, E., and S. Gächter 2000. "Fairness and retaliation: the economics of reciprocity," *Journal of Economic Perspectives* **14**: 159–81.

Feyerabend, P. K. 1975. *Against Method: Outline of an Anarchistic Theory of Knowledge*. London: Verso.

Fine, B. 2006. "Addressing the consumer", in F. Trentmann (ed.). *The Making of the Consumer: Knowledge, Power and Identity in the Modern World*, 291–310. London: Berg.

Finn, A., and J. J. Louviere 1992. "Determining the appropriate response to evidence of public concerns: the case of food safety," *Journal of Public Policy and Marketing* **11**: 12–25.

Flynn, T. N., J. J. Louviere, T. J. Peters, and J. Coast 2007. "Best–worst scaling: what it can do for health care research and how to do it," *Journal of Health Economics* **26**: 171–89.

Fodor, J. A. 1983. *The Modularity of Mind: An Essay in Faculty Psychology.* Cambridge, MA: MIT Press.

Forsyth, D. R. 1980. "A taxonomy of ethical ideologies," *Journal of Personality and Social Psychology* **39**: 175–84.

Frankfurt, H. G. 1971. "Freedom of the will and the concept of a person," *Journal of Philosophy* **68**: 4–20.

Freling, T. H., and L. P. Forbes 2005. "An empirical analysis of the brand personality effect," *Journal of Product and Brand Management* **14**: 404–13.

Friedman, J. M. 2003. "A war on obesity, not the obese," *Science* **299**: 856–8.

Garone, S. J. 1999. *The Link between Corporate Citizenship and Financial Performance.* New York: Conference Board.

Gogoi, P. 2006. "Wal-Mart's organic offensive," *Business Week*, March 29; available at www.businessweek.com/bwdaily/dnflash/mar2006/nf20060329_6971.htm.

  2007. "Organics: a poor harvest for Wal-Mart," *Business Week*, April 12; available at www.businessweek.com/bwdaily/dnflash/content/apr2007/db20070412_005673.htm.

Grande, C. 2007. "Ethical consumption makes mark on branding," *Financial Times*, February 20.

Gregg, A. P., B. Seibt, and M. R. Banaji 2006. "Easier done than undone: asymmetry in the malleability of automatic preferences," *Journal of Personality and Social Psychology* **90**: 1–20.

Gunnthorsdottir, A. 2001. "Physical attractiveness of an animal species as a decision factor for its preservation," *Anthrozoös* **14**: 204–15.

Gunnthorsdottir, A., K. McCabe, and V. Smith 2002. "Using the machiavellianism instrument to predict trustworthiness in a bargaining game," *Journal of Economic Psychology* **23**: 49–66.

Gurney, P. M., and M. Humphreys 2006. "Consuming responsibility: the search for value at Laskarina Holidays," *Journal of Business Ethics* **64**: 83–100.

Harrison, R., T. Newholm, and D. Shaw (eds.) 2005. *The Ethical Consumer.* London: Sage.

Hart, S. L., and M. B. Milstein 2003. "Creating sustainable value," *Academy of Management Executive* **17**: 56–69.

Hartley, E. L. 1946. *Problems in Prejudice.* New York: King's Crown Press.

Hauser, M. D. 2007. *Moral Minds: The Nature of Right and Wrong.* New York: Harper Perennial.

Hays, C. L. 2000. "Ben & Jerry's to Unilever, with attitude," *New York Times*, April 13; available at www.nytimes.com/2000/04/13/business/ben-jerry-s-to-unilever-with-attitude.html.

Heinlein, R. 1999 [1961]. *Stranger in a Strange Land. The Science Fiction Classic Uncut*. London: Hodder and Stoughton.

Hiscox, M. J., and N. F. B. Smyth 2008. "Is there consumer demand for improved labor standards? Evidence from field experiments in social product labeling." Unpublished working paper, Department of Government, Harvard University, Cambridge, MA.

Hodgson, G. M. 2003. "The hidden persuaders: institutions and individuals in economic theory," *Cambridge Journal of Economics* **27**: 159–75.

Holt, D., and C. J. Thompson 2004. "Man-of-action heroes: the pursuit of heroic masculinity in everyday consumption," *Journal of Consumer Research* **31**: 425–40.

IGD 2008. *Ethical Shopping: Are UK Consumers Turning Green?* Watford: IGD.

Inman, J. J., L. McAlister, and W. D. Hoyer 1990. "Promotion signal: proxy for a price cut?," *Journal of Consumer Research* **17**: 74–81.

Johnston, J. 2008. "The citizen-consumer hybrid: ideological tensions and the case of Whole Foods Market," *Theory and Society* **37**: 229–70.

Jubas, K. 2007. "Conceptual con/fusion in democratic societies: understandings and limitations of consumer-citizenship," *Journal of Consumer Culture* **7**: 231–54.

Kahneman, D., and A. Tversky 1979. "Prospect theory: an analysis of decision under risk," *Econometrica* **47**: 263–91.

Keane, J. 2009. *The Life and Death of Democracy*. New York: W. W. Norton.

Klandermans, B. 1997. *The Social Psychology of Protest*. Oxford: Basil Blackwell.

Kysar, D. 2004. "Preferences for process: the process/product distinction and the regulation of consumer choice," *Harvard Law Review* **118**: 525–642.

Laury, S. K., and L. O. Taylor 2008. "Altruism spillovers: are behaviors in context-free experiments predictive of altruism toward a naturally occurring public good?," *Journal of Economic Behavior and Organization* **65**: 9–29.

Lazzarini, M. 2007. "The challenge of being an ethical consumer," *Consumers International*; available at www.consumersinternational. org/shared_asp_files/GFSR.asp?NodeID=96623.

Leake, J. 2009. "Whitehall snipes at Prince Charles's 'misguided' green thinking," *Times*, July 12; available at www.timesonline.co.uk/tol/news/environment/article6689978.ece.

Lee, J. A., G. N. Soutar, and J. J. Louviere 2007. "Measuring values using best–worst scaling: the LOV example," *Psychology and Marketing* **24**: 1043–58.

2008. "The best–worst scaling approach: an alternative to Schwartz's values survey," *Journal of Personality Assessment* **90**: 335–47.

Lévi-Strauss, C. 1983. *Structural Anthropology*. Chicago: University of Chicago Press.

Levitt, S. D., and J. A. List 2007. "What do laboratory experiments measuring social preferences reveal about the real world?," *Journal of Economic Perspectives* **21**: 153–74.

List, J. A., P. Sinha, and M. H. Taylor 2006. "Using choice experiments to value non-market goods and services: evidence from field experiments," *Advances in Economic Analysis and Policy* **6**: article 2.

Louviere, J. J., D. A. Hensher, and J. D. Swait 2000. *Stated Choice Methods: Analysis and Applications*. Cambridge: Cambridge University Press.

Louviere, J. J., and G. G. Woodworth 1983. "Design and analysis of simulated consumer choice or allocation experiments: an approach based on aggregate data," *Journal of Marketing Research* **20**: 350–67.

Low, W., and E. Davenport 2006. "Mainstreaming fair trade: adoption, assimilation, appropriation," *Journal of Strategic Marketing* **14**: 315–27.

Lyons, M. T., and S. J. Aitken 2008. "Machiavellianism in strangers affects cooperation," *Journal of Evolutionary Psychology* **6**: 173–85.

Macleod, L. 2006. "Amazon delivers lesson on powers of market segmentation," *Portland Business Journal*, March 17; available at http://portland. bizjournals.com/portland/stories/2006/03/20/smallb4.html.

Malinowski, B. 1992. *Magic, Science, Religion and Other Essays*. Long Grove, IL: Waveland Press.

Marley, A. A. J., T. N. Flynn, and J. J. Louviere 2008. "Probabilistic models of set-dependent and attribute-level best–worst choice," *Journal of Mathematical Psychology* **52**: 281–96.

Marley, A. A. J., and J. J. Louviere 2005. "Some probabilistic models of best, worst, and best–worst choices," *Journal of Mathematical Psychology* **49**: 464–80.

Martin, N. 2008. *Habit: The 95% of Behavior Marketers Ignore*. Upper Saddle River, NJ: Pearson.

Mather, D. W., J. G. Knight, and D. K. Holdsworth 2005. "Pricing differentials for organic, ordinary and genetically modified food," *Journal of Product and Brand Management* **14**: 387–92.

Mather, D. W., J. G. Knight, D. K. Holdsworth, and D. F. Ermen 2007. "Acceptance of GM food: an experiment in six countries," *Nature Biotechnology* **25**: 507–8.

Maynard, M. 2007. "Say 'hybrid' and many people will hear 'Prius,'" *New York Times*, July 4; available at www.nytimes.com/2007/07/04/business/04hybrid.html?scp=5&sq=prius&st=cse.

Mill, J. S. 2002 [1859]. *On Liberty*. Mineola, NY: Courier Dover.

Morwitz, V. G., J. Steckel, and A. Gupta 2007. "When do purchase intentions predict sales?," *International Journal of Forecasting* **23**: 347–64.

Murray, S. 2005. "Ethical consumers: where trust is all-important," *Financial Times*. 5 July.

Nagle, T., and R. Holden 2001. *The Strategy and Tactics of Pricing: A Guide to Profitable Decision Making*, 3rd edn. Englewood Cliffs, NJ: Prentice-Hall.

Newholm, T., and D. Shaw 2007. "Studying the ethical consumer: a review of research," *Journal of Consumer Behavior* **6**: 253–70.

Nicholls, A., and C. Opal 2005. *Fair Trade: Market-driven Ethical Consumption*. Thousand Oaks, CA: Sage.

O'Rourke, D. 2004. *Opportunities and Obstacles for Corporate Social Responsibility Reporting in Developing Countries*. Washington, DC: World Bank.

O'Shaughnessy, J., and N. J. O'Shaughnessy 2008. *The Undermining of Beliefs in the Autonomy and Rationality of Consumers*. Oxford: Routledge.

Orme, B. 2009. *Anchored Scaling in MaxDiff Using Dual-response*. Sequim, WA: Sawtooth Software.

Payne, A. F., K. Storbacka, and P. Frow 2007. "Managing the co-creation of value," *Journal of the Academy of Marketing Science* **36**: 83–96.

Petty, R. E., and J. T. Cacioppo 1986. "The elaboration likelihood model of persuasion," in L. Berkowitz (ed.). *Advances in Experimental Social Psychology*, vol. XIX, 123–205. New York: Academic Press.

Polonsky, M. J., P. Q. Brito, J. Pinto, and N. Higgs-Kleyn 2001. "Consumer ethics in the European Union: a comparison of northern and southern views," *Journal of Business Ethics* **31**: 117–30.

Prasad, M., H. Kimeldorf, R. Meyer, and I. Robinson 2004. "Consumers of the world unite: a market-based response to sweatshops," *Labor Studies Journal* **29**: 57–80.

Radin, P. 1950. "The basic myth of the North American Indians", in *Eranos-Jahrbuch 1950: Der Mensch und die Mythische Welt*, Band XVII, 359–419. Winterthur, Switzerland: Rhein-Verlag Zurich.

Rajecki, D. W. 1982. *Attitudes: Themes and Advances*. Sutherland, MA: Sinauer Associates.

Rawwas, M. Y. A. 1996. "Consumer ethics: an empirical investigation of the ethical beliefs of Austrian consumers," *Journal of Business Ethics* **15**: 1009–19.

Rawwas, M. Y. A., Z. Swaidan, and M. Oyman 2005. "Consumer ethics: a cross-cultural study of the ethical beliefs of Turkish and American consumers," *Journal of Business Ethics* **57**: 183–95.

Reich, R. B. 2008. *Supercapitalism: The Transformation of Business, Democracy, and Everyday Life* (reprint edn.). New York: Vintage Books.

Rode, J., R. M. Hogarth, and M. Le Menestrel 2008. "Ethical differentiation and market behavior: an experimental approach," *Journal of Economic Behavior and Organization* **66**: 265–80.

Rook, D. W. 1988. "Researching consumer fantasy," in J. N. Sheth and E. C. Hirschman (eds.). *Research in Consumer Behavior*, vol. III, 247–70. Greenwich, CT: JAI Press.

    2001. "Typology of projective techniques," in M. C. Gilly and J. Meers-Levy (eds.). *Advances in Consumer Research*, vol. XXVIII, 253. Valdosta, GA: Association for Consumer Research.

Sagan, C. 1987. "The burden of skepticism," *Skeptical Inquirer* **12**: 38–46.

    1995. *The Demon-haunted World: Science as a Candle in the Dark.* New York: Random House.

Sagoff, M. 1988. *The Economy of the Earth: Philosophy, Law, and the Environment.* Cambridge: Cambridge University Press.

Sassatelli, R. 2006. "Virtue, responsibility and consumer choice: framing critical consumerism," in J. Brewer and F. Trentmann (eds.). *Consuming Cultures, Global Perspectives: Historical Trajectories, Transnational Exchanges*, 219–50. Oxford: Berg.

Schudson, M. 2006. "The troubling equivalence of citizen and consumer," *Annals of the American Academy of Political and Social Science* **608**: 193–204.

Schwartz, S. H., and W. Blisky 1987. "Toward a universal psychological structure of human values," *Journal of Personality and Social Psychology* **53**: 550–62.

Schwarz, N. 1999. "Self-reports: how the questions shape the answers," *American Psychologist* **54**: 93–105.

Schwarz, N., C. Grayson, and B. Knäuper 1998. "Formal features of rating scales and the interpretation of question meaning," *International Journal of Public Opinion Research* **10**: 177–83.

Sen, A. 1997. *On Economic Inequality*, 2nd edn. Oxford: Oxford University Press.

Sherif, M., O. J. Harvey, B. J. White, W. R. Hood, and C. W. Sherif 1961. *Intergroup Conflict and Cooperation: The Robbers Cave Experiment.* Norman, OK: University of Oklahoma Book Exchange.

Simon, H. A. 1957. *Models of Man: Social and Rational.* New York: John Wiley.

Smith, A. 2000 [1776]. *The Wealth of Nations.* New York: Modern Library.

Smith, C. N. 1990. *Morality and the Market: Consumer Pressure from Corporate Accountability.* Oxford: Routledge.

Solomon, M. R. 2009. *Consumer Behavior: Buying, Having, and Being*, 8th edn. Upper Saddle River, NJ: Pearson Prentice Hall.

Soon, C. S., M. Brass, H.-J. Heinze, and J.-D. Haynes 2008. "Unconscious determinants of free decisions in the human brain," *Nature Neuroscience* **11**: 543–5.

Soper, K. 2004. "Rethinking the 'good life': the consumer as citizen," *Capitalism Nature Socialism* **15**: 111–16.

2007. "Rethinking the 'good life': the citizenship dimension of consumer disaffection with consumerism," *Journal of Consumer Culture* **7**: 205–29.

Sriram, V., and A. M. Forman 1993. "The relative importance of products' environmental attributes: a cross-cultural comparison," *International Marketing Review* **10**: 51–70.

Srnka, K. J. 2004. "Culture's role in marketers' ethical decision making: an integrated theoretical framework," *Academy of Marketing Science Review* **1**: 1–32; available from www.amsreview.org/articles/srnka01-2004.pdf.

Stigler, G. J., and G. S. Becker 1977. "De gustibus non est disputandum," *American Economic Review* **67**: 76–90.

Street, D. J., and L. Burgess 2007. *The Construction of Optimal Stated Choice Experiments*. Somerset, NJ: Wiley InterScience.

Street, D. J., L. Burgess, and J. J. Louviere 2005. "Quick and easy choice sets: constructing optimal and nearly optimal stated choice experiments," *International Journal of Research in Marketing* **22**: 459–70.

Tadajewski, M., and S. Wagner-Tsukamoto 2006. "Anthropology and consumer research: qualitative insights into green consumer behavior," *Qualitative Market Research: An International Journal* **9**: 8–25.

Tenbrunsel, A. E., and K. Smith-Crowe 2008. "Ethical decision making: where we've been and where we're going," *Academy of Management Annals* **2**: 545–607.

Tetlock, P. E., O. V. Kristel, B. S. Elson, M. C. Green, and J. S. Lerner 2000. "The psychology of the unthinkable: taboo trade-offs, forbidden base rates, and heretical counterfactuals," *Journal of Personality and Social Psychology* **78**: 853–70.

Thompson, C. J. 1997. "Interpreting consumers: a hermeneutical framework for deriving marketing insights from the texts of consumers' consumption stories," *Journal of Marketing Research* **34**: 438–55.

2004. "Marketplace mythology and discourses of power," *Journal of Consumer Research* **31**: 162–80.

Thompson, C. J., H. R. Pollio, and W. B. Locander 1994. "The spoken and the unspoken: a hermeneutic approach to understanding the cultural viewpoints that underlie consumers' expressed meanings," *Journal of Consumer Research* **21**: 432–52.

Thurstone, L. L. 1927. "A law of comparative judgment," *Psychological Review* **34**: 273–86.

Tiltman, D. 2007. "Who is the ethical consumer?," *Marketing*, 10 July; available at www.marketingmagazine.co.uk/news/669623/ethical-consumer.

Triandis, H. C. 2009. *Fooling Ourselves: Self-deception in Politics, Religion, and Terrorism*. London: Praeger.

Uusitalo, O., and R. M. Oksanen 2004. "Ethical consumerism: a view from Finland," *International Journal of Consumer Studies* **28**: 214–21.

Vargo, S. L., and R. F. Lusch 2004. "Evolving to a new dominant logic for marketing," *Journal of Marketing* **68**: 1–17.

Vogel, D. 2005. *The Market for Virtue: The Potential and Limits of Corporate Social Responsibility*. Washington, DC: Brookings Institute Press.

Von Mises, L. 1996 [1949]. *Human Action: A Treatise on Economics*, 4th edn. San Francisco: Fox & Wilkes.

Walsh, C. 2006. "Big Mac tops 'unethical' poll: McDonald's beats Nike to unwelcome accolade in new survey that reveals UK consumers' concerns about the things they buy," *The Observer*, April 16.

Warren, M. 2006. "Lightbulb giveaway is switched off," *The Australian*, October 14; available at www.theaustralian.news.com.au/story/0,20867,20578570-2702,00.html.

Watson, M. 2007. "Trade justice and individual consumption choices: Adam Smith's spectator theory and the moral constitution of the fair trade consumer," *European Journal of International Relations* **13**: 263–88.

Wedel, M., and W. S. DeSarbo 1995. "A mixture likelihood approach for generalized linear models," *Journal of Classification* **12**: 21–55.

Wedel, M., and W. A. Kamakura 2000. *Market Segmentation: Conceptual and Methodological Foundations*, 2nd edn. Dordrecht: Kluwer.

Weiss, H., and D. J. Beal 2005. "Reflections on affective events theory", in N. M. Ashkenasy, W. I. Zerbe, and C. E. J. Härtel (eds.). *Research on Emotion in Organizations: The Effect of Affect in Organizational Settings*, vol. I, 1–21. Oxford: Elsevier.

Wilson, D. S., and M. Csikszentmihalyi 2007. "Health and the ecology of altruism," in S. G. Post (ed.). *Altruism and Health: Perspectives from Empirical Research*, 314–31. Oxford: Oxford University Press.

Wilson, D. S., D. Near, and R. R. Miller 1996. "Machiavellianism: a synthesis of the evolutionary and psychological literatures," *Psychological Bulletin* **119**: 285–99.

Wolfers, J., and E. Zitzewitz 2004. "Prediction markets," *Journal of Economic Perspectives* **18**: 107–26.

Yergin, D., and J. Stanislaw 2001. "Commanding heights; interview of Manmohan Singh"; available at www.pbs.org/wgbh/commandingheights/shared/minitextlo/int_ manmohansingh.html.

Zimbardo, P. 2007. *The Lucifer effect: Understanding How Good People Turn Evil*. New York: Random House.

Žižek, S. 2008. *Violence*. New York: Picador.

Index

a priori segmentation of consumers
    53–4, 114–15
actions *see* consumer behavior
activists
    effects of pressures on firms 34
    ethics of power and influence 34
    firms' responses to pressure from
        32–3
    protests and demonstrations 10–11
    social persuasion 30–1
adaptive unconscious model 42–3, 46–8
    consumer as evolved ape 46–8
affective events theory 52
AT&T 30
attitude–behavior gap, implication for
        measurement 56
attitudes
    linear model of consumer behavior
        48–50
    recursive model of consumer behavior
        51–3
Australia, cross-cultural research 124–6
authorities, desire to pass responsibility
        to 133

Becker, Gary 167, 171
behavior motivation models
    55–6 *see also* consumer behavior
beliefs
    linear model of consumer behavior
        48–50
    recursive model of consumer behavior
        51–3
    see also values and beliefs
Ben & Jerry's 3, 33, 34–5
Best Buy 31–2
best–worst (BW) experimental
        approach 141–2
Betfair 44

Bono (U2) 1, 2
boycotts of products or companies
        10–11
brands and logos
    influence of 30
    value to the consumer 19–20
British Union for the Abolition of
        Vivisection 39
Burger King 30

Calvin Klein 30
Caribou Coffee 3
Carnegie, Andrew 138
Carrefour 31–2, 36
categorization of consumers from
        survey information 53–4
China, cross-cultural research 128–32
citizen-consumer
    concept 139–40
    estimating general societal
        preferences 152–62
    linking social and consumer
        preferences 162–5
    measuring social issue priorities
        140–52
    moral citizen myth 163–5
    trade-offs between social causes
        140–52
C_NSR (consumer social responsibility)
    definition 9
    vs ethical consumerism 9–11
    evolution of 35–6
    impact on corporate economic profit
        23–4
    implications of ethical consumption
        research 39–40
    means of expression 10–11
    purchasing or non-purchasing
        behavior 10–11

relationship to corporate social
 responsibility 27, 33–5
revealed social preferences 10–11
role in consumer decision making
 11–13
role of interpretive research 118–20
stated social preferences 10–11
value in the study of consumption
 186–7
and willingness to pay 18–23
C$_N$SR enhancement strategies 179–83
 allow the consumer to learn and
 co-produce 180–1
 approaches to social consumption
 investigation 179–80
 focus on behavioral outcome 180
 focus on ties and interactions with
 functionality 180
 link behavior back to motivations
 181–2
 logical premises 182–3
 persuasion and behavior
 reinforcement 181–2
 use small-scale experimental
 steps 180–1
Co-operative Group (UK) 39
cognitive simplification 186
comparability problem in research
 57–8
consumer, a priori segmentation 53–4,
 114–15
consumer-as-voter model of social
 consumption 43–6
consumer behavior
 archetypes 41–3
 consumer as evolved ape 46–8
 consumer-as-voter model of social
 consumption 43–6
 consumer as *vox populi* 43–6
 economic voter model of
 consumption 43–6
 evolutionary biological view 46–8
 importance of understanding 64–6
 linear model of consumer behavior
 48–9, 51
 link with knowledge and beliefs 133
 recursive model of consumer behavior
 51–3
 social, economic, and political
 implications 64–6

consumer behavior archetypes
 adaptive unconscious model 42–3,
 46–8
 quasi-rational co-producer of value
 42, 43
 quasi-rational reactive purchaser
 41–2, 43
 rational informed processor 41, 43
 see also social consumer behavior
 models
consumer behavior research
 approaches 40–8
 empirical approaches 40–1
 models underlying empirical
 approaches 40–1
 respondent bias issues 40
consumer choice
 dilemma in ethical consumerism
 168–9
 and taste 166–72
consumer decision making, role of
 C$_N$SR 11–13
consumer depth interviews, cross-
 cultural research 120–3
consumer preferences
 coevolution with products and
 services 29–30
 constrained preferences 31–3
 and CSR 33–5
 evolution of 33–5
 influence of brands and logos 30
 influence of product advertising 30
 influence of social persuasion 30–1
 linking with social preferences 162–5
 manipulation of the shopping
 experience 31–3
 persuasion strategies 30–1
 pressure on firms from activists 32–3
 revelation to firms 29–30
consumer social behavior, review of
 studies 67–71
consumer social responsibility *see* C$_N$SR
consumer surplus 17–18
consumer value 17–18
 market scenarios for social
 consumption 24–8
consumerism *see* ethical consumerism;
 social consumerism
consumption activity, testing for a social
 component 21–3

context
  importance of 114, 177
  interaction with values and beliefs
    173–4
  problem in research 58–9
  and salience bias 137–9
core social value 20
corporate activity
  economic profit in light of C$_N$SR 23–4
  economic profit motive 17–18
  and social consumerism 16–28
corporate social responsibility (CSR)
    16–17
  and the ethical consumer 35–6
  and evolution of customer preferences
    33–5
  relationship with C$_N$SR 27, 33–5
  role of the consumer 27
  value creation 33–5
corporations
  coevolving system of supply and
    demand 28–35
  constraining consumer preferences
    31–3
  control of product mix on offer
    31–2
  ethics of power and influence 34
  experimentation for and with
    consumers 29–30
  influence of pressures from activists 34
  influence on the social consumption
    context 28–35
  manipulation of the shopping
    experience 31–3
  motives for offering ethical products
    34–5
  persuasion strategies 30–1
  response to pressure from activists
    32–3
  revelation of consumer preferences
    29–30
  scenarios of effects of social
    consumption 24–8
counterfeit goods market 11
cross-cultural research
  Australia 124–6
  China 128–32
  comparison with the mythical ethical
    consumer 134–6
  consumer depth interviews 120–3

desire to pass responsibility to
    authorities 133
developmental realist justifications
    128–32
economic rationalist justifications
    124–6
Germany 126–8
governmental dependent
    justifications 126–8
hostility toward social policy
    initiatives 133–4
India 128–32
information not a motivator 133
link between knowledge and
    behavior 133
rationales for consumption behaviors
    123–32
Spain 124–8
Sweden 126–8
trends in logic and justification 132–4
Turkey 128–32
USA 124–6
CSR *see* corporate social responsibility
culture
  and ethical consumerism 8
  impact of cultural differences
    108–9
  and rationalization of behavior 8
  role in social consumption 175
  see also cross-cultural research
customer *see* consumer

David Jones (department store) 30
de gustibus non est disputandum
    (there is no accounting for tastes)
    166–72
decision making, Kantian versus
    Humean approach 42–3
demographics
  and ethical consumerism 7–8
  experimental study 99, 100, 106
developmental realist justifications
    128–32
discrete choice experimentation (DCE)
    72–4
dolphin-safe tuna 64
domicile, and ethical consumerism 8
Drummond, John 173
Durex, annual sexual well-being
    survey 57

economic exchanges, as prediction
    markets 44
economic profit 17–18
    in light of C$_N$SR 23–4
economic rationalist justifications
    124–6
economic voter model of consumption
    43–6
Economist, The 30
elaboration likelihood model of
    persuasion 52
emotive social value 20–1
empirical truths
    consumer responses to product social
        features 178–9
    context interacts with values and
        beliefs 173–4
    convenient truths 176–9
    effectiveness of active persuasion 177
    function trumps ethics 176
    importance of context 177
    inconvenient truths 172–6
    ineffectiveness of passive information
        provision 177
    influence of other social choices 177–8
    intentions without trade-offs are
        suspect 173
    role of culture 175
    role of the group is overstated
        174–5
    role of the individual in understated
        174–5
    social consumption follows the law of
        demand 175–6
    values and beliefs are overrated
        173–4
empowerment dilemma in ethical
    consumerism 168–9
ethical consumer
    assessing the myth 116
    categorization from survey
        information 53–4
    challenges to simplistic
        characterization 6–9
    and the citizen-consumer 163–5
    comparison with real consumer
        behavior 134–6
    evolution of the concept 1–2
    as heroic ideal 134–6
    interpreting the myth 134–6

jettisoning the myth 183–7
    and the moral citizen myth 163–5
    mythical attributes 4–6
    notions of what is ethical 4–5
Ethical Consumer Research
    Association 168
ethical consumerism
    assumptions behind surveys 2–3
    beliefs about consumer behavior
        2–3
    cognitive simplification 186
    consumer choice dilemma 168–9
    consumer empowerment dilemma
        168–9
    vs consumer social responsibility
        9–11
    and corporate social responsibility
        35–6
    and culture 8
    demographics 7–8
    and domicile 8
    ethical judgment of individual taste
        166–8
    illusion of free will 36
    implications of experimental studies
        112–16
    informing consumers 168–9
    myth and self-deception 14–15
    narrowness of studies 8–9
    non-social aspects 21–3
    overgeneralization of studies 8–9
    possible motives for 21–3
    review of studies 67–71
    self-deception 186
    surveys contradicted by purchasing
        behavior 9–13
ethical consumption
    implications of consumer behavior
        models 43
    linear model of behavior 48–51
    myth of 60–3
ethical consumption research
    implications for the ethical consumer
        39–40
    inability to predict consumer
        behavior 37–40
    possible sources of bias 39
ethical disposition inventory 76–9
ethical judgment of individual taste
    166–8

ethical products
  extent of the market for 1–2, 3
  firms' motives for offering 34–5
  firms' strategies toward 32–3
  lack of public support for 1–2
  low levels of purchase 11
  niche markets 3
evolution of C_NSR 35–6
evolutionary biological view of the
  consumer 46–8
experimental studies
  assessing the ethical consumer
    myth 116
  effects of providing information 116
  implications for ethical consumerism
    112–16
  importance of context 114
  individual-level analysis 115
  ineffectiveness of a priori
    segmentation 114–15
  issues addressed 66–7
  level of influence of social features
    113–14
  picture of social consumption 112–16
  review of ethical consumerism studies
    67–71
experimental study no. 1 72–97
  comparison of trade-offs 72–4
  discrete choice experimentation
    (DCE) 72–4
  effects of providing information 86, 87
  ethical disposition inventory 76–9
  experimental approach 72
  Forsyth's ethics position
    questionnaire 78–9
  functionality trade-offs against ethics
    77, 94–7
  influence of social features on choice
    79–86
  link between surveys and experiments
    87–94
  Machiavellianism scale 76–8
  MORI poll 79
  product categories 72
  structure of the experiment 72
  study aims 72
  study components 74–9
  study sample 72, 79, 80
  survey results and true preferences
    87–94

  willingness to consider/purchase
    79–86
  willingness to pay 79–86
experimental study no. 2
  (global segments) 98–112
  choice of countries 98
  cross-cultural context 98
  demographics 99, 100, 106
  impact of cultural differences 108–9
  influence of previous purchasing
    decisions 109–12
  latent class (finite mixture) regression
    analysis 102
  product categories 98–9
  product features 99–102
  recall of features of previous
    purchases 109–12
  segment size and country
    differentiation 108–9
  social segment position across
    product categories 106–7
  structure of experiments 102
  structure of the study 98–9
  study aims 98
  study sample 98, 99, 100

Fairtrade movement 3, 11, 19
Forsyth's ethics position questionnaire
  (EPQ) 78–9
function
  priority over ethics 176
  trade-off against ethics 77, 94–7
functional components of value 18–20

G8 133
Gap 1
Germany, cross-cultural research,
  126–8
Giorgio Armani 1
global segments, experimental study
  102–6
Globescan 39
Gore, Al 35, 55–6
government
  desire to pass responsibility to 133
  leading social change 35
governmental dependent justifications
  126–8
Greening America 168
Greenpeace 31

group, role in social consumption 174–5
guilt, socially induced 20–1

Harrods 30
Heinlein, Robert 166–7, 170
Hollywood Stock Exchange 44
Humane Society 39
Humean approach to decision making
    42–3
Huxley, Thomas 184
hybrid automobile market 3 *see also*
    Toyota Prius

Ikea 36
image signifier value 19–20
incentive compatibility problem in
    research 56–7
India, cross-cultural research 128–32
individual level of analysis 115, 174–5
inferences problem in research 58
influence marketing 31
information
    as motivation 133
    effectiveness of active persuasion 177
    effects of providing 86, 87, 116
    and ethical consumerism 168–9
    ineffectiveness of passive provision 177
intentions
    effects of trade-offs 173
    increasing predictive validity 59–60
    linear model of consumer behavior
        48–9, 51
    recursive model of consumer behavior
        51–3
International Labour Organization
    (ILO) 133
International Right to Know campaign
    55–6
interpretative research
    interpretative approach to C_NSR
        120–3
    role in understanding C_NSR 118–20
Ipsos MORI 39

Kantian approach to decision making
    42–3
Kirk, James 47
knowledge and behavior 133 *see also*
    information
Kroger 31–2, 36

latent class (finite mixture) regression
    analysis (LCRA) 102
law of demand and social consumption
    175–6
linear model of social consumer
    behavior 48–51
logos *see* brands and logos

Machiavellianism scale 76–8
market research surveys
    a priori segmentation of consumers
        53–4
    failure to predict purchasing behavior
        2–3, 9–13, 37–40
    implications for C_NSR 39–40
    methodological flaws 56–9
    narrowness 8–9
    overgeneralization 8–9
    possible sources of bias 39
    relationship to true preferences
        87–94
    see also consumer behavior research;
        social consumption research
market scenarios, reactions to social
    consumption 24–8
McDonald's 30
measurement, implications of consumer
    behavior models 53–6
MediaMarkt 31–2
Mill, John Stuart 44
models of consumer behavior
    archetypes 41–3
    empirical approaches based on 40–1
    see also social consumer behavior
        models
Monsanto 55–6
moral citizen myth 163–5
MORI poll, use in experimental
    study 79
motives for apparent ethical
    consumerism 21–3
MTV 30
Murphy, Thomas 44
myths, and scientific objectivity
    185–6 *see also* ethical consumer

Nader, Ralph 36
Nestlé 28–9
Nike 30, 114
Nokia 31

organic food 19
Oxfam Shop 33

People for the Ethical Treatment of
    Animals (PETA) 30, 65–6
persuasion
    effectiveness of active persuasion 177
    elaboration likelihood model 52
    strategies 30–1
Procter & Gamble 28–9
producer surplus 17–18
producers, market scenarios for social
    consumption 24–8
product advertising strategies 30
product mix on offer, control of 31–2
product social features, consumer
    responses to 178–9
Project Red 1–2
protest groups *see* activists
pseudo-opinions 58
purchasing (or non-purchasing)
    behavior
    and C$_N$SR 10–11
    disconnect with stated preferences 9–13

quasi-rational co-producer of value
    model 42, 43
quasi-rational reactive purchaser model
    41–2, 43

rational informed processor model 41, 43
recall of features of previous purchases
    109–12
recursive model of social consumer
    behavior 48, 51–3
reputational value 19–20
research *see* consumer behavior
    research; ethical consumption
    research; market research surveys;
    social consumption research
respondent bias in consumer behavior
    research 40
retailers, supply chain systems 31–2
revealed social preferences, and C$_N$SR
    10–11

Sagan, Carl 186
salience bias in social consumption
    research 137–9
Saturn 31–2

scientific objectivity, dangers of myths
    185–6
Scott, Lee 34
segmentation of consumers from survey
    information 53–4, 114–15
self-deception 186
self-perception theory 52
Shakespeare, Stephan 2
Shriver, Bobby 1
signal value 19
Singh, Manmohan 133
Smith, Adam 43–4
social change, role of government 35
social component of consumption
    activity 21–3
social consumer behavior models 48–56
    assumptions about how people
        behave 55–6
    consumer-as-voter model 43–6
    factors affecting decision making 48
    implications of models 53–6
    linear model 48–51
    models of what motivates behavior
        55–6
    recursive model 48, 51–3
    and research approach 54–5
    segmentation of consumers 53–4
    ways to influence behavior 55–6
social consumerism 9–11
    and corporate activity 16–28
    evolution of 35–6
    and firm profitability 16–28
    firms' strategies toward 32–3
    see also C$_N$SR (consumer social
        responsibility)
social consumption
    impacts on aggrieved third parties
        24–8
    implications of consumer behavior
        models 43
    market response scenarios 24–8
    picture from experimental studies
        112–16
    potential economic effects on
        producers 24–8
    reality of 60–3
    role of interpretive research 118–20
    testing for 21–3
    see also C$_N$SR (consumer social
        responsibility)

social consumption context, influence of corporations 28–35
social consumption rationales 123–32
  comparison with the mythical ethical consumer 134–6
  developmental realist 128–32
  economic rationalist 124–6
  governmental dependent 126–8
  trends in logic and justification 132–4
social consumption research 56
  abstract nature of the context 58–9
  attitude–behavior gap 56
  citizen-consumer concept 139–40
  comparability problem 57–8
  comparison with the mythical ethical consumer 134–6
  context problem 58–9
  cross-cultural consumer depth interviews 120–3
  desire to pass responsibility to authorities 133
  effects of trade-offs 137–9
  general societal preferences 152–62
  hostility toward social policy initiatives 133–4
  implications for C_NSR 39–40
  inability to predict consumer behavior 37–40
  incentive compatibility problem 56–7
  increasing the predictive validity of intentions 59–60
  inferences problem 58
  influence of context 137–9
  information not a motivator 133
  interpretative approach 120–3
  link between knowledge and behavior 133
  linking social and consumer preferences 162–5
  measuring social issue priorities 140–52
  methodological flaws 56–9
  possible sources of bias 39
  problems related to informational content 57–8
  pseudo-opinions 58
  rationales for consumption behaviors 123–32
  salience bias 137–9
  "social desirability" bias 56–7

trade-offs between social causes 140–52
  trends in logic and justification 132–4
  wording and meaning issues 57–8
  see also empirical truths
social features, influence of on choice 79–86
social intent, specific nature of choices 7–8
social issue priorities, measurement 140–52
social networks, use in marketing 31
social persuasion, influence on consumers 30–1
social policy initiatives, hostility toward 133–4
social preferences
  and C_NSR 10–11
  linking with consumer preferences 162–5
social segment position across product categories 106–7
social value for the consumer 20–1
socially induced guilt, responses to 20–1
societal preferences, estimation 152–62
socio-political nature of consumption 163–5
Sony 28–9
South Park cartoon series 19
Spain, cross-cultural research, 124–8
Starbucks 3, 11, 36
stated social preferences
  and C_NSR 10–11
  disconnect with purchasing behavior 9–13
status goods 19–20
Stigler, George 167, 171
surveys *see* market research surveys
Sweden, cross-cultural research 126–8

Target 31–2
tastes
  and consumer choice 166–72
  de gustibus non est disputandum 166–72
  ethical judgments about 166–8
  nature and complexity of 166–72
  role of values in determining 171–2
Tesco 31–2, 36
third-party value (TPV), market scenarios 24–8

Toyota 28–9
Toyota Prius 3, 19–20, 135–6, 181
trade-offs 8–9, 173
    and ethical consumerism 137–9
trade-offs between social causes
    estimating general societal
        preferences 152–62
    individual 140–52
truths *see* empirical truths
Turkey, cross-cultural research 128–32

unconscious consumption 119
Unilever 28–9, 33, 34–5
University of Iowa, Iowa Electronic
    Market 44
USA, cross-cultural research 124–6

value
    branding 19–20
    changes with market scenarios 24–8
    components of the individual's
        valuation equation 18–23
    core social value 20
    customer value (consumer surplus)
        17–18
    economic model 17–18
    economic profit (producer surplus)
        17–18
    emotive social value 20–1

functional components 18–20
image signifier 19–20
pure social value 20–1
reputational 19–20
signal value 19
status goods 19–20
willingness to pay 17–23
values and beliefs
    influence of 173–4
    interaction with context 173–4
    linear model of consumer behavior
        48–9
    recursive model of consumer behavior
        51–3
    role in consumption decisions 6–7
    role in determining tastes 171–2
    role of context 7
viral marketing 31
Vogue 30
von Mises, Ludwig 169

Wal-Mart 28–9, 31–2, 34–5, 36
willingness to consider/purchase,
    experimental study 79–86
willingness to pay (WTP)
    and C_NSR 18–23
    definition 17–18
    experimental study 79–86
World Trade Organization (WTO) 133